ADVANCED
SURVEILLANCE

The Complete Manual of Surveillance Training

BY

Peter Jenkins

Published by

Intel Publications

Advanced Surveillance
The Complete Manual of Covert Surveillance

Copyright: Peter Jenkins 2003

1st Edition

Intel Publications
The Sett
Yate Lane
Oxenhope
Keighley
BD22 9HL
United Kingdom
info@intelsecurity.co.uk

A CIP catalogue is available from the British Library.

Printed and bound in Great Britain by:
Bell & Bain Limited, Thornliebank, Glasgow

Typesetting: Eye Spy Publishing Ltd, Skipton
Cover Design: Mark Ian Birdsall

ISBN: 0 9535378 11

Dedication

For Frank,
for showing me the way

Frank Jenkins

CONTENTS

Acknowledgements

Introduction

ACKNOWLEDGEMENTS

This project has been very hard work and I would like to acknowledge and thank the following for their support, their ideas, criticisms and assistance in bringing this book to its conclusion.

First and foremost, Mark Ian Birdsall, the editor at Eye Spy Publishing Ltd for his enthusiasm, hard work and effort during the typesetting and production stage.

Those many individuals who passed on their ideas and comments and assistance in the recent past.

And in no particular order:

Erik and the Team at Sector Protection AB, Sweden
Chris Mills at South East Solutions Ltd
Robert Armstead at RP & H Associates Ltd
Peter Consterdine at Chase Consultants
Sonic Communications Ltd
Audiotel International Ltd
Law Enforcement Picture Library (Steve McManus Photography)
Flight Images Ltd
Manorlands Sue Ryder Home, Oxenhope
Peter Barritt - if it wasn't for you, I would have no graphics
Janet Hadwin for the proof reading, thank you

The Trojan Project Training Team for their support who have helped make the past year an interesting one, now let's get our feet wet!

And finally, my family for their patience whilst working on this project and whilst being on the road.

Introduction to Advanced Surveillance

Three years ago, I wrote and published 'Covert Surveillance' as a basic manual of surveillance training. The book has been immensely popular within the security industry, with copies being distributed to many law enforcement agencies, investigators, security consultants and various military units all over the world. Since it's publication, over three thousand copies have been sold.

The reasons for producing this second and more advanced book are many. Some readers considered that the first book was too basic and wanted more comprehensive information on techniques and methods and so these have now been included. All of the chapters have been rewritten and extended, which includes plenty of more detailed information and there are also new chapters concerning; Legal Aspects, Anti and Counter Surveillance, Video Photography and also Technical or Electronic Surveillance.

Within the last two years in the United Kingdom, we have seen the introduction of the Human Rights Act 1998 and more importantly the Regulation of Investigatory Powers Act 2000. At the time of writing, these laws do not directly concern the private sector surveillance operator. However, if you are from a government enforcement agency or public body (or a private individual sub-contracted by a public body) you should be aware of these regulations and procedures and how they relate to surveillance operations.

Surveillance work is still a growing business. In the UK there is no legal requirement to be licensed to operate as a surveillance operator or as a private investigator. A number of security and trade organisations are currently lobbying the government to introduce licensing, something that is desperately needed to bring the security industry up to a professional standard by training and vetting.

This book is not only aimed at the person who is new to surveillance but also to those experienced operators who require a reference book and training manual. Surveillance cannot be taught and learnt by reading a book alone; it is a skill that requires the correct teaching and plenty of practice and experience.

Although an advanced training manual, this book is by no means complete as there are still some covert methods and techniques that have been deliberately left out which may compromise surveillance operations by their inclusion. All the methods and techniques mentioned here in this book are already 'out there' in the public domain, either by written material, on the internet, featured on television or appeared in films.

Covert Surveillance is a means of gathering evidence and information. It is a skill when put to good use, can provide the investigator with vital information when other avenues have failed. It therefore follows, that careful planning and preparation must take place before hand and surveillance should not be entered into lightly. Any course of action taken during a surveillance could be made available to the courts as part of advance disclosure if it is a legal issue that you are investigating.

Surveillance can be either from a static point, on foot or from a vehicle. In most cases a combination of all three is usually the case with the target even possibly taking public transport.

Everyone in the surveillance team has an important role to play, none less than the person who is actually watching the activity and reporting on it to the rest of the team. He or she is the eyes and ears of the surveillance and is in effect painting a picture. The more accurate the description, the better the evidence and the better response from the team as a whole. The most important factor for any surveillance team is communication. Without any form of communication between the team members (such as radios) you will have no surveillance team. As far as surveillance equipment is concerned, your radio sets are probably the most important asset that you will have in addition to your camera.

Prior to carrying out a surveillance, it is up to the investigator to educate and convince the client for the need of two or more operators to do the job properly. Although more expensive, it is cheaper in the long term and your evidence will be that much better. You should certainly highlight the problems that will be encountered when operating on your own such as; losing the target in traffic and/or having a compromise, which could cause embarrassment to yourself and consequently to your client.

Due to requests, I have included a section on 'single handed surveillance' but strongly recommend that this is not carried out, especially by the novice. However, even as part of a team, you will often find yourself on your own with no back up and so having to operate on your own for a period of time is inevitable. Acting as a team, surveillance is 'imposed' on a target but when on your own a target is 'followed' and there is a vast difference between the two as this book will explain.

Throughout the manual I have referred to the Surveillance Team and the Surveillance Operator. Within the Police, Military, Customs and other Enforcement Agencies, surveillance teams of eight or more operators can be used at any one time. It is appreciated that in the Commercial Investigation environment there are restrictions in both cost and manpower and it may not be possible or wise to use such a large surveillance team. However, I consider a team of three operators to be sufficient for most practical tasks and it is a three man team that I have based the techniques and methods described in this book.

Surveillance work is not all excitement! Very often the amount of time spent waiting for something to happen far outweighs the amount of time that the target is active. Long periods of boredom and frustration have to be overcome and this can only be achieved by personal discipline and experience. A mobile surveillance is not a 'pursuit' with the need to drive at excessive aggressive speeds, but is carried out in a calm, relaxed, professional manner and most importantly, with self control.

The surveillance operator is often tasked to obtain evidence. This evidence may be used in legal proceedings and the operator may have to give evidence in court. The defence (or prosecution) may attempt to discredit you, your evidence and how it was obtained in order to assist their case. As a professional you must be a credible witness and be able to justify your actions at all times which means keeping within the law. If you are acting on behalf of an Enforcement Agency or Public Body, you should be aware of the legislation and procedures regarding the Regulation of Investigatory Powers Act 2000.

There are no rules in surveillance. We cannot say that when a target comes to a halt then 'this operator does this and another does that', as every situation is different. However, there are guidelines which help us, there are certainly things that we should do and there are others that we should not.

Everyone charged with carrying out investigations and undertaking a surveillance in order to obtain evidence, should find this book both informative and educational. Surveillance cannot be taught by reading a book alone. It is a practical subject that requires realistic training, practice and most of all experience. This book is a guide and reference to support that training and practice.

A Word on Training

If you wish to learn more and put these skills into practice, then come and see us on one of our training courses. Over the past seven years we have been successfully providing surveillance training to many individuals and organisations from quite a diverse background. Essentially there are two types of courses that we run, those that are 'open' where any paying member of the public can attend and those that are 'closed' which are normally geared to Public Bodies or Enforcement Agencies where the paying public are not permitted to attend.

Course students having a roadside debrief

Four Day Basic Foot and Mobile Surveillance Course

Our basic four day course is very practical in content and over the years we have had students from various backgrounds, many of which have had no experience in the security industry but have used the course as a footing to enter into it.

Over the years we have trained:

> Experienced Private Investigators
> Novice Private Investigators
> Close Protection Officers (Bodyguards)
> UK Government Enforcement Agencies
> Institute of Trading Standards
> Environment Agency
> Allied Foreign Military Units
> Local Housing Authorities
> Students with no security background
> Investigative Journalists
> Security Consultants
> Researchers
> Professional Witnesses

As far as surveillance training is concerned in the Police or Military, the courses are run over a period of months, not days. We, or any other civilian training

company could not be expected to provide this type of training on a budget that your average person could afford and so a fine line has to be drawn when calculating costs and training time.

Courses are normally held over a four-day period with up to eight students. Four days is sufficient to teach and practice the basics (and some advanced techniques) for the student to go away and put into practice what he/she has been taught. All of the instructors are either former regular military, police or security service with a surveillance background. We also run two-week and four week advanced training courses for some specialist units and also a rural surveillance course that concentrates on all aspects of rural observation posts or OPs.

Unlike some security training courses, we do not carry out any type of physical training or the giving of abuse to those who appear to be below standard. Physical training is a personal thing and so if the students want to go for a run or do training circuits, they can do so after the day's instruction. Nor do we scream and shout at slow learners, if a student is weak on a subject he is brought up to speed in a manner that is condusive to learning. The student's time and money is better spent on learning covert techniques than running up hills and being verbally abused.

Open courses are normally held at a training facility in West Yorkshire for both men and women. It is an obvious advantage to be able to drive a car but we have had students on the courses that do not. This does not cause any real problems as they can still carry out every activity as the others, except get behind the wheel of a car! Quite often courses are held at the clients' venue, especially for larger security firms or Enforcement Agencies.

The course content is quite heavy as you will see from the training programme and some periods are spent in the classroom. This is unavoidable and essential to teaching the basic tactics and procedures that will be later practised on the street. We try to spend as much time as possible on the ground, be it on foot, mobile surveillance exercises, or carrying out recces. Surveillance is a practical subject and so you would not be expected to spend four days in a classroom.

We also provide all of the equipment, which includes covert radios, cameras, vehicles and fuel, so all the student has to do is turn up on the day with plenty of enthusiasm. By the end of the final exercise there is normally a good team spirit and the course is actually working as an effective surveillance team, it is surprising how steep the learning curve rises on the final day. In addition, many students meet like minded people and often 'network' and keep in touch after the course has finished. We cannot and do not promise any offer of employment after the course but we can recommend particular investigation companies to approach.

The four day course covers everything described in this book and below is a copy of the training programme.

One Day Electronics Surveillance Course

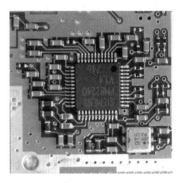

Another popular course is the one-day instruction on electronic surveillance. The aims of the course are to:

- Give an insight to the techniques used by the buggist

- Demonstrate how the devices operate and their limitations

- Demonstrate the reality from the hype

- Provide knowledge of concealment methods and how to avoid detection

- Provide knowledge of counter surveillance measures

- Improvised bugging

- Teach how to set up covert video systems

- Provide knowledge of the respective law

- Provide details of suitable equipment suppliers

This is not specifically a course in Electronic Surveillance Countermeasures (ECM) but rather the opposite which complements training for the ECM specialist. We teach the methods of how audio, video, telephone and computer eavesdropping takes place. If you are considering offering an ECM service to your clients, then this training is a must as a 'first step' course prior to spending money on ECM equipment.

The course covers a variety of topics and is crammed with vital information, as you will see in the training programme.

Rural Surveillance Course

This specialised course concentrates on all aspects of planning and carrying out a surveillance in a rural OP. Camouflage, concealment and stalking is taught and practised in a rural setting and students are also taught how to insert, occupy and work in an OP whilst being in uncomfortable conditions.

This course has been well received by those enforcement agencies operating in a predominantly rural area and covers:

- Planning, preparation and reconnaissance

- Camouflage and concealment

- Stalking

- Construction of a rural hide

- Map reading skills

- Insertion, occupation and extraction from rural OPs

- Still and video photography

- Preservation of evidence

This course was designed for the need for carrying out surveillance primarily from static rural OPs.

Professional Witness Training

This course has been attended by private investigators and local authority housing officials that carry out surveillance in relation to anti-social behaviour and nuisances on housing estates.

The course covers:

- Planning, preparation and reconnaissance

- Static surveillance methods

- Report and log writing

- Covert CCTV

- Preservation and continuation of evidence

- Eye witness testimony

- Legal procedure (RIPA, PACE and CPIA)

Not only does the course teach urban static surveillance techniques but also involves legislation relating to the recording of evidence that will be accepted by the Court. References are made to the Regulation of Investigatory Powers Act 2000, Criminal Procedure and Investigations Act 1996 and the Police and Criminal Evidence Act 1984.

ISS Training Ltd training venue in West Yorkshire

PETE'S TIP: Learn from the mistakes of others and not your own.

Course Training Programmes

Four Day Foot and Mobile Surveillance Course

Day One - Introduction & Foot Surveillance

DAY	LOCATION	TIME	EVENT
Day 1	Class	0900-0930	Opening Address
	Class	0930-1045	Intro To Surveillance
	Rest Room	1045-1100	Break
	Class	1100-1200	Communications
	Rest Room	1230-1300	Lunch
	Class	1300-1415	Foot Surveillance Tactics
	Training Area	1415-1630	Foot Surveillance Pt1
	Class	1630-1700	De Brief & Finish

Day Two - Foot Surveillance

DAY	LOCATION	TIME	EVENT
Day 2	Class & Area	0900-0930	Trigger Platforms
	Class	0930-1030	Planning & Recce' Reports
	Rest Room	1030-1045	Break
	Class & Local Area	1045-1200	Mobile Surveillance Tactics
	Rest Room	1200-1230	Lunch
	Training Area	1230-1630	Mobile Surveillance Practice
	Class	1630-1700	Exercise Debrief
	Class	1700	Finish
	Local Area	Night	Local Recce' Exercise

Day Three - Mobile/Foot Surveillance

DAY	LOCATION	TIME	EVENT
Day 3	Class	0900-1030	Legal Issues & Evidence
	Rest Room	1030-1045	Break
	Class	1045-1130	Video Photography & Covert Video
	Class	1130-1200	Mobile To Foot Technique
	Training Area	1200-1630	Mobile & Foot Surveillance Exercise
	Class	1630-1700	Exercise Debrief
	Class	1700	Exercise Brief & Finish

Day Four - Combined Skills

DAY	LOCATION	TIME	EVENT
Day 4	Class	0900-1000	Exercise Brief
	Area	1000	Deploy Exercise
	Exercise Area	1000-1545	Exercise
	Class	1500-1530	Return Stores/Vehicles
	Class	1530-1615	Exercise Debrief
	Class	1615-1630	Course Discussion
	Class	1630	Course Disperses

Training Programme

SURVEILLANCE TRAINING
ELECTRONIC SURVEILLANCE ONE DAY COURSE

DAY	LOCATION	TIME	EVENT	EQUIPMENT	REMARKS
Monday	CLASSROOM	0900-0915	OPENING ADDRESS		Admin
	"	0915-0930	TYPES OF TECHNICAL SURVEILLANCE	White Board	
	"	0930-1045	COVERT CCTV	Time Lapse, Covert	Body Fits
	TEA ROOM	1045-1100	BREAK		
	CLASSROOM	1100-1230	ROOM MONITORING		Analogue & Digital
	TEA ROOM	1230-1300	LUNCH		
	CLASSROOM	1300-1330	TELEPHONE MONITORING		Digital Systems
	TRAINING MODEL	1330-1500	PRACTICAL TELEPHONE MONITORING	Wiring models	Analogue Systems
	TEA ROOM	1500-1515	BREAK		
	CLASSROOM	1515-1545	COMPUTER SURVEILLANCE		
	CLASSROOM	1545-1615	LEGAL ISSUES		
	CLASSROOM	1615-1700	DISCUSSION / OTHER MATTERS		
	DISPERSE	1700	FINISH	Certificates	

Chapter One
Covert Surveillance

In this first chapter, we define the types and methods of surveillance, detail the qualities of a good surveillance operator and describe the areas that provide a grounding for the chapters to follow. First of all, what is surveillance?

DEFINITION

Surveillance is the continuous watching or listening (Overtly or Covertly) of persons, vehicles, places or objects to obtain information concerning the activities and identities of individuals

• Continuous

If we break this definition down, we say that surveillance is the 'continuous' watching. By this we mean that the period of observations have to go unbroken unless this fact is recorded. For example, if we commence surveillance at 7.30am follow the target for a number of hours, then at 10.00am we accidentally lose contact in heavy traffic. Half an hour later we manage to relocate him again and continue with the surveillance. This in effect has not been a continuous surveillance as the target has been out of your control for a period of time.

• Watching or Listening

Surveillance can be the watching or listening as defined in the Regulation of Investigatory Powers Act 2000 (RIPA 2000). The majority of our surveillance relies on what we see, therefore your eyesight (aided or unaided) has to be perfect. If we are obtaining information by using our ears, this can be carried out technically using audio listening devices or by being close to the target so that we can overhear conversation and obtain good intelligence.

*Camouflaged Observations
in a rural setting*

• People

Invariably we are concerned with individuals. There are many reasons why we put people under surveillance but essentially we need to record:

> • **Where they go**
> • **What they do**
> • **Who they meet**
> • **When they do it**
> • **How do they do it**
> • **Why they do it**

• Vehicles

Surveillance is often carried out in motor vehicles. This could be to monitor deliveries made by vehicle or because our particular target gets about by vehicle.

Although many people drive today, do not always assume that you will be following a target in a car. If a target leaves a house, a number of options are open to them, they can walk, cycle, get picked up, take a taxi, use public transport such as a bus, or as happened on one occasion leave on a pony.

• Places

Sometimes the surveillance of a place or premises could be the primary source of information and the activities of individuals may be secondary.

This could be a target's house or even business premises. We have often put surveillance on commercial premises in order to record what deliveries are made and by which company. In this case, we have not been concerned with the actions of any individuals at this time.

• Objects

We may carry out observations on an object. In the past we put a number of aluminium containers under surveillance that were illegally stored and stacked up in a garden. It was anticipated that certain individuals would take the containers to a scrap metal merchant for smelting down. It took many days of observations until the individuals were identified and caught moving them.

TYPES OF SURVEILLANCE

Overt Surveillance

Overt surveillance is an open observation where we deliberately let the target know that a surveillance is being conducted. This type of surveillance is not carried out often and normally acts as a deterrent to an illegal or illicit activity.

In the past we carried out an overt surveillance on a milkman who would purchase his milk from a cheaper dairy farmer rather than from the dairy franchise, he belonged to. He had been served an injunction forbidding him from buying his milk from anywhere but his franchise and as we could not maintain surveillance on him covertly (he drove an electric milk float at five mph in the dark at 4.00am) we went 'overt'. He was aware he was being observed and adhered to the injunction. One of the major disadvantages to this type of surveillance is confrontation with the target.

This police officer is totally overt. Note the video camera mounted alongside the SLR stills camera.

Closed circuit television cameras (CCTV) found in town centres and car parks could be considered as overt because we can see that they are there and therefore act as a deterrent.

Covert Surveillance

Covert Surveillance is a secretive watch where the target is not aware of our presence or activities. We are trying to be totally covert, not only should we be hidden from the target but also from anyone else not connected with the surveillance team. This 'anyone else' we call the 'Third Party' and we have to be very 'Third Party' aware whilst carrying out observations. Many surveillances are compromised not because a team member has been seen by the actual target but by other third parties such as local residents and passers-by, but more about third party awareness is covered later.

OBJECTIVES OF A SURVEILLANCE

Surveillance can be carried out for a variety of reasons, but essentially the following purposes could be considered:

• **To obtain evidence of a crime or unauthorised activity**

You may be obtaining evidence of a theft, fraud or other criminal act. Your evidence may be used in legal proceedings and so you have to preserve the integrity of that evidence which has to be obtained fairly and justifiably.

• **To obtain detailed information about the targets activities**

In order to build up 'the big picture', surveillance may have to be carried out in order to identify other 'players' or associates, their habits and routines.

• **To develop leads and information received from other sources**

Surveillance should provide the investigator with other sources or leads that can be followed up to provide further intelligence.

• **To know at all times the whereabouts of an individual**

Surveillance operations may be carried out on a target's premises the night prior to, and the same morning that a search or arrest warrant may be executed. It has happened by some agencies in the past where they have gone along to an address to execute a warrant, only to find no one at home after they have burst through the door.

• **To confirm the reliability of informant information**

At times we are trying to establish the truth and to prove or disprove facts. If information is received from an informant of an accusation, we cannot take it for granted that it is the truth. Therefore we will embark on an investigation to prove whether the accusation is true or simply malicious.

• **To obtain information for later use in an interview**

Enforcement agencies often interview suspects or targets (in accordance with the Police And Criminal Evidence Act (PACE)). A good interviewer should be confident and there is nothing better to boost that confidence than to have a surveillance report and photographs/video of the suspect carrying out the 'illicit act' up your sleeve. If there is denial from the suspect or a not guilty plea, you will be at an advantage.

• **To locate persons (by watching their haunts and associates)**

Quite often, people provide false addresses if they suspect that they may be under investigation or have a reason to suspect that they may be under surveillance. Keeping observations on a known place that the target frequents, like a pub for example, will provide us with a 'starting point' for a surveillance. From this surveillance we may establish where the target is residing. In a similar fashion, if we know that an associate frequently meets with the target, it may be easier to put surveillance on the associate.

• To obtain information for search warrants

Enforcement Agencies cannot simply apply to a Magistrate for a search warrant. Good evidence needs to be obtained to substantiate the need for such a warrant. Surveillance logs, covert video or photographs could provide the evidence required to obtain a warrant.

• To obtain evidence for use in Court

Much of the information obtained by investigators and surveillance operators is for legal purposes having been tasked by a solicitor or a commercial company. This evidence will often be used in criminal and civil proceedings. Because of this, our evidence has to be accurate, truthful and beyond reproach.

• To identify people

Quite often we may carry out a surveillance in order to know what a person looks like, so that further investigations or surveillance can be carried out at a later date. We may have to identify people to eliminate and/or discount them.

METHODS OF SURVEILLANCE

Surveillance can be conducted in various ways but are primarily divided into five groups. They can be conducted separately or in combination with others. Regardless of which method of surveillance is used, all rely heavily on teamwork. Surveillance should never be carried out single handed. It is a team effort and to have effective teamwork you require good communications such as radios.

Carrying out a single handed foot or mobile surveillance has many risks and would be considered foolish. Two problems you will encounter; being compromised, and also having a loss of contact. If you are on your own, there is a high probability that the target will spot you (especially if he is aware). To avoid being seen, we would tend to hang back and keep our distance, by doing this we now risk losing sight of the target and also risk losing contact altogether.

Single handed surveillance is not at all recommended but even in a team we often find ourselves the only person in the follow, as the other members have been held up or detached. At the end of this chapter there is a section on single handed surveillance for that reason.

VARIOUS METHODS OF SURVEILLANCE

• Foot Surveillance

• Mobile Surveillance

• Static Surveillance

• Technical Surveillance

• Combined Surveillance

Foot Surveillance

If we have planned our surveillance correctly we should have an idea whether our target will be going about his business on foot and so we have to prepare for this. The majority of our information and intelligence may be obtained whilst out on foot. A mobile surveillance by car is only a mode of transport which takes the target from A to B. It is only when he gets out of the car at the other end when we need to get in close and obtain detailed information.

Do not always expect your target to drive everywhere. Be prepared for him walking, taking a bus, train, taxi or even by bicycle.

There are two main reasons why an operator gets compromised, **multiple sightings** by the target and **unusual behaviour,** these two combined will definitely get you noticed. Therefore it is essential that foot surveillance is carried out in a team (more than one operator) both communicating with covert radios. Foot surveillance is covered in more detail in Chapter Six.

Mobile Surveillance

As mentioned, we do not advocate carrying out a mobile surveillance single handed. Mobile Surveillance is carried out to follow moving targets by car or other motorised vehicle, motorbike, or by boat and this should always be carried out in a team.

An essential ingredient in mobile surveillance is communication. Communication and radio voice procedure is **vital** to the success of a mobile surveillance. The mobile operators must be able to observe the target, provide radio commentary, navigate, and record information simultaneously whilst also driving safely.

The operator must be flexible, and be prepared for ever changing situations such as the target leaving his car and proceeding on foot, using public transport or meeting with others.

Static Surveillance

Static Surveillance is where the surveillance operator(s) are in a static position from where they can keep observations such as: a car, a building, hedgerow, surveillance vehicle, or even whilst on foot. Static Observation Posts (SOPs) can be **long term** or **short term** and may be divided into a further two groups Urban and Rural OPs depending on the local topography.

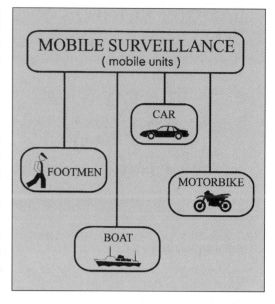

We may wish to conduct surveillance on factory gates to monitor the vehicles that leave or arrive. Initially we may consider sitting in the front of our car from where we can observe. If this is too risky, we may then consider using a surveillance van as an OP. If we cannot park in the street, there may be some form of building or structure from where we can watch. If this is still not possible but there is a thick hedgerow and a ditch we may be able to observe from here although this takes skill and experience. On a short term basis an operator on foot could also keep observation, providing he has a reason for being there, such as using a phone box or waiting at a bus shelter.

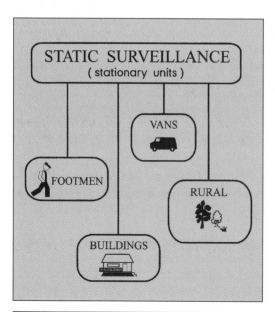

Static OPs are used when the target comes to your area of observation and you therefore await their arrival to be photographed. The Static OP is also used as a 'trigger platform' to inform mobile operators that the target is departing or arriving at a particular area such as the home or office. The different forms of Static OPs are covered in detail in a Chapter Eight.

Technical Surveillance

Technical or (electronic surveillance) is a means of gathering information with the use of technical devices such as:

> • **Radio Microphones (bugs)**
> • **Tape Recorders & Microphones**
> • **Telephone Monitoring Devices**
> • **Covert Video Recording**
> • **Vehicle Tracking**
> • **Computer Intercepts**

Each item will have its limitations, but used purposefully can be a very effective tool in gathering information and providing technical support to the other types of surveillance. Technical Surveillance is detailed in a Chapter Nine.

Combined Surveillance

The make up and formation of a surveillance team will be decided at the planning stage. The team leader should be able to make an appraisal and may decide what resources are required. For example, on a large task with a budget to suit, the team leader may decide to use a van for the 'trigger', two cars and a motor-bike for the follow. It may be expected that the target may go out on foot in a busy city centre, therefore an extra foot person may be carried in one of the cars.

So effectively we are using various resources in order to make up a combined surveillance team.

THE 'IDEAL' SURVEILLANCE OPERATOR

A good standard of surveillance by an individual or team can only be acquired by training, practice and most of all, experience. It is important not to stand out in a crowd and the operator should fit in with his surroundings at all times. His dress code should suit the area in which he is operating and his vehicle should be given the same consideration.

The ideal surveillance operator could be described as:

'Not too tall, too short, too fat or too thin, with no outstanding features, characteristics or mannerisms'.

And as being:

A Mr 'Nobody' but a Mr 'Everybody' who looks like Mr 'Average'.

Personal Qualities

Not everyone is born as the 'ideal' surveillance operator. The making of a good operator will depend upon that persons aptitude, training, practice and most of all experience. The ideal surveillance operator should ideally have the following qualities:

• Confidence

Confidence comes with training, practice and experience. A person on a surveillance that lacks in confidence will be a liability to himself and to the team. Regardless of what skills we have in life, if we are proficient in what we do we will have confidence in doing it and will operate that much better.

• Be quick thinking and quick to react

The surveillance target can be very unpredictable in his movements and actions, therefore we have to adapt very quickly to ever changing situations. We also have to react very quickly when using a radio in order to direct the team and let the team know of the targets movements and intentions.

• Have patience

Many people consider surveillance as being an exciting occupation. From the operator's point of view, many hours are spent doing absolutely nothing, waiting for things to happen and this waiting requires much discipline. When the action starts, you have to put yourself into gear and be where you are supposed to be, doing what you are supposed to be doing.

• Be capable of acting naturally at all times and move unobtrusively

What will get you noticed in surveillance more than anything else is unnatural behaviour especially whilst on foot, you should be seen but not noticed. On surveillance courses we see students standing in doorways quite often whilst trying to keep observations on the doorway across the other side of the street. After 30 seconds or so, the inexperienced operator starts to get itchy feet and shuffles about, craning his neck and generally moving about acting unnaturally, when all he had to do was stand still and do absolutely nothing.

In a similar manner, if there is a park bench nearby then why not use it and sit on it rather than stand beside it. If there is a telephone box, get into it and use it as cover but don't forget to pick up the receiver remember, we are trying to act naturally.

The way that we carry ourselves and move about is also important. In surveillance, we never run. If we run, we start to attract attention, not only by the target but also by third parties. The only time you should run is when you have a reason for doing so, such as running across a road, for example.

Whatever you do in surveillance give yourself a reason for being there and act naturally whilst doing it.

• Be able to fit and merge into a variety of backgrounds

The way you dress and act (including the type of vehicle you use) must suit the area in which you are operating. Carrying out a surveillance wearing a suit and driving a new vehicle will soon show out in a rough housing estate. Conversely, wearing scruffy jeans and T shirt and driving a wreck of a car would soon be noticed in a more *up-market suburbia.*

This does not mean that we cannot wear a suit during surveillance. If our target is expected to drive into the city and enter an office block, then we have to be similarly attired, common sense prevails.

• Have good eyesight and good hearing

The majority of our evidence comes from what we actually see, therefore our eyesight has to be good. It does not matter whether we wear glasses or contact lenses but as long as we can see clearly.

At times we may be very close to the target where we can overhear conversation and so our hearing has to be very good also. Remember, following a target on foot or by car is a means to an end, it gets us from A to B. It is only when they actually arrive at B when we are more likely to be out on foot in order to get close and obtain our evidence.

• Have a good memory

Combined with good eyesight and hearing, we must be able to remember facts and sequences of events. We may not always be in a position to write down events as they happen or commit them to dictaphone tape and so our memory and the information we remember has to be accurate.

• Be a good talker and actor

For a number of reasons we have to converse with the general public. It may be to satisfy the curiosity of a concerned member of the public (third party) who has seen you parked in a particular place. It may be to quiz a member of the public for information during your enquiries. As far as the target is concerned, you may have to speak to him to obtain information although this is not often done. However, he may even approach you if his suspicions are aroused and so you need to be able to act and talk your way out of a situation. Always have a cover story ready.

• Be physically fit and healthy

We do not necessarily have to be at peak fitness but at least reasonably fit so as not to be out of breath on a long foot surveillance. If you are taking part in an OP you also need to be reasonably healthy. Coughs and sneezes not only will get you noticed but will also impair your effectiveness as a team member.

• Be able to work on ones own initiative as well as a team

Surveillance is all about teamwork and communication. The longer that you work together with the same team, the better you will perform which will reflect in your results. However, as an individual, you must draw on your knowledge, skill and experience to act on your own initiative in order to make a contribution to that team.

• Be a confident and proficient driver with good navigational skills

Surveillance operators within the police and military must pass an advanced driving course prior to carrying out any mobile surveillance. In the commercial world, your driving skills have to be good in order to operate safely and effectively. After all, you would not expect a person who has just passed a driving test to be able to operate effectively as part of a mobile team.

If you are held-up by a slow driver, it is best to pass as soon as possible (safely!).

Within some Police Forces and Enforcement Agencies, mobile surveillance is often carried out with two operators per car (two up). One operator will drive and control the vehicle whilst the other operates the radio and deploys on foot when required. This way the responsibilities are shared between the crew and in some respects makes life easier for each individual, although going 'two up' does have its drawbacks. Within military surveillance organisations and especially on the private and commercial surveillance circuit, surveillance is often carried out single-handed or 'one up'.

When working 'one up' all of your skills have to be on the ball. You have to navigate, consider the targets intentions or movements, provide a radio commentary whilst simultaneously driving in a safe manner.

• Be astute to the local situation where he is working

A mobile surveillance can move at a fast pace and cover a large area. When entering an unfamiliar area, take stock of the situation and consider any 'third party'. You may have entered a rough inner city housing estate; crime could be rife, drugs being dealt and high unemployment. Many people may be on the look out for anything or anyone that does not fit in or looks suspicious. If you do not notice this quickly as you drive around the estate, you will soon find yourself being chased out or at worse attacked.

• Be proficient in the use of all equipment such as cameras and radios

This is an important factor and the surveillance operator has to be an expert in all the equipment that he uses. A professional soldier will know his weapon and radio inside out because he has to rely on them for his survival. A surveillance operator has to be able to handle and operate his camera and radio in a similar

fashion, it is his livelihood at the end of the day and many of us are paid for results.

Being able to follow a target and take him to a destination is only a means to an end in most cases, it is what actually happens at the 'other end' that provides the evidence and the results. If you miss that vital piece of evidence because you were unfamiliar with your camera or you did not know how to change batteries at the critical time, the job may have been a complete waste of time. Do not let your team or your client down by providing poor excuses because you were unable to operate your equipment properly.

Many people reading this book will pay 'lip service' to what I have just stated above, but I can assure you that equipment failure or rather failing to operate it correctly will be their downfall.

• Have a 'sixth sense', borne by experience

After training, the most important quality a surveillance operator can possess is experience. An experienced operator will get a 'feel' for the job and the way it is progressing. He will be able to predict possible outcomes, purely because he has 'been there' and seen it before. What we try not do in surveillance is assume what the target will do. An inexperienced operator will regularly guess and assume what may happen. This is dangerous, if you expect a target to do one thing, he will probably do something totally different.

PERSONAL APPEARANCE AND DRESS SENSE

The way that we appear and dress is very important, especially when operating on foot. The area in which you are working should govern your dress sense. The team should all be dressed differently, if we were all to wear black T shirt, blue jeans and black trainers we may as well carry out the surveillance on our own or at worst wear a uniform as we would all look the same.

Try to avoid clothing with contrasting colours or bright colours, also clothes with large logos may be remembered by the target. You should be seen but not noticed, it is advisable not to wear white trainers as these can also stand out especially at night.

If the target sees you once, unless you are wearing something outrageous, he should not be able to remember you. If he sees you a second time and a third time, again he should not be able to remember you; he will of course, if your dress is distinct.

If operating on foot at night, consider wearing darker clothing and be aware of faded jeans as these can shine like a beacon under fluorescent light or a cars headlights. Ensure that you also dress for the weather. The last thing you want to do is leave your car to carry out a foot surveillance on a wet and windy day when you have forgotten to take a jacket or coat with you. You will be the only one in the street getting wet and consequently stand out in the crowd.

In a similar manner, you should dress for the occasion if at special events. On a recent surveillance at a trade fair, the surveillance team all wore business suits because that was the dress of the day in order to fit and blend in. Jeans and trainers or casual dress would not have been acceptable in this instance.

It may be wise to carry a change of clothing with you, such as a lightweight or reversible jacket or a hat. A plastic carrier bag in your pocket can be used to put your jacket in, thus changing your overall appearance. If you have long hair, you could wear it down and then tie it back with a bobble.

You may wish to change your appearance by wearing a baseball cap, this is okay but do not continually put it on and off. The target may notice these frequent changes in appearance and so confirm suspicions. Be aware of wearing black 'bobble' hats or rolled up balaclavas, this will make you look shifty and be the focus of attention.

A change of outline is recommended by the removal of a hat or scarf, the putting on or off of a jacket, plain glass spectacles, or even putting your hands in pockets to change your overall appearance. Do not use disguises, especially wigs (even the best look obvious), an alert target will notice a change of appearance and again, will only help to confirm any suspicions. Do not wear sunglasses unless everyone else about you is also wearing them.

Always carry an amount of change and money with you. If the target gets onto public transport or takes a taxi he will have to be followed. If he enters a pub or café you may have to go in with him. Do not forget money for car parking, also some trolleys at supermarkets, airports, specialist stores require coins.

A baseball cap can alter your outline and appearance if worn at the correct time

TYPES OF TARGET WHO COME UNDER SURVEILLANCE

Many people can be the target of a surveillance for many different reasons and can come from all walks of life. Listed below are the various categories of awareness that the target may fall into. When obtaining a brief from a client, it is very important to know whether the target has been put under surveillance in the past, so do not forget to ask at the briefing stage. If they have, you should be told of the outcome, especially if there was a compromise, as you will have to be on your guard and adapt your tactics.

• Aware

The aware target disciplines and trains himself to look for 'watchers' and 'followers' and he may carry out anti-surveillance tactics as a matter of course every time he appears in the open. This type of target is usually from the criminal element that has knowledge of surveillance procedures or is a subject who expects to be followed.

They can be tricky to put under surveillance but a larger team and more covert tactics will enable you to control such a target.

• Unaware

This target does not consider or think about being watched or followed, and can be very complacent about his activities and is easily caught out. This does not mean that they are not up to no good. We have put people under surveillance in the past who were carrying out serious criminal acts but because they have been carrying out these activities for so long without being caught out, they become complacent.

• Semi-Aware

The target categorised as being semi-aware would expect to be followed or watched as they have a reason for doing so. For example, they are up to no good. This target will be alerted by noticing things that are out of the ordinary and unusual without having to look too hard. They may adopt some anti-surveillance tactics to identify whether they are being followed but may not really know what to look out for.

• Hidden

The target we consider 'hidden' is more likely to be the hard criminal such as the drug trafficker or terrorist. Rather than appear out in the open to carry out their dirty work, they would remain out of sight and have their 'foot soldiers' to carry out their work for them. If they do appear out in the open, (as everyone has to do at sometime) they will carry out counter surveillance measures and have a team of minders in order to protect them. This type of target is difficult to put under surveillance and can only be infiltrated by undercover operators or informants.

On a recent investigation we were asked to follow a sales manager. After asking the client if the target had been under to surveillance in the past we were told "no." The sales manager carried out some unusual manoeuvres as he left work in his lunch hour, but had no reason for doing so as we had no reason to suggest that we had been compromised. After talking to the client again, he stated: "Well, one of our staff did try to follow him in his lunch hour a couple of weeks ago but he was noticed, which is why we have called you in!"

The target is more likely to be aware in three specific places or times.

> **• When he is leaving his home or his base**
> **• When he is about to commit a crime or act**
> **• When he returns to his home or base**

Be alert and aware at these times and treat with caution.

• A 'Lost' Target

Losing contact with the target of surveillance is inevitable from time to time even when working with large teams. Losses occur for many reasons, for example, traffic congestion, busy roundabouts, traffic lights and lack of concentration. When this occurs the surveillance team must adopt a search pattern, (as described in Chapter Seven). It assists greatly if the operators draw on knowledge and background of the target in an effort to pick him up and continue the surveillance. The type of target who expects to be followed will undoubtedly attempt to lose the tail. Never let over-enthusiasm in not wanting to lose the target result in 'showing out' and compromising the surveillance.

If you find yourself following a lost driver he may carry out manoeuvres that you may consider to be 'anti-surveillance'. This could include; changing speed, suddenly stopping, making 'U' turns or going around a roundabout a few times. These are classic anti-surveillance manoeuvres but are also the signs of a lost driver, so you should decide at an early stage, is the target lost or is he trying to catch you out.

> **Losses happen, they are a fact of life and an occupational hazard in surveillance**

THIRD PARTY AWARENESS

Most surveillance work is considered 'covert'; we are being secretive about what we are doing and we do not want the target to know that they are under surveillance. More importantly, we need to remain unobtrusive from the general public and anyone else who is not connected with the surveillance whom we call the 'Third Party' and we have to be third party 'aware' at all times. It is the third party who causes at least 80% of all compromises and if not careful, the surveillance can be blown well before the target has appeared out in the open. These compromises are not unique to Neighbourhood Watch areas, whether we are working on the roughest estates, the remotest rural areas or the sleepiest suburbs, we have to have to be astute to the area in which we are working.

You may be quite a distance from the target's house or premises (possibly acting as back-up to the trigger) but you still have to take precautions when deciding where to 'plot up'. During a mobile or foot surveillance act accordingly, never run about or drive erratically and try not to be the focus of attention.

When Static

Your vehicle has to fit in with the area in which you are working in order not to attract unwanted attention. A scruffy beat up old car may soon invite curiosity if it is parked in a very *up-market* residential area, conversely, a brand new Cavalier on a 'rough' estate will not only be noticed but likely to be approached with no sympathy. If you are not using a surveillance van or an OP to 'trigger' the surveillance it may be that you have to remain sitting in your vehicle. In this event you have to be far away enough from the target for them not to notice you but close enough for you to identify them. There are a number of precautions that we can take to minimise bringing attention to ourselves. Some of them are common sense but they are easily forgotten.

• The colour and appearance of the vehicle should be nondescript, no *go faster stripes,* no headlight clusters, the obvious furry dice, nodding sheep, dogs or whatever animal of the week. The vehicle should be seen but not noticed.

• Do not carry out multiple 'drive pasts' of the targets address. If you have to take another look at the property get out of the car and walk, or ask another team member to do it.

• When parked turn your engine off, don't forget your lights and square off your wheels, you do not want to appear as if you are on a mission! Park pretty, a vehicle parked 'unnaturally' will stand out and if you are the only vehicle in the street, you will not last long.

• Park the vehicle where houses or offices do not overlook you. Use cover such as hedges, walls and other vehicles. If working on industrial estates be aware of CCTV cameras that may be present.

• Consider sitting in the passenger seat, any passer-by or local would naturally presume that you are waiting for the driver to return. Maybe sit in the rear seat with a jacket on a hanger over a window to provide some temporary cover, especially when taking photographs if there are people about. The small roller sun blinds that you get from motor spares stores can be useful.

Align your wheels. Do not give the appearance that you are on a 'mission'.

• Always have your 'working tools' close to hand so that they can be used at short notice. Your camera, binoculars, dictaphone, notebook and pen should always be within easy reach but remember not to have them in view so that passing third parties can see them. This does not mean that the car is clean and sterile but it needs to look natural and used.

• In warm weather when windows are open, keep your radio volume turned down, passers-by may hear transmissions.

After a while you may feel that you have to move your position or bring in a replacement because you've been there too long. Do not position your replacement in the same spot, this will only confirm the locals' suspicions and will possibly compromise another vehicle.

You may be part of a surveillance team and not even be the person that has 'eyes on' whilst waiting for the 'Standby'. The position where you park up and how you act is equally important, taking in the above same considerations. Take a good look around you and try to see yourself from the 'third parties' perspective.

"Nice cup of tea, dear?"

Be prepared to be approached and have a cover story ready. Remember in surveillance, that in everything we do we must always act naturally, adopt an identity and have a reason for being there. Cover stories are many and may be left to the imagination but ensure that your reason for being there is realistic and probable. I have got away without being approached for hours just by wearing a fluorescent vest or having the vest thrown over the dashboard. Also in the past I have told enquirers that I intend serving a Divorce Petition on someone who is trying to avoid me and am awaiting for them to return.

Have the right attitude with enquirers, being off hand with people will only irritate them and attract further attention. Be confident and try not to act 'shifty'. Whatever you do, do not pretend to be the Police, not only it is illegal, it will attract more attention than you wished for.

The Burglar, the Fraudster, the Nutter and the Lover

Remember that your target may not be the only person in the street who has a reason to be under surveillance. I am sure that in an average street of sixty properties there is at least one fraudulent Social Security claim, a personal injury insurance claim, a drug dealer, a matrimonial affair, someone that was recently burgled and the local 'paranoid' expecting the men from Mars. All of whom have reason to be on their guard. Just because you are watching one property, it does not mean that all the other properties are considered safe.

During Mobile Surveillance

Whilst taking part in a mobile surveillance we have to drive in a manner that will not attract attention. Aggressive, high speed driving is not only dangerous but you will be noticed and reported. If you are in a situation where you are directly behind the target and held at a junction, act naturally and avoid eye contact in the mirrors. Do not slowly creep up behind the target vehicle hoping that he will not notice you, he will. You are a member of the public on a public road and have every right to be there and so act normally.

When Stopping

If your target comes to a halt, do not stop directly behind without any cover and definitely do not screech to a halt. You may need to get your camera up and running so have a quick look about you before you start filming including above you. Most passers-by may not even notice you or even care, but it only takes one person to see that you are up to something. Consider jumping into the back seat using a jacket on a hanger as cover.

Deploying on Foot

If you have to get out on foot, don't ever run (unless you're crossing a road or wearing a pair of running shorts!). Anyone seen running in a public place attracts attention, people are naturally curious and they will want to know why. Again, act naturally and give yourself a reason for being there.

Rural Areas

Plotting up in rural areas can be difficult and the fluorescent jackets come in handy once again. On one occasion I pretended to be a 'check point' for a Scouts hike (complete with scout badge on the dashboard, maps, flask and radio) and got away with it three weekends in a row because the 'cover' was realistic for the area.

To summarise, in order to minimise 'showing out' to third parties, adopt the following procedures:

• Be aware of the area and situation in which you are operating.

• Be extremely observant of your surroundings when close to and away from your target. Do not forget to look above you at buildings.

• Be aware of Neighbourhood Watch Schemes or criminal elements.

• Keep all equipment such as radios and cameras out of view and covered up, This also applies to any paperwork, files or photographs. Do not let radio transmissions be heard through an open window.

• When using the radio, camera or binoculars, be discrete.

• Use the other team members to keep a look out and back you up if you have to do something you consider risky; for example, photographing items in the rear of the target vehicle.

• Adopt an identity always give yourself a purpose and reason for being there.

• Have a convincing cover story ready if a member of the public challenges you, make it realistic. Curious neighbours will not tolerate excuses such as 'mind your own business'. This will arouse their suspicions further and they are likely to inform the Police.

> **Never inform a member of the public that you are the Police or intimate that you are the Police. It is a criminal offence to impersonate a Police Officer.**

Do you inform the Police of your presence and of the investigation?

There are many different trains of thought on this matter, both have their advantages and disadvantages but as a rule we do not usually inform the Police of our activities and this decision has been borne by past experience, unless it is to our advantage.

When working in 'rough areas' where there is a high risk of crimi-nal element and the operators

could be under threat, we would inform the local Police of our presence providing them with our vehicle details. In the past we have provided the Police with our details when working in particular areas. Not long after being on the ground, a Police patrol car would arrive in the area searching and trying to spot us. This has happened on many occasions and does nothing to assist our cause but to alert the locals.

You will undoubtedly be stopped and questioned by the Police on occasions, therefore always carry some form of identity card to prove to them that you are an investigator. You are not obliged to give specific target details, but politeness and common sense prevail.

Short Story

A few years ago we carried out a surveillance on a sales manager who was suspected of skiving off work and so he was put under surveillance in order to see what he did during the day.

We carried out the job by triggering the surveillance with a van, which I was in. Covering the left option some half a mile away was Mick in a car, he was parked up in a country walk car park where members of the public would arrive in order to walk their dogs. Half a mile covering the right option was Keith on a motorbike who used a lay-by to lie up in. The target did not leave until 12.30pm and drove for about six miles to his place of work, when he arrived, the team re-plotted. As we were doing so, Mick and I were separately 'hemmed' in by the Police using plain cars and were questioned as to who we were and what we were doing, they were obviously upset and on a mission, at this time.

It turns out that the Police were from the regional Drugs Squad and they had had Mick under surveillance through no fault of his own. Unbeknown to us, the Police had an OP in a public house that overlooked the country car park and were waiting for their targets to arrive. From their OP they would have seen this person arrive early morning (Mick) who would just sit in his car and do nothing, now and again he would take a drink from his flask or be seen to talk on his mobile phone.

After a while another person (Keith) would arrive at the car park dressed in black and riding a motorbike, he would exchange words with the driver of the car for a few minutes and then disappear. Half an hour later or so the rider would return for another chat and a share of a flask of coffee. To the Drug Squad, this was 'it', Standby Standby!

When our target went mobile, so did the Police! During the journey, the Police obviously switched on to the fact that Mick was not alone as he was backed by me in the van and Keith on the bike. It was revealed that the Police suspected that Mick was driving with his own 'counter surveillance' team behind him and so they decided to 'strike' and stop us when they did.

As team leader, I was given a telling off from the Police sergeant and was asked if I ever tell them when we operate in certain areas. I said 'No' and told him my reasons, 'We always get the 'nosey copper' who comes looking for us' and so compromises the job. The sergeant was sympathetic and agreed, we were asked to stay away from the country car park for the remainder of the week.

Being Compromised *(Showing Out)*

During any covert operation there is always the risk of 'showing out' and being compromised, experience and training will help to minimise this risk. You will either show out personally, your vehicle will be noticed or it will be your actions that draw the targets (or a third parties attention). As an operator you will only have so many 'lives' and having too much exposure will lose them one by one.

As we have already discussed, it is imperative that you are aware of the targets surveillance awareness level before embarking on the job. Consider what your aims and objectives are, as these will dictate how you operate on the ground and will not put you at unnecessary risk. For example, if we are on foot surveillance in a city centre, investigating a target who is suspected of fraudulently copying music CD's we do not want to go in too hard and too close when it is not necessary. He may go into a newsagent, a clothes shop, and a chemists. When he does stop, although you have to keep control over him (by covering the door to the shop) you have to decide whether it will be of an advantage to go in with him. Unless you are going to achieve anything, then I would recommend that you stay out. If he was to visit HMV or Virgin Megastore then (remembering the aims and objectives) I would most certainly get an operator in close if it was of evidential value. What you have to decide is:

What am I going to <u>gain</u> against what am I going to <u>lose?</u>

By going in close you may gain some good intelligence but in doing so, you will lose a number of lives. Guard your exposure levels if you have had a 'close encounter' with the target. If it is necessary that you get in close again, let the team know that you are 'warm' and so a different operator can go in close, remember, it is all about teamwork.

An experienced team member will know if he has been seen or noticed. Often we are very sensitive when the target looks in our direction and we are over cautious to the extent that we think we may have shown out. Should this be the case, you should make a quick decision whether the operator or team should pull out of the surveillance.

There are two main reasons why we may be compromised. You constantly have to be aware of:

- **Multiple Sightings**
- **Unusual Behaviour**

• Multiple Sightings

As previously mentioned, you should be seen but not noticed and be the ultimate 'grey' person. After the target has seen you on several separate occasions he will remember you, especially if you give him a reason to, by the way you dress or act. Therefore, if you are working as a team, each member should have their share of taking the eyeball and thus sharing the exposure levels. Always ensure that you are behind or to the side of the target (out of his 10 to 2 o'clock of vision) and never in front, avoid eye contact at all costs.

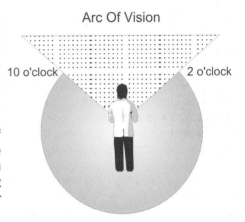

Arc Of Vision

10 o'clock   2 o'clock

If you can see the target, the target can see you.

• Unusual Behaviour

They way we act and carry ourselves is very important and if not checked will soon have us noticed. During the early stage of surveillance training courses we find that the hardest thing for a student to do whilst on foot is to stand still and do absolutely nothing. The target may have entered a shop, and so the team are plotted up waiting for him to emerge. We see them hiding behind shop doorways

'peeping' out, suspiciously leaning against lamp posts, pretending to look in a shop window which has not been used for years or standing against a park bench rather than sitting on it.

Their actions are unnatural and therefore come to the attention of others. Admittedly, it is not easy trying to act naturally whilst having a hidden agenda (the surveillance) and this only comes with practice and experience.

Be aware of 'fiddling' underneath your jacket if adjusting your radio settings, a passer-by may notice the radio set. In addition, try to avoid constantly touching your earpiece, as it is unnatural and an aware target will notice you.

At the end of the days surveillance, give yourself a score out of ten to establish your 'heatstake'. Nine out of ten would suggest that you have had hardly any exposure to the target, whereas a four out of ten would put you at a high risk level. If it gets to this stage you would want to consider not getting too close the next day or involved at all.

Standing Down

If you feel that you may lose contact with the target, and by keeping close you risk showing out, then it is better to let him continue and experience a loss. If you are compromised you may not be able to return to that target for a number of weeks, it is far better to let the target run and remember...

There is always another day

Teamwork

Any experienced person trained in surveillance, would tell you that to carry out a surveillance single-handed is not only difficult but down right foolish. Not only do you run the risk of losing contact with the target in traffic but also and more importantly, you run the high risk of compromise and possible confrontation. As a rule, I do not carry out single handed surveillance, if I did, I would feel that I would not be doing my client any favours, I would not be acting professionally, and feel that I would be deceiving the client into handing over their money when the odds are against me.

What do I do if a client says, 'I can't afford for more than one person?' I turn the job down and let some other person in the phone book take it on and bid them good luck.

Teamwork is essential in surveillance and in order to have effective teamwork you require effective communication. The team have to be fully conversant with radio voice procedure and radio discipline, you have to trust the other members of the surveillance team and act on your own initiative without being told where to go and what to do.

A team leader has enough to think about and should not have to continually direct the surveillance. If the target stops, the team should carry out a set rehearsed drill in order to control him (covered in Chapter Seven), the team leader should not have to direct individuals with particular tasks unless he has to.

In the early stages of training, all three members of a three man foot surveillance team tend to get 'eyes on' the target all at once. This is expected, as we are keen and it is only natural that we all want to be in control of the target. Remember, only **one person** has to see the target at any one time, the 'eyeball', who is giving a radio commentary and painting this picture of events for the benefit of those that are out of view of the target. During this time, if you are not the eyeball, you have to listen to the commentary and totally trust what is said.

PRINCIPLES OF SURVEILLANCE

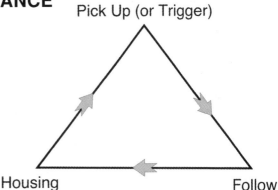

Principle Stages or Phases

The surveillance operation can be broken down into the following three stages which we will discuss in detail.

The **pick up,** the **follow** and the **housing** is a continuous cycle of events or phases of a surveillance.

What this means is that the team plot up in the area and obtain a trigger. The target comes out of his house and gets into his car (the Pick Up phase). He then drives for two minutes (the Follow phase) and stops at a newsagent shop and enters (the Housing phase). The cycle then starts again, we obtain a trigger on the newsagents door, the target comes out and gets into his car (the Pick Up) and drives away (the Follow), after a short while he arrives at his place of work (the Housing). So you see this sequence of phases can happen many, many times during the days surveillance.

The Pick Up Phase

The start of the surveillance can be the most difficult and critical part and is known as the *Trigger* or *Stake Out.* The whole operation can go wrong at the outset if the target cannot be 'triggered' and initiated away from his house or premises. It is the task of the trigger person to keep the target house or premises under observation in order to alert the remainder of the team when the target departs. It goes without saying that if we don't have a trigger and a pick up, then we will not have a follow.

There are various types of trigger to consider, more detail of which is described in Chapter Two on foot and mobile surveillance:

- Static Trigger

- Mobile Trigger

- Technical Trigger

- Informant

Static Trigger

The trigger 'platform' can be from a car, a van, building, hedgerow or any other static point from where the target's premises can be covertly observed, he could easily be out on foot if he has a reason for being there (such as in a bus shelter). During this phase the trigger man plays the most important role in the team, he has to be alert at all times and have total concentration on the target premises. The operator has to be covert and should not be in a position that is obvious. An aware target is more likely to be alert at the pick up phase and anything unusual will be noticed, remember this will be his territory and his domain and he will know it better than you.

At the first sign of possible movement by the target, the trigger man puts the team on 'Standby'. He should provide the team with a radio commentary of the targets actions such as getting into a vehicle or any other activity. He should also state the targets intended route, the route being taken and a description of the target or what he is wearing.

This is probably the most crucial part of surveillance, especially if you have no knowledge of the target or his intended movements. A target is likely to know short cuts and back street routes in the local vicinity to his house and may well take them to avoid heavy traffic. Therefore the target is more at risk of being 'lost' in the first few minutes of the surveillance than at any other time.

Mobile Trigger

If, for a number of reasons, the target premises are not able to be kept directly under static observation you will not be able to provide a static trigger. This situation normally occurs when a mobile target stops somewhere unexpectedly or stops in a cul-de-sac of a housing estate or industrial estate.

The only option open to you would be to place an operator at each possible exit of the route that the target may take on his departure (this is what we call a secondary stake out). If the options are many, the team leader should decide on which exit is the most likely to be taken. All the team members should know the whereabouts of their colleagues and the exits that they are covering.

Do not pretend to break down in order to get a trigger - it looks too obvious!

In this instance all the operators have to be alert and observant at all times, as the target may be travelling at speed or suddenly depart in a different vehicle. Once the target has been identified as being mobile, the other team members should be informed immediately to ensure that they close up and continue the surveillance.

Whatever you do, don't simulate a breakdown! I know that it works well on the TV but that's TV. If I were to pretend to break down and put the car bonnet up I would expect the target to drive past laughing at me or at least offer a hand to fix the problem. If the target does not offer to help, I am sure that a kind-hearted neighbour will, and before you know it you will have a 'standby' but your engine has been stripped down and is spread out all over the pavement.

Take up a position where you will not be noticed or attract unwanted attention. Consider sitting in the passenger seat, any passer-by would naturally presume that you are waiting for the driver to return.

Technical Trigger

Electronic devices may be utilised to provide a trigger to alert the team that the target is going mobile. These technical triggers can either be audio or video operated and are discussed in Chapter Five on specialist equipment.

Audio Trigger

A simple audio transmitter can be covertly placed in the target area (such as a garden hedgerow) in order for you to listen (via a receiver) to what is happening in the area, such as doors opening/closing and vehicle engines starting.

On one occasion we had to trigger a target out of a block of flats where we could not observe the front doors or the car park. A cheap VHF transmitter was concealed in the foyer of the flats which transmitted the sounds of people walking down the stairs and using the main doors. We were able to listen in and put the team on 'standby' every time we heard the main door slam shut. This provided us with the extra time we needed to put a footman in position to cover the exit, in order to check and confirm the target leaving.

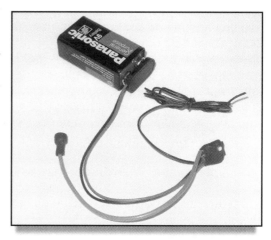

A similar system can be used whereby a signal being transmitted to a receiver will warn of a vehicle being started. The device is covertly attached to the under-side of a vehicle by magnets, where it remains dormant until the vibration of the starting engine switches it on and activates a transmitter. The transmitted signal is received on a scanner or dedicated receiver (held by an operator), which gives a beeping tone when activated. The operator can then put the surveillance team on standby and await the target going 'mobile'. More information on this device is found in Chapter Nine that deals with electronic surveillance.

Video Trigger

A video camera located in a hedgerow or concealed in a car and pointing at the target, can transmit video pictures by UHF/VHF or Microwave signals. An operator, (located nearby in a safe area) can trigger the surveillance by watching the target area on a small television monitor. When activity is viewed on the screen, the team can be put on standby. The camera will be able to tell you what direction the target is travelling and possibly what he is wearing and any other relevant details.

A hollow tree log conceals a transmitting video camera

These devices are not extremely expensive and can be used to good effect when other conventional means fail or are considered too risky. Cameras are now available that can transmit over the mobile phone network (GSM) and therefore have an unlimited range.

The Informant

If the team can be informed on an imminent move of the target, this could greatly assist their effectiveness at the pick up stage. We had a surveillance not so long ago where we had to follow a company vehicle suspected of making unscheduled stops. It was difficult to 'trigger' without risking compromise but the client was able to telephone us and give prior warning. He would ring saying that the vehicle was loaded and would be departing within the next five minutes. This allowed the team to relax somewhat in safe areas until we were put on standby, the team would then close in and take up their positions for the follow.

To have a client or person to inform you of a standby is a luxury that is rare but very welcome when the chance arises.

The Follow Phase

The Follow is the term used when the target is on the move. He is considered 'mobile' if he is in a vehicle and 'foxtrot' if he is on foot. At this stage you know where the target is and he should be under control at all times so the team can be deployed to the best advantage.

During this phase we do not always follow like ducks in a line but surveillance is 'imposed' upon the target and there is a vast difference, especially when on foot. The various techniques and methods used during the follow are discussed in Chapters Six and Seven. Do not always assume that the target will drive a car, he could travel by taxi, bus, train, bicycle or any other mode of transport.

The Housing Phase

Housing the target after a follow can often be a tricky part of any surveillance and could be the most important. The housing could be a very short stop or could be a long wait. Obviously the length of the stop will not be known until the next 'standby', therefore on a stop, the team have to act with a sense of urgency, re-trigger the target and re-plot at the location straight away. Once this is established (pick up/trigger phase) only then can the team settle down and relax a little.

By identifying the address or premises that the target enters may provide that final, vital piece of information you have been waiting for throughout your surveillance. You may have observed the target for many days but he now suddenly arrives and parks his vehicle in an unknown street. It is imperative that an operator is close enough to identify the property that he enters and this may possibly mean deploying an operator on foot as quickly as possible to identify the address. Whilst doing so the team have to hold their positions in the event he goes mobile again.

In the next chapter, we will cover the various methods of planning and preparation that is required before deploying on the ground.

PETE'S TIP: *Generally speaking, if the team has a good pick up, they will have a good follow.*

Chapter Two
Planning & Preparation

It is essential that detailed planning and preparation should be carried out prior to any surveillance taking place. It would be foolish to just turn up at the target address on the morning of surveillance and hope that it goes well, because it probably won't. It is true to say that the old cliché below is fact:

Prior Planning and Preparation Promotes Peak Performance

Is Surveillance the Solution?

When obtaining your brief, decide whether surveillance would provide the answer to your clients' problem. There are many reasons why a surveillance should be carried out but could the answers to your investigation be found out by other means?

Pretext telephone calls, pretext visits to neighbours, or even speaking to the target of inquiry on a pretext can often lead to the results that you require. In addition, covert video cameras or controlled audio monitoring may provide you with information that you can act upon, without having to resort to lengthy and costly surveillance.

The Regulation of Investigatory Powers Act 2000

Law enforcement agencies or a public body such as local authorities in the United Kingdom are unable to carry out a surveillance at will on a target that is of interest to them. They have to act within the Regulation of Investigatory Powers Act 2000 (RIPA) which is the legal enforcement arm of the Human Rights Act 1998 (HRA). Prior to the surveillance taking place, correct authority and permission has to be obtained by an authorised person of rank or grade. More information regarding RIPA 2000 is covered in Chapter Three.

What are your objectives?

Look at the whole picture. You may have to break the investigation down into phases or objectives so that each one can be realistically achieved, do not expect to achieve the result that you want all at once.

For example, you may be tasked to investigate possible copyright infringement of your clients' product, you may be asked to establish:

> **Where the target premises are?**
> **Who is involved, how many staff?**
> **How are they manufacturing the product?**
> **What materials are used to make the product?**
> **Who is supplying the materials?**
> **What is the level of sales and distribution?**
> **How are they marketing the product?**

Each objective could be tackled individually or put into groups or phases of the investigation. With forethought and planning at this stage, you should be able to achieve your aims in a logical order an often achieving one aim will provide information leading into another.

The Surveillance Option

Considering that surveillance is the option that you have decided to take, to formulate a plan, you will require as much information as possible from the client concerning the target of enquiry and the circumstances.

It is essential that you establish whether the target has been under surveillance in the past and that you establish his 'awareness level'. It will affect how you plan and conduct your own surveillance.

Having decided on your aims and objectives, you should then work in a methodical approach to arrive at a viable plan. Regardless of whether the task is a simple short single handed affair, to a complex team task requiring the use of static and mobile operators. All require some form of detailed planning and essentially there are two main areas that we need to look at, prior to going out on the ground, the **target himself** and the **start point.**

If we can gather as much information about the target at the clients briefing or before we leave the office the better prepared we will be. Every surveillance needs a 'start point', we have to start somewhere. This is often found to be the target's home address, his place of work or a place where you intend to pick him up and we can look at the two as different issues.

THE TARGET

Attempt to obtain as much information about the target as possible, this can be provided by the client or by your own enquiries. Ensure that you get as much as possible from the client, with a bit of thought you may be able to gain more information from them, they have a habit of forgetting important facts or they do not understand our methodology.

Points to consider are:

• **Target's name, nick-name or aliases**

Ensure that you know what the target is known by. Your target may be called Paul but all his life he may have been known by his middle name or nickname. If you have to make pretext enquiries and you have his name wrong you could arouse suspicion.

• **His address and associated addresses**

Ensure that the address that the client provides is correct; you do not want to be watching the wrong property. Double check with the Electors Register if at all possible and the phone book. Invariably, if you telephone directory enquiries and ask for the person by name, they should tie it up with the address you have. You will be told either; the telephone number, whether it is ex-directory or that the number is not listed. If the latter is the case you will know that the target is not responsible for the bill and/ or may no longer be resident. If you have to ring directory enquiries, do so on a landline or

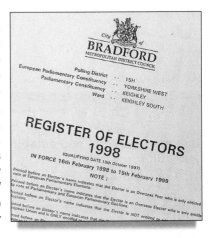

payphone rather than from a mobile phone. Mobile directory enquiries are often a couple of months behind in their information.

If there are any associated addresses you should have information relating to these such as work places, family or colleagues.

• **Telephone number**

It is always handy to have the target's telephone number. If you arrive at the address for the surveillance and there has been no movement after four or five hours, the curtains have not opened or the milk is still on the doorstep, you would be thinking, 'Is anyone at home?' A realistic pretext call to the house would tell if there is anyone about and at worst, hear an answering machine providing a mobile number that you did not have.

On a past surveillance we could not identify whether it was our target or his son that had left the address but we decided to follow him just in case. The trigger person was left in situ in the event that we were wrong but whilst there, he telephoned the target's address and asked for him by name. We were lucky as the reply from a female was, 'I'm sorry but you have just missed him, he left two minutes ago'. Bingo!

In another enquiry we could not identify the target who was with two other similar looking men. By having his mobile phone we were able to video all three of them at once whilst another member of the team rang him on his mobile. The one that pulled out his mobile to answer it was our target.

If you do talk to someone on pretext, make the call realistic and never hang up on anyone they only get suspicious. What would you think if someone did it to you?

> **PETE'S TIP:** *If the target is ex-directory, visit the local library and search the historical Electors Register for the name of the person that lived there before. If you cross-reference this name with the phone book of the same year, you may find out their telephone number. This same number may be used by the target who has since gone ex-directory.*

• Description

A full up to date description of the target should be obtained. In Chapter Three we deal with how a description is given use this as your checklist.

• Is a photograph or video available of him?

If you can get a photograph or a piece of video tape then use it. Ensure that the photograph is up to date and there have been no changes (hair styles, facial hair and so on). Make sure that you study the picture, take it with you and do not pay 'lip service' to it. I have often seen investigators with photographs but they have not really looked at them or compared it with the subject.

A few years ago, we carried out a surveillance on the Isle of Man and we were armed with a photograph that was some 15 years old (taken when the target was 18). It was difficult to identify the target at first but certain characteristics could be seen in the picture and so it proved useful.

• Mode of Transport

Not everyone drives a vehicle; therefore you need to know the targets mode of transport as you will have to prepare for travelling by the same means. He could use public transport, get a lift, walk, or ride a motorbike.

If he uses a vehicle you need to know the vehicle, make, model, shape, colour, registration and any other identifying features.

• Family details or other occupants of the household

The Electors Register should identify all the adults in the household, although it is accepted that the records are not always accurate. It would help to know how many male adults lived in the house (if your target is male), you do not want to follow the first one that leaves which may be the wrong person.

In addition, if there are children known to be living at the house, you can expect them to leave for school on their own or have them taken on the 'school run'. This is a time when the team need to be on the alert for possible movement.

Families often live in areas we call 'tribal'. By this we mean that other members of the family live in the same area or estate. You may find that the target's sister lives three doors down, the parents live two streets away. This is handy to know, especially if you have a loss as it is somewhere to search. In addition, if the target stops at one of the addresses, you know whether to go in hard or not, as it may not be that important to the investigation.

• Employment

The details of the targets work or trade are required. The type of job, his workplace or area, his position, the shifts and hours he works including overtime. If he is unemployed, the day, time and place he signs on for unemployment benefits may also be of use, especially if you have to pick him up there.

• Habits or Routines

You should be aware of any habits or routines, that the target may have. Recently, a target of ours would leave his house and religiously stop at a nearby newsagent in the morning to buy his paper and cigarettes. On the third and fourth day of surveillance, we never plotted up at his home address (which was difficult to cover) but at the newsagents and had no problems picking him up.

You should also know the targets haunts such as pubs, clubs and also information relating to his friends or associates.

SOURCES OF INFORMATION

There are various sources of information that can assist us at the planning stage:

• The Client's Brief

Obtain as much information from the client that you can. Be aware of the client that is over zealous with information that can often be misleading or inaccurate. You should decide what is important and what is not.

• A pretext visit to the target's address to identify him

If you have to call at the target's address, do so only as a last resort and preferably use someone that will not be involved in the surveillance. If you do, do so with caution and have a realistic reason for being there. Enquiries to locate the previous occupant (who's details you have obtained from the Electors Register) are a reasonable excuse for a visit. Do not make up an elaborate story or deliver the worlds biggest bunch of flowers, people only get suspicious.

• Telephone Directories

There are many directories available which contain information, BT Directories, Thompson's Directory, Yellow Pages, Business Pages and so forth.

• Trade Directories

Trade Directories that list specific professions such as Kelly's and Dunn and Bradstreet are available in most reference libraries .

• Electors Register

As mentioned above, this is a good source of information but soon may no longer be available to the general public. Treat the register with caution as the information contained can be inaccurate. At the time of writing, some libraries in the UK are being advised not to divulge Electors Register information to a person unless it relates specifically to them. This has come about due to a member of the public taking the local authority to court for a breach of their human rights. The local authority were accused of this breach because they were selling on personal information to commercial organisations for advertising purposes.

• County Courts Register

Information can be found as to the targets credit history and whether they have a history of debt.

• On Line Computer Searches (Equifax & Experian)

Organisations such as Equifax and Experian collect financial data such as credit history and credit ratings that may be of use to you, and this information can be obtained 'on-line' to those who subscribe or via the Internet. They also have a 'locate' facility, which can be used to trace a person if they have moved. Quite often, a person will move house and then obtain a credit card or other form of credit, when they apply they have to provide their previous address. When the data is entered into a computer, the new address gets tied in with the old address.

• The Internet

A wealth of information can be obtained from the Internet. There are websites such as **www.192.com** which lists the Electors Register and phone book all in one. There is **www.upmystreet.co.uk** and **www.multimap.com** where you can enter a postcode and you will see a map of the area together with an aerial photograph. You will also be able to find out the cost of property, the nearest schools and pubs in the immediate area.

Information can also be obtained from the many directories and information providers such as Companies House.

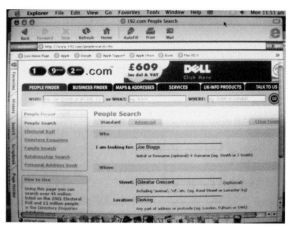

• Local Press

The local press can often help you with information, especially if you have a particular date or point of reference. Many local newspapers also have a website, have a look at these in the event that they also have their own search engine. If you search for your target's name, if he has been written about in the paper, it should come up with the story.

• Companies House

By applying direct or going via the internet, you can obtain information about limited companies, their accounts and the directors. It is possible to provide them with a name and address and they will be able to tell you if that person has any appointments within any companies.

• Local Enquiries & Local Knowledge

It may be necessary to make some local enquiries from local shops or neigh-bours but do so with caution and remember to have a realistic cover story ready.

TRIGGER POSITIONS

Prior to mentioning recce reports we will spend some time discussing the various trigger options that are available to us. Every mobile or foot surveillance will need an operator to trigger the surveillance and call the 'standby' in order to put the team into action.

Only one person needs to trigger the target away and the remainder of the team have to rely on this person to call a standby. They have to trust him to be alert, not to fall asleep or be distracted.

What normally makes a surveillance operation difficult or easy is the way that it is triggered.

Triggers are in some way the same as Observation Posts (or OPs), but they are primarily used to trigger away a mobile or foot target rather than keep a continuous static observation. Some similarities in this chapter will also be found in Chapter Eight regarding Observation Posts as much of the principles are the same.

Regardless of which type of trigger you choose to use, for each one you must consider the following from your position:

• Can you see the Target?

From your position you must have a clear and unobstructed view of the target, be it the front door of the house, the gate, vehicle or a road junction. Be aware if the view is likely to become obstructed by passing or parked vehicles or pedestrians.

You need to be close enough to identify the target but far away enough for him not to see you.

• Can you observe the approaches?

The approaches to the target should also be able to be observed. This will help when waiting for a target to arrive and give you that extra time you may need to have your camera up and running. When the target departs you will need to inform the team of his direction of travel. Additionally you may need to observe if any third party approaches your location.

• Are you overlooked?

Be aware of people above you in buildings or offices. If they are constantly looking down on you, you do not want to attract any attention. Be aware of CCTV cameras, especially on industrial estates.

• Can the target see you?

In surveillance we say: *'If you can see the target, the target can see you'.* [Unless you are behind oneway glass or buried in a hedgerow]. You do not want to make your trigger position obvious or have it attract attention. The trigger position should not be right outside the target's front door but out of his '10 to 2' o'clock arc of vision.

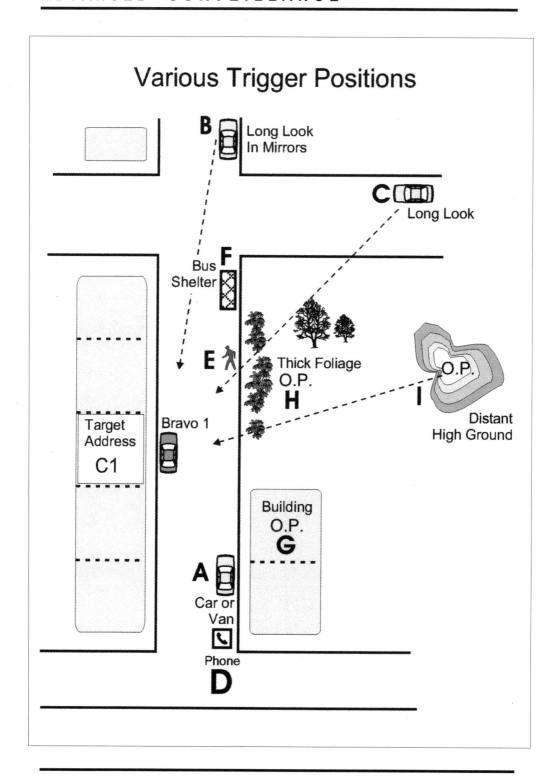

Various Trigger Positions

B Long Look In Mirrors

C Long Look

F Bus Shelter

E

Thick Foliage O.P. **H**

I O.P.

Distant High Ground

Target Address C1

Bravo 1

Building O.P. **G**

A Car or Van

Phone **D**

This area may be the target's home, his domain and territory, therefore he may notice anything that is unusual or out of place.

• Can you move in and out safely?

You will need to move in and out of this position without attracting attention or curiosity. Remember, for everything that we do in surveillance, we have to act natural and have a reason for being there.

TRIGGERS FOR A MOBILE SURVEILLANCE

Together with the street plan opposite, we can look at the various trigger positions open to us. The scenario is that we would expect the target to leave the house by the front door, depart on foot or get into his vehicle and go mobile.

Trigger Positions

A From a car in this position we are behind the target and so he does not have to pass you when he goes mobile. You can see the front of the house, the car and also the next junction so that you can call a change in direction. When on plot, ensure:

- You are out of the '10 to 2' arc

- You are not overlooked

- Not parked right outside someone's window

- Do not appear as if you are on a mission (turn off lights, engine and square your wheels)

- Sit in the passenger seat

- Have a reason for being there

- Have a cover story ready

A We could also insert a surveillance van (see Chapter Eight on Observation Posts) where we can afford to get a little closer to the target. Ensure:

- All of the above points

- You are driven in and extracted, do not drive in yourself then jump in the back of the van if it is risky

B   From your car you are well away from the target. You could position yourself to look directly at the target or use your mirrors. If using your mirrors, rehearse to yourself what you will say on the radio if the target goes mobile. Even experienced operators often give the wrong commentary as through the mirrors everything is back to front. Consider:

> • When the target goes mobile he will be towards you

C   Still using our car or van, we do not necessarily have to be in the same street, from this 'long look' position, we can see from across the park or waste ground. Consider:

> • This 'long look' is good if the target is aware

> • If you have been on the surveillance previously and it is not necessary to go in close in order to identify

> • Be aware of obstructions to your view

D   A foot person could be deployed to provide the trigger although this is usually a short term measure. Many phone boxes have advertising graphics over the windows, through which you can see through from the inside but cannot look into the from the outside which provides us with good cover. If using the phone box consider:

> • You will have a good all-round view

> • If someone is in it, then wait. It will provide you with additional time to hang about on the street

> • Once in the box, **Pick Up The Phone!** You have to act naturally and someone in a phone box not using the phone looks suspicious

> • If you cannot hold the position for too long, get another team member to take over

> • After the Standby, you should be able to be picked up by a mobile unit or return to your own vehicle

E   If there is no cover but you still have to deploy a footman, do so with caution. You will get away with it so long as you have a reason for being there.

On a previous surveillance, we had to identify the driver of a car as he left a cul de sac. The only way to get close enough was to actually stand on the curb side, so one of the team, dressed in overalls, clutching a sandwich box and a rolled up newspaper giving the appearance of waiting for his early morning lift, was able to identify the driver and call a 'standby'.

An OP was located these chevrons in order to trigger a target in this rural area

F In a manner similar to the telephone box, the bus shelter gives you a reason for being there. Again this is only short term as you can only let one or two buses go past without getting on. If there is a queue then get into it, what better cover. If a queue starts to build up behind you then let it. If a bus arrives, all you have to do is step back and let everyone else get on. Do not feel out of place doing this, everyone else will be in their own little world and minding their own business as they get on the bus and probably not notice you.

G If there is a building opposite (used or unused) then this could make an ideal trigger location. Caution should be used when entering and leaving the location and you have to decide whether to extract the trigger when the target goes mobile.

H Surveillances become tricky or difficult when you cannot get a decent trigger. In the past 13 years in the private sector, I have carried out many surveillances where we have had to use a 'rural' trigger from a hedgerow, ditch or thick foliage, even in built up areas.

It works, but it takes skill, planning and discipline and for obvious reasons is specially suited to former military personnel with training in covert movement, camouflage and concealment. Once your trigger is in position, he has to consider what to do after the target goes mobile. Does he:

• Stay where he is until the end of the day, he may have to trigger the target in and out numerous times during the day

- Should he self extract, return to his vehicle and attempt to re-join the team

- Should he be extracted by another team member and go with his vehicle.

I   A distant rural trigger could also suit your purpose, why get in close if you do not have to?

Three years ago, we carried out a three-man team job in Ireland; the target lived in a very rural area, which was criss-crossed with single track roads. The only place to trigger the target from was on a small hill some 600m from the house. The team had nowhere to lie up as there were no lay-bys and there was no real reason to be in the area and so they had to keep on the move. With the aid of a spotting scope (powerful telescope), I was able to trigger away the target who was picked up by the rest of the team. Once they housed him, I was extracted and picked up.

Attempt to trigger from as far away as possible. It is not necessary to be in close proximity to the target.

PETE'S TIP: *When checking the tyres pressure on your car, do not forget to check the spare!*

TRIGGERS FOR A FOOT SURVEILLANCE

Together with the street plan of a precinct shopping area, we can look at the various trigger options open to our foot team. The scenario is that we would expect the target to leave the burger bar where he works by the front door in order to establish where he goes during his lunch hour. There are no rear exits to the premises, he normally leaves for lunch at 12.30pm.

Trigger Positions

A Having a person trigger from inside the burger bar has its advantages and disadvantages. On the plus side:

> • You can obtain a good identification, the staff may wear uniforms and look similar, so identification is important
>
> • You should not miss the target out, as you are fairly close
>
> • You should be able to give a direction, when he leaves
>
> • You may be able to cover any other exits if there are any

On the minus side:

> • You may be in close and so a sighting may cause you to lose a 'life'
>
> • If the shop is very busy, you do not want to miss him out

B The phone box would be an ideal option as it is short term, but we know roughly when we can expect the target to leave. From the telephone box:

> • You will have a good all-round view
>
> • If someone is in it, then wait. It will provide you with additional time to hang about on the precinct

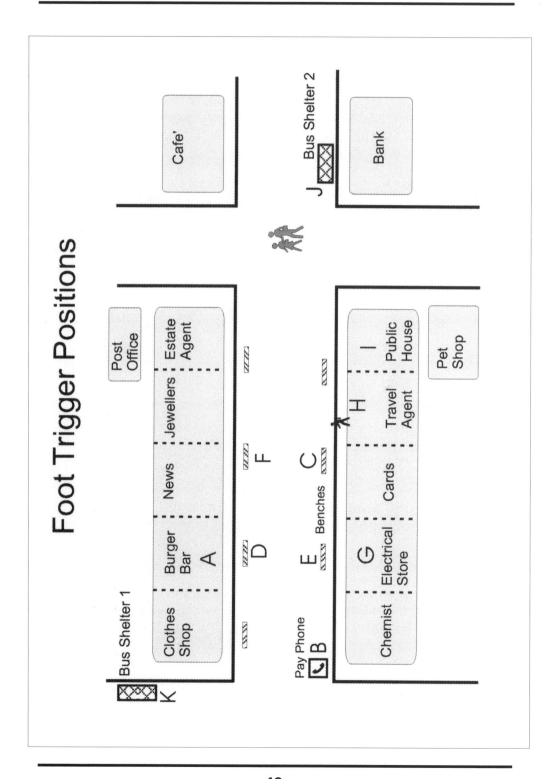

Foot Trigger Positions

• Once in the box, remember to pick up the phone

• If you have outstayed your welcome, get another team member to take over

C   There is no reason why we cannot sit on this bench as it is out of the '10 to 2' arc of vision. If using benches:

• Make sure you sit on them; it is what they were designed for! If you are stood up and leaning against it, it may look unnatural

• If the bench is occupied but there is a space, then use it, what better cover to have than other people. It may be difficult to talk on the radio in close proximity of others but there are ways around it, as described in Chapter Four on communications

• Just sit there and do absolutely nothing. Do not get fidgety after a few minutes and then look for another position, just stay where you are, and act naturally. Remember, you are a member of the public in a public place and you have a right to be there

D   This bench offers a number of disadvantages:

• You are too close

• You will be in the '10 to 2' as the target exits

• You will have to constantly turn your head around to look at the door, which would appear odd and unnatural

E   From this bench you have a direct line of sight to the front door but you are at a disadvantage due to the reasons listed above.

F   From this bench, you will be in the '10 to 2' if the target comes out and turns left (his left remember). In addition, you will be constantly looking over your right shoulder to look at the door, which would not appear natural.

G   You could place the trigger in the Electrical Store but:

• You are in the '10 to 2', although you may have cover from within the shop

- It may be difficult to pretend to browse and keep your eye on the target. Remember, as soon as you look away, the target will be out and gone

- If you are not acting naturally, you will become the focus of attention of store assistants and store detectives

H From outside the travel agents (or any other shop doorway), there is no reason why you can't just stand and wait. STAND STILL, do not *bob and weave* about or you will attract attention. This sounds obvious but we find many inexperienced students moving about as if they have ants in their pants!

- You are out of the '10 to 2'

- You have a clear view across the street

- You have a reason for being there (you are waiting)

- Do not 'peep' around corners

- A travel agents window is designed to be looked into (similar to an estate agents)

- If you use a shop doorway, make a cursory check of what the shop is selling. Loitering outside jewellers is not recommended

I If you have a clear and unobstructed view of the doorway from the pub, then there should be no reason why you should not consider this trigger position.

- You do not really want to consume alcohol, so keep to soft drinks

- Obtain a position where you would look naturally in the targets direction

Other Team Members Positions

Once you have established a trigger, that person will have control over the target. You may have another two members on the team. They have to be positioned away from the target, remember, only one person has to see the doorway. These team members should be off the street but for now we will place them in the following locations, as we will cover this aspect in more detail in Chapter Six that focuses on foot surveillance.

J   At the bus shelter you are far enough away from the target and you give yourself a reason for being there. If the target walks away from you, you can take up the follow. If he walks towards you, you can take control from where you are as you do not have to move to anywhere.

K   From this bus shelter, you are 'off the plot' which is good. You will be listening in to your radio for a standby and a direction of travel. If the target comes out and goes left (his left remember), you can take up the follow. If he walks towards your corner, you can take control at the corner without you having to move.

We now have the beginnings of teamwork and are 'imposing' surveillance on the target rather than just following him.

The Start Point

Prior to any surveillance being carried out a reconnaissance visit should be made of the target location, it is visited to enable you to plan and organise the task. This could be residential, business premises or an area in which the target is going to be or likely to visit.

You will carry out a pre-surveillance (or Recce) in order to help you decide:

- The size of the team
- The make up of the team and which type of vehicles to use
- What equipment you may need such as cameras and radios
- Dress code to suit the areas and target
- The time spent on the surveillance, which affects the budget
- Length of time spent on the ground
- Likely trigger points
- Any possible hazards

There are certain things that we can do before actually going out on the ground. By looking at a map, be it an A-Z or an Ordnance Survey, we can establish what type of area we will be operating in such as urban town or rural village. If we use the internet and a web site such as **www.multimap.com** we will get various scales of mapping together with aerial photographs.

Once we have arrived in the area, there are certain things that we should look out for and a sample of a recce report is found below detailing the factors that should be known or considered.

Aerial Photographs

Aerial photographs can be a very useful aid to planning if they can be obtained. Many parts of the United Kingdom can be found on the Internet site **www.multimap.com** some of which have a very good detailed scale. As part of our pre-surveillance routine, this site is checked for aerial photographs.

Use the photographs with caution as shadow will make features look different, and check the age of the photograph as buildings and roads can change very quickly. Consider also the seasonal change, a photograph taken in the summer will not show a true likeness during the winter.

PETE'S TIP: Ensure that your vehicle first aid kit is regularly checked and replenished

Ref: PB/1212   **RECCE REPORT**   C/S Zulu
                                                          0935hrs 7/8/03

A1:   Kenneth Minter

          Description:- Age 32yrs, short black hair, slim build.

B1:   Black V.W. Golf   Reg: YG03 GKL

B2:   Dark Green Landrover Discovery   Reg: ??

C1:   3 The Bank, Haworth Road, Fulford, York, YO9 6CB.   Tel: Ex-Directory.

A-Z: O.S North Yorkshire Page 74, D/5.   O.S. Grid 068363

Route: From the junction of the A64 and A19 (south of York), head north on the A19 for 1 mile until you reach a roundabout for Sainsbury's supermarket. Take the third option at this roundabout onto Haworth Road. 'The Bank' is 200m further down on the nearside

RV: Sainsbury's supermarket - Fulford.

Area: 'The Bank' is a short cul-de-sac comprising of 3 newly built properties located on a slope and set back from the road in an older part of the town. Haworth Road runs along the bottom of a small valley and is a fairly busy street with local shops either side and a number of rows of Victorian style terrace houses. It is a neighbourhood watch area.

C1:   C1 is a detached property in the the top right corner as you enter the cul-de-sac. There is no access to the rear. To the left of the house is a garage with a white painted door and there are flower baskets hanging from the front porch.

Escape Route: There is only one way out onto the main Haworth Road by car or foot.

Bravos: A black VW Golf Reg' YG03 GKL has been seen on the drive. In the garage was a dark green Landrover Discovery, no registration noted.

Trigger: **Primary:** Trigger can be given from a car in the lay-by on Dark Lane (see sketch) from here you have a clear unobstructed view of C1 and can give a direction of travel.

Secondary: A van can be positioned on Haworth Road (see sketch) with no problems. However, you will only be able to see the entrance to 'The Bank' but not get 'eyes' directly on C1.

Back Up: There are many locations for mobile units to lie up safley and cover the options.

Sightings: A male was seen at the time fitting the description of A1. Wearing a white T shirt and red shorts.

Misc': 192.com lists Kenneth and Alice Minter only.

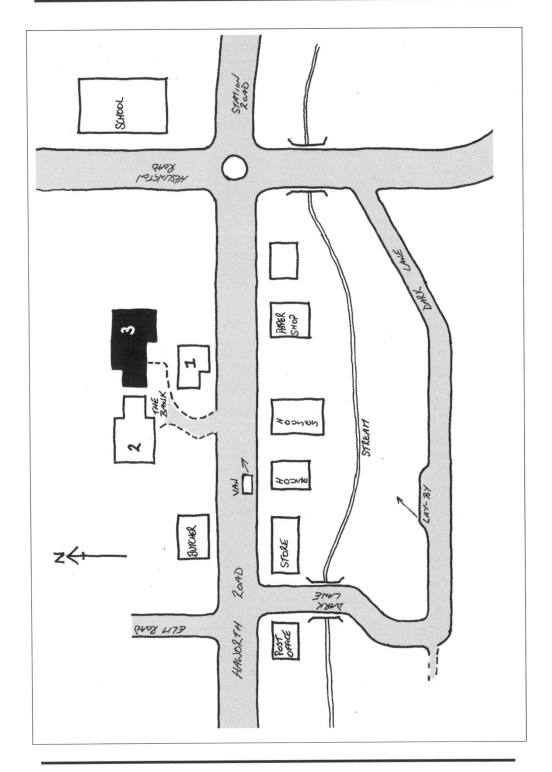

Views from layby on Dark Lane. C1 on the right with open garage door

View from Haworth Road towards entrance of 'The Bank' on the nearside

RECCE AND PRE-SURVEILLANCE REPORT

This should comprise of a report together with a sketch map or diagram of the area.

A-Z

Provide details of the A-Z map book including page and grid reference.

Approach and Route

Operators may have to make their own way to the target's location rather than be led there by the team leader. Directions should be taken from a main local landmark to the target or to a central RV (rendezvous point) and include the distance. In this example we have used Junction 36 of the M62 Motorway.

Rendezvous

The team do not want to meet up in the target's street for obvious reasons, therefore an area within a short distance should be selected where you can RV on the morning prior to the job starting such as in a car park or lay-by. Ensure that the RV is safe so that the team would not look suspicious by meeting at this location early in the morning.

This RV or another may be selected as an emergency rendezvous (ERV). In the event the team have to split up and meet at a later time such as after a loss or a compromise.

Area in General

Ensure the address is correct and provide a description of it, especially if it is difficult to locate. If there isn't a number on the door double check. Carry out a recce 360 degrees surrounding the target premises (do not just consider the front of the premises, there may be hidden access to the rear).

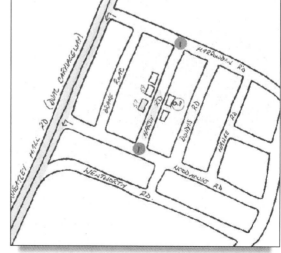

Draw a sketch plan of the immediate area indicating all routes in and out by vehicle or on foot and consider how many observation (trigger) positions are available and their locations.

Target Address

Provide a detailed description of the address; it may be that you can only carry out one 'drive past' and so the more information you have, saves wasting valuable 'lives'. Point out any identifying features that can easily be recognised from a distance such as prominent satellite dishes, window frames or painted porches.

Escape Routes

The possible routes that the target can take must be identified. Do not just carry out your recce from your car, get out and have a look around. You must identify all mobile (road) routes and any *foxtrot* (footpath) routes that he can possibly take. Do not forget to look 360 degrees surrounding the target address and check for exits at the rear as these may also have to be covered.

Vehicles (Bravos)

List the details on any vehicles sighted at the time of carrying out the recce. You may have to pay a visit early morning or late evening to establish further vehicles. Note how they are parked as this will not only tell you which direction they my go in, but also tell you from which direction they have arrived.

Trigger Locations

Every surveillance needs a trigger. Therefore you need to decide how you are going to get an 'eyeball' on the house and how you will trigger the surveillance. Consider all the options that have already been discussed but keep it simple, there is no need to have a complex plan in order to get a trigger.

Covering at nearby junction may be the only option available (secondary trigger)

Position for Back Up & Support

Locations could be identified where the mobile units could 'lie up' in a safe area (Lie Up Position or LUP) whilst waiting for a 'standby'. This is often personal preference and left to individual operators once they are on the ground. The position has to be within radio range and should not attract attention from 'third parties'.

Sightings

Sometimes you will see the target or any other person during the recce. Make a note of descriptions and of any timings.

Miscellaneous

Note anything else of interest that may be of value to the team. Note any particular hazards that may present themselves such as: parking problems, traffic conditions, security patrols and neighbourhood watch. Carry out a radio check from where you intend to put your trigger or OP.

Get Out of Your Car!

A number of years ago we carried out a surveillance on behalf of a firm of solicitors who specialised in personal injury insurance claims. They had asked us to carry out a surveillance on a particular claimant who was claiming some £250,000. They stated that a surveillance had been carried out by a private investigation firm in the past and that they had more or less stated that the job was impossible to do having been compromised.

This particular agency, headed by a former Police officer claimed to be 'surveillance experts' and were members of a professional association. Below is an extract from their report.

Dear Sirs,

Thank you for your instructions in the above matter.

Further to our telephone conversations in respect of this case. I would advise that we have had little success on this operation, and have not been able to catch Mr. Lewis engaging himself in any untoward physical exertion in contravention to his claim.

As I stated at the outset, we were always going to experience problems due to the location of the subjects home address. It is an isolated property on a minor, but relatively busy road running between Romanby and Cleves. There are numerous isolated properties along this stretch of road, the residents of which use the road frequently. Consequently any parked vehicles soon attract unwanted attention from the locals and the 'jungle telegraph' soon goes into action. I am fairly certain that we have blown out at least four vehicles in attempting to carry out static observations on this man.

We have managed to obtain a very short passage of film showing him walking his dog at the rear of the premises, but this is really no more than what he states he is able to do when interviewed recently by Mr. Boyle.

We have observed him driving but again this was only whilst visiting local farms, and on one occasion a brief journey into Cleves and back which I suspect was merely an attempt to 'draw' the observation vehicles.

We have given passing attention to the property whenever we have been in the area, in the hope of obtaining some random evidence, unfortunately we have had no success on this aspect either.

Regrettably, for the reasons outlined, I do not feel that we will be in a position to achieve any positive result for you in this matter as we have reached the authorised fee limit, I cannot justify incurring any further costs.

We took a look at the area and instantly realised why the investigators were compromised, the target lived at a farm house set back from a very long straight Roman road in a rural setting, any vehicle parked along here would have been treated as suspicious.

However, the job was very easy to carry out using a little imagination. By putting in a rural OP in the edge of a wood some 200m from the rear of the farm you could observe the garden, the vehicles and the end of the driveway.

A target that lives in a tower block can be difficult to trigger

By using a three man team, one in the OP and the other two in cars located in the vicinity, we were able to successfully carry out surveillance of this particular target. We obtained much video evidence of him in his garden and also away from home which contradicted his claim, he lost his £250,000.

If carrying out a recce, look at the whole picture. Check 360 degrees around the target property and think, 'How can we trigger this?'

The Plan

On completion of the recce, you will have to formulate a plan of action in order to carry out the task, within the bounds or restrictions placed on you by the client. Points to consider are:

- The size of the surveillance team

- The make up of the team, male or females or both

- Team vehicles, such as cars, vans, motorbikes

- Communications and radios

- Any specialist equipment required, such as night vision optics

- How you will record your findings and evidence (surveillance logs, dictaphone tape)

- Calculate the man-hours into actual costs to provide an estimate of costs including mileage, accommodation and incidentals

It is essential that a recce is carried out at the target's address and that as much information is obtained about him in order to plan and carry out a successful surveillance.

REMEMBER - KEEP IT SIMPLE

Chapter Three
Evidence & Law

If we are going to carry out a surveillance, we obviously have a reason for doing so and the ultimate aim may be to gather information that will be used in a court of law as evidence. That evidence has to be accurate, fair, credible and accounted for. We must record our observations in a manner that is accepted by the courts and in particular the Criminal Procedures Investigations Act 1996 (CPIA) especially as our evidence will most likely be disclosed to the 'other side'.

We may have carried out a surveillance which required detailed planning, had taken place over a number of days and a positive result achieved. But if we had not recorded our evidence correctly (especially if it is a criminal matter) then the whole case could be thrown out of court on a procedural matter.

European Convention on Human Rights

In the United Kingdom we recently saw the introduction of the Human Rights Act 1998 (HRA). In relation to surveillance, there is the legal and enforcement arm of the HRA, so called the Regulation of Investigatory Powers Act 2000 (RIPA). In simplified terms, this means is that any 'Public Body' has to be accountable for carrying out surveillance in order to prevent a persons human rights being violated.

By Public Body we mean:

- Police
- Customs & Excise
- Inland Revenue

- Department for Work & Pensions (Social Security)
- Institute of Trading Standards
- Environment Agency
- Local Authority
- Social Services

Or any other organisation that comes under the public umbrella. Private Investigators, Surveillance Operators or Security Consultants are not public bodied and so technically they do not have to seek any approval or authorisation in order to mount a surveillance. If a private investigator is carrying surveillance work on behalf of a public body, that body should still obtain authorisation in accordance with RIPA.

By being accountable, surveillance by a public body has to be:

- A last resort when all other investigative means have failed

- Authorisation for surveillance has to be applied for

- Authorisation for the surveillance operation has to be granted by a person of rank or grade

- Authorisation and the actual surveillance has to be carried out in accordance with RIPA 2000

When a Public Body seeks authorisation, the Act requires you to follow human rights principles. In particular, you will be required to justify why you propose to use the powers in terms of **legality, necessity** and **proportionality.** You must ask yourself the following questions:

- Is my proposed action lawful?
- Is it necessary?
- Is it proportionate? (using a sledgehammer to crack a nut)
- Is my action non-discriminatory?

KEY DEFINITIONS

Surveillance (under RIPA 2000 (Section 48 (2))

> • Monitoring, observing or listening to persons, their movements, their conversations or their other activities or communications

> • Recording anything monitored, observed or listened to in the course of surveillance and

> • Surveillance by or with the aid of a surveillance device

• Covert

> • If, and only it is carried out in a manner that is calculated to ensure that the persons who are subject to surveillance are unaware that it is or may be taking place

• Directed Surveillance

Surveillance is **directed** if it is covert but not intrusive and is undertaken:

> • For the purposes of a specific investigation or specific operation

> • In such a manner as is likely to result in the obtaining of private information about a person and

> • Otherwise than by way of an immediate response to events or circumstances, the nature of which is such that it would not be reasonably practicable for an authorisation under this part to be sought for carrying out the surveillance

• Intrusive Surveillance

Surveillance is **intrusive** if, and only if, it is covert surveillance that:

> • Is carried out in relation to anything taking place on any residential premises or in any private vehicle and

• Involves the presence of an individual on the premises or in the vehicle or is carried out by means of a surveillance device.

• **Residential Premises**

• Any premises occupied or used by a person however temporarily, for residential purposes or otherwise as living accommodation including hotel or prison accommodation that it is so occupied or used. Such accommodation might be in the form of a house, yacht, a railway arch or other makeshift shelter. It includes hotel rooms, bedrooms in barracks and prison cells but not any common area to which a person is allowed access in connection with his or her occupation of any accommodation.

• **Private Vehicle**

• Any vehicle which is used primarily for the private purpose (family, domestic & leisure use) of the person who owns it or of a person otherwise having the right of use to it. This does not include a person whose right to use the vehicle derives only from having paid, or undertaken to pay, for the use of the vehicle and its driver for a particular journey. A vehicle includes any vessel, aircraft or hovercraft.

CODE OF PRACTICE

Pursuant to Section 71 of the Regulation of Investigatory Powers Act 2000

This code applies to every authorisation of covert surveillance or of entry, on or interference with property or with wireless telegraphy carried out under section 5 of the Intelligence Services Act 1994, Part III of the Police Act 1997 or Part II of the Regulation of Investigatory Powers Act 2000 by public authorities which begins on or after the day on which this code comes into effect.

PETE'S LINK:
www.homeoffice.gov.uk/ripa/code_of_practice/covert_surveillance.htm

Although Article 8.2 of the HRA uses the phrase 'Public Authority', private individuals should be aware of the Article which deals with the **Right to Respect For Private and Family Life** (Article 8.1).

8.1 Everyone has the right to respect for his private and family life, his home and his correspondence.

8.2 There shall be no interference by a public authority with the exercise of his right except such as in accordance with the law and is necessary in a democratic society in the interests of national security, public safety or the economic well being of the country, for the prevention of disorder or crime, for the protection of health or morals, or for the protection of the rights and freedoms of others.

We mention these Acts as the private surveillance operator should be aware of them in the event that he is asked to carry out surveillance on behalf on a public body. Any public body or enforcement agency involved in investigation or surveillance work should already be familiar with procedures involved with obtaining authorisation, the HRA and RIPA 2000.

Privacy

In a recent court case relating to a 'personal injury' surveillance, private investigators had obtained video film of their target carrying out physical activities which contradicted his claims. The conclusion made by the district judge at the court hearing, was to the effect that the claimant (target) was exaggerating his claim in view of the video evidence.

The video film was taken from a public place but detailed activity filmed through his front door and windows. The claimant and his legal team used this as a basis to apply for an appeal against the district judge's decision, on the grounds that the video film was inadmissible as it infringed the claimants human rights under Article 8.1 (as it was a contravention to his right to privacy). The judge added that the evidence (video tape) **was** justified under Article 8.2 and added that, so long as the surveillance operative did not trespass onto private property to obtain the film of what can be seen with the naked eye, then that evidence is lawfully obtained. Thus the application for appeal was not granted.

The Human Rights Act 1998 together with the Regulation of Investigatory Powers Act 2000 can be a minefield and very confusing to the lay person. In summary, I would suggest that you continue with your surveillance as you have been in the past but keep in mind what you would consider as morally acceptable, fair and how **you** would expect to be treated in the same circumstances.

PROTECTION FROM HARASSMENT ACT 1997

This Act is briefly mentioned as a number of investigators have been threatened with being taken to court for harassment by a target who had compromised them.

This act has often been referred to as the 'Stalker's Act', and is designed to catch all types of harassment, not just offences such as stalking. It can also include neighbourhood disputes, anti-social behaviour, racial hatred, bullying and domestic violence. Extracts here are taken from the Protection from Harassment Act 1997, Chapter 40.

The Act states that a person must not pursue a course of conduct which he/she knows (or ought to know) amounts to the harassment of another.

It is not necessary to prove that the person intended that his/her conduct amounted to harassment. The test is whether a reasonable person, who had the same information would think that it amounted to harassment. It does not apply to a course of conduct if the person who pursued it shows:

- That it was pursued for the purpose of preventing or detecting crime

- That it was pursued under any enactment or rule of law or to comply with any condition or requirement imposed by any person under any enactment, or

- That in the particular circumstances the pursuit of the course of conduct was reasonable

Definition

Harassment is not defined by the Act, the courts will probably have to rely upon the dictionary definition (to worry, pester, annoy, distress). The factors which may be taken into account include:

- Where and when the conduct (harassment) occurred
- The relationship between the harasser and victim, and
- The previous dealings between the parties

In criminal proceedings, harassment must have occurred on at least two occasions, although a civil claim may succeed where there has only been one incident, especially if there are reasonable grounds to believe that the harassment may occur again.

Criminal Offence of Harassment

The Act creates two criminal offences:

• Harassment

It is an offence to pursue a course of conduct which amounts to the harassment of another and the harasser knows (or ought to know) his conduct amounts to harassment. The offence is arrestable and is dealt with in the Magistrates Court. If convicted a person can be sentenced to up to six months imprisonment or fined up to £5,000 or both.

• Causing Fear of Violence

This is a more serious offence. The offence is committed if a person's course of conduct causes another person to fear, on at least two occasions, that violence will be used against him/her.

This offence can be tried at the Crown Court. The maximum sentence is five years imprisonment, unlimited fine or both.

Civil Offence of Harassment

A person who is or may be the victim of a course of conduct amounting to harassment can bring a civil action. This claim will be heard in the County Court or in the High Court. The Court can award damages including damages for anxiety and any resulting financial loss.

The victim or potential victim can also ask the Court to grant an injunction restraining the person from any conduct which amounts to harassment. If the person does anything which is prohibited by that injunction, he or she can be sentenced to imprisonment for contempt of Court.

In Your Defence

It is a defence to show that the person's course of conduct was done for the prevention or detection of crime, or was authorised by statute (bailiff), or it was reasonable for purposes of protecting him/herself or another person or property.

If the Secretary of State certifies that in his opinion anything done by a specified person on a specified occasion related to:

- National security
- The economic well-being of the United Kingdom, or
- The prevention or detection of serious crime

was done on behalf of the Crown, the certificate is conclusive evidence that this Act does not apply to any conduct of that person on that occasion. The Act, like any other, is quite heavy going but nevertheless, quite important.

Criminal Procedure and Investigations Act (CPIA) 1996

Surveillance may be carried out in any public place so long as trespass is not committed (see below). A public place can be defined as a place or premises to which the public has access or has access subject to conditions, and where a reasonable person would have no general expectation of privacy, or would expect privacy to be significantly reduced.

This extends to private land which is capable of being overseen by the general public such as driveways and gardens. A public place also includes private areas that are open to the public such as parks, zoos and fairgrounds, whether by free admission or by payment.

Not so much for the private individual, but a public body when carrying out surveillance should be familiar with the R -v- Johnson 1988 rules where there are set guidelines for carrying out surveillance in public places. This is essential when carrying out surveillance from a observation post on someone's private property such as a house, and with special regards to the disclosure of the evidence obtained. All evidence obtained must be revealed, as it will be required to be disclosed to the 'other side'. However, surveillance methods, tactics and in particular the location of Observation Posts do not have to be disclosed.

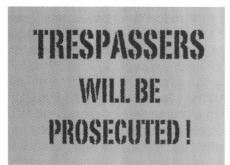

Trespass

We can take photographs or carry out our enquiries in a public place. We can also be in a public place and take photographs looking into a private place if it would be deemed reasonable that we did not have to make an effort to do so, such as climb up a ladder to look over a wall.

The distinguishing feature of trespass in modern law is that it is a direct and immediate interference with person or property, such as striking a person, entering his land or taking away his goods without his consent. The act of trespass is a 'tort' (a civil wrong) not a crime and therefore it is not necessary to prove that it has caused damage. The sign *'Trespassers will be Prosecuted'* is therefore usually misleading and should actually read, 'Trespassers will be Sued'.

There are three types of trespass: to the **Person,** to **Goods** and to **Land.** Trespass to land, usually takes the form of entering it without permission. Remaining on land after the owner has withdrawn his permission for you to be there is also a trespass.

Data Protection Act 1998

The Data Protection Act 1998 came into force on 1st March 2000. It sets rules for processing personal information and applies to some written paper records as well as those held on computers. The Act applies to 'personal data' that is about **identifiable living individuals.**

The Data Protection Act is extremely complicated and therefore only the fundamentals are covered here as it would effect the surveillance operator.

In the United Kingdom, any person who compiles or holds private information, whether you are a private investigator, security consultant or even the owner of a video rental shop (who may store names and addresses) you are required by law to be registered with the Data Protection Registrar. Failure to do so can result in heavy fines and/or imprisonment.

Anyone processing information or personal data (be it on computer, video, photographic or written on paper) must comply with the eight enforceable principles of good practice, which states that information is:

- Fairly and lawfully processed
- Processed for one specific and limited purpose

• Adequate, relevant and not excessive

• Kept accurate and up to date

• Not kept for longer than necessary

• Processed in accordance with the data subject's rights

•Acceptable security measures are used to prevent unauthorised use or misuse of data

• Not transferred to foreign countries without adequate protection

The person holding the information is referred to as the 'Data Controller', the person which has information stored about them is referred to as the 'Data Subject'.

Personal data covers both facts and opinions about the individual and also includes information regarding the intentions of the Data Controller towards the individual.

The Data Subjects Rights

The reason and concept of the Data Protection Act was to partially provide some sort of fairness and security for the 'Data Subjects' or 'us', the general public. As so much information is being stored and processed by many organisations, it was deemed that this information should be kept accurate, truthful and fair. The Act also makes provision for the 'Data Subject' so that he or she is able to find out what information is held about themselves on computer and/or on paper files. This is known as the 'right of subject access'.

The Act also allows individuals to apply to the Court to order a Data Controller to rectify, block, erase or destroy personal details if they are inaccurate or contain expressions of opinion which are based on inaccurate data.

PETE'S LINK: www.dataprotection.gov.uk

Access to information and data held about you

Any person can apply for a copy of the information held about them. Requests must be made to the person or organisation (Data Controller) who you think processes the information to which you want access. You must apply in writing and must be accompanied by the appropriate fee of £10.00 and proof of your identification. The Data Controller should respond within 40 days of receiving your request.

Individuals are entitled to be told if any personal data is held about them and if so:

- To be given a description of the data

- To be told for what purposes the data are processed

- To be told the recipients to whom the data may have been disclosed

You are also entitled:

- To be given a copy of the information with any unintelligible terms explained

- To be given any information available to the controller about the source of the data

Theoretically speaking, if a target of surveillance were to find out which investigation agency or person has them under surveillance, they are legally entitled to view any information or data (surveillance logs, video tapes) that they have obtained about them. There are various exceptions to this rule which includes surveillance by a public body. So if you get compromised, ensure that the target does not identify you and keep your fingers crossed that he is unaware of the DPA!

Again, this subject can be a minefield, the Data Protection website is very clear and helpful. To register you have to notify that you are a Data Controller by submitting the relevant forms with a fee of £35.00 per year. Failure to do so is a criminal offence and can result in a fine and/or imprisonment.

PETE'S TIP: Consider delivering a 'circular' or a newspaper by placing it half way into the letterbox. Should it be taken in, you will know that someone is up and about.

EVIDENCE GATHERING

Let us no examine various aspects, which help us to notice events, recognise and describe people.

Target Detail

On arrival at the target address, make a note of the surrounding details. Should you be keeping a house under surveillance, it is possible that you may not see any sign of life for many hours. This can be disheartening for the investigator and puts doubt that there is anyone at home, the target could be a late riser or he could have left home prior to you arriving.

Rather than make a pretext visit or phone call to the house, your powers of observation will tell you if anyone is present. Things to look out for are:

- The state of the curtains and windows
- Are there any lights on?
- Chimney smoke
- Milk on the doorstep
- Dry patch on the driveway after rain
- Cats waiting to be let in or dogs barking
- Steam from bathroom window or vents
- Birds flying off when disturbed
- Noise from machinery such as tools or lawnmowers

You may not always be in a position to observe any of the doors and so any of the above indicators will tell you that someone is present and may give you prior warning of them leaving.

Should there be two exits from the property you may have to put a 'trigger' on each. Alternatively, consider putting some sort of 'tell tale' marker on the rear gate/door such as a stone or stick against the gate. If the gate is used it will be disturbed.

In addition to being visually aware, you should also rely on your hearing. You may probably hear the sound of doors and gates opening, car alarms being unset for example. This will give those extra seconds warning to have your camera up and ready or to put the surveillance team on standby.

DESCRIBING PEOPLE

It is not always possible to obtain a photograph of your target and so a full description of him should be taken from those instructing you, so that he is immediately recognisable. In addition, you may need to describe the target in your written reports and so the list below should help you memorise the identifying characteristics.

Photographs of Targets

Whenever possible obtain photographs or video of your target, obviously the more recent the picture the better and establish whether your target has changed since it was taken, for example, has grown a moustache, now wears glasses or has altered their hair style. Do not pay lip service to identification photographs, study them and examine facial detail and bodily details so that the target is instantly recognisable when being seen for the first time.

Sometimes comparisons can be difficult, so carry the photograph with you on the task and use it. There is no point in having a photograph if it is going to be left at the office or the car, especially when identification is not easy.

The description details you will require are:

- Sex/Gender
- Ethnic Origin
- Age
- Height
- Build
- Weight
- Hair, (style, length, colour)
- Features (shape of face)
- Facial Hair
- Accessories (spectacles or jewellery)
- Tattoos, scarring or blemishes
- Speech (accent)
- Gait
- Clothing
- Resemblance's
- Overall Appearance

Quite often you will have to describe certain persons in your reports. Even if you recognise your target from a photograph, it is always wise to add a description of that person to your log or report. The descriptive list shown above should be sufficient for most purposes.

Characteristics and features vary and could be described in the following ways:

• **Ethnic Origin**

Your description of origin should be treated as being descriptive rather than a guess. Terms to be used could be: White, Negro, Asian, Arabic, Hispanic, Oriental, Latin, Scandinavian, East European. In Chapter Four on communications, you will note a system we call the 'I.C. Code', which puts these origins into a naming order.

• **Age**

To estimate age, compare the target's age with your own or someone that you know. If you find this difficult, try to 'bracket' their age. If you feel that they can not be older than 50 but are not as young as 40, we can estimate that the target is approximately 45 years old. When making notes such as your surveillance log, do not be too accurate when estimating ages and put them down in brackets (35-40 years). Be aware that beards and baldness can make men to appear much older than they really are.

• **Height**

Height can be estimated in a similar manner as we would for ages. Compare the target's height to yourself or someone you know and bracket accordingly. In addition, you can compare the target against his surroundings such as a door frame (6 feet 6 inches) or a car roof. Height can sometimes be difficult to estimate as the persons build can often alter our perception especially if they are higher up than you, such as on a doorstep.

• **Build**

Build could be considered as: Slim, Medium, Heavy, Well Built, Proportionate, Stout, Stooped, Small, Athletic, Muscular and Wiry. Be aware that peoples clothes can often alter your perception of build, especially heavy coats.

• **Hair**

Hair can be described in many ways but we divide hair styles into three sub-categories:

• **Colour** Light, Dark, Fair, Streaked, Bleached, Tinted, Coloured, Black, Brown, Grey

• **Length** Cropped, Short, Balding, Collar Length, Shoulder Length, Long

• **Style** Tidy, Scruffy, Wavy, Permed, Straight, Thick, Thin, Curly, Receding, Greasy, Fringed, Styled, Spiky, Bobbed

• **Facial Features**

• **Complexion** Pale, fair, tanned, olive, rashy, weathered, dark

• **Shape of Face**

When looking at faces there are many features that make up the face apart from the overall shape

Facial shapes could be described as: Round, Fat, Thin, Pointed, Angular, Square, Oval, Sallow, Small

• **Eyes**

Large, Small, Squint, Slanted, Bloodshot, Piggy, Piercing, Hooded Lids, Wide

• **Eyebrows**

Thick, Thin, Bushy, Arched, Plucked, Narrow, Joined, Slanted, Straight

• **Noses**

Small, Large, Button, Hooked, Roman, Fat, Bumpy, Snub, Bulbous, Wide, Pointed, Squashed

• **Chins**

Square, Round, Pointed, Long, Double, Angular

- **Facial Hair**

    Moustaches: Military, Droopy, Handlebar, Bushy/Thick, Toothbrush, Mexican, Thin, Walrus, Clipped, Waxed

    Beards: Stubbly, Unshaven, Pointed, Long, Straggly, Short, Designer

- **Spectacles and Jewellery**

    - Spectacles: Round, Square, Horn Rimmed, Metallic, Bi-Focal, Tinted

    - Jewellery: Rings, Necklaces, Medallions, Broaches, Earrings, Hairslides

- **Tattoos or Skin Marks**

    Obtain the design of the tattoo and their locations. Tattoos are designed for showing off and are often found on the forearms. Some people have very distinguishing marks such as birthmarks, blemishes and scars

- **Speech**

    Regional accents are not always distinct but attempt to put the accent to an area, even if it is only North, South, Midland or West Country. Consider the tone and volume such as quiet, soft, loud, slurred, educated, clipped

- **Gait, Stride and Posture**

    Most people have a unique and identifiable gait in the way they carry themselves and move whilst walking

    - Posture / Bearing: Upright, Slouched, Stooped, Round Shouldered, Head Drooped, Lethargic

    - Gait and Pace: Fast, Slow, Bouncy, Marching, Skipping, Plodding, Springy, Dainty, Lethargic, Limping

- **Clothing**

    Smart, scruffy, casual, business-like, sporty, industrial

• **Overall Appearance**

Smart, Tidy, Untidy, Professional, Scruffy, Casual

Resemblance's

Does the target resemble anyone famous? A television personality, a politician, for example. If you use this method to describe a person, ensure that it's someone that most people could recognise! To hear, *'Standby, Standby, that's the target out and he's a dead ringer for my uncle Albert!* is no use to anyone unless they know what your Uncle Albert looks like!

On one particular investigation, we were tasked to establish that a particular character worked in a busy car garage and obtain photographs or video of him working there. The client did not have very good powers of description but stated that the target looked very similar in appearance to the entertainer Bruce Forsyth, by having a long prominent chin.

On arrival at the garage, there were approximately 16 male staff working there and the target was instantly recognised. Should we not have had this descriptive 'resemblance' our task would have been made much more difficult by having to ask pretence questions.

PETE'S TIP: On occasions it may be necessary to identify whether a car or vehicle has remained parked in the same position overnight or over a period of time without moving. In order to do this, place a small chalk mark on the ground and also on the tyre so that they are in line with each other. In the morning you can casually walk past and examine the marks, if the two chalk marks are not aligned it would indicate that the vehicle has been moved during the night.

The military use a pneumonic 'A to J' in order to describe people:

A Age
B Build
C Clothing
D Distinguishing Marks
E Elevation (Height)
F Face
G Gait
H Hair
I I.C. Code
J Just Like (resemblances)

Vehicle Details

Any vehicle detail that you can obtain regarding the target is extremely useful. When vehicles arrive on the scene of an observation, or you arrive there to find a

vehicle for that matter, it is important that you record as much detail as possible about it. Today, many vehicles are designed by computer and consequently appear to be a similar shape such as the Laguna, Mondeo or Corolla. Therefore it is also important to recognise the car's logos and badges.

• Make and Model

The make could be either a Ford or a Vauxhall, the Models possibly being an Escort or Astra respectively.

• Shape

In addition, there are variants such as estates, saloons, hatchbacks and convertibles. If you do not know what make it is, provide a detailed description.

• **Colour**

Colours are fairly straight forward with variants in shades and metallic finishes. Make a note of the state of repair and body work, does it have any modifications?

• **Registration Marks and Numbers**

Registration numbers are unique to every vehicle and is the best means to recognition.

In the United Kingdom there is a new style of registration number, the old style registration was in the form of:

Where the 'S' identified the year of production (1998/9) and the letters 'TN' identified the area in which the vehicle was first registered. In this instance 'TN' relates to Newcastle.

The new registration system introduced in 2001, sees a registration number in the form of:

The first two letters are a local identifier or 'tag' to show where the vehicle was first registered. The tag 'YG' relates to the Leeds area, the letter 'Y' indicating Yorkshire.

The two figure number is an age identifier which changes every six months in March and September. In this case, '51' relates to 1st September 2001 to 28th February 2002. The age identifier which comes after this will be '02', the next period will be '52', the next '03' and so on. The three letters are generated randomly to give a unique identity to the vehicle.

PETE'S TIP: A small pebble placed on top of a tyre can be used to determine if a vehicle has been driven. The pebble can be viewed on a walkpast.

Identifying Features

Note any unusual marking or ornaments such as stickers, furry dice, nodding dogs and tow bars. In busy traffic you may only get a brief sighting of a sticker in a rear window when the car is way ahead of you, this may be the only indicator to provide his location in a long queue of traffic.

Remember, if the target drives a powerful car, it will be necessary for the surveillance team to use similar powered vehicles also.

NIGHT VISION

After being in a well lit area and then moving into the dark, it takes approximately 20 minutes for your eyes to get accustomed to the dark and about 40 minutes to become fully adjusted. This adjustment is what we call 'night vision' or getting used to the dark.

Photograph taken through image intensifying night-sight

At the back of the eye is the retina which is made up of cells, these cells (of which there are two types) are formed in the shape of rods and cones. The cones (in the centre) are sensitive to coloured light but not shades of grey. Alternately, the rods (surrounding the cones) are not sensitive to colours but are sensitive to shades of grey. During the daytime, the cones cells are used to transmit light to the brain, as darkness takes over, so do the rods.

If you are observing at night, do not stare directly at the object, but look slightly to one side so that you are using the area of the rods. If you look directly at the target, it will be covered by the cones and in effect causing a blind spot.

When we go from one extreme to another such as a light area into dark, it takes some time for the cells to change role and so we have this 20-40 minute period of 'getting used to the dark'. The suggestion that carrots help you to 'see in the dark' is true to some extent. Carrots are rich in Vitamin 'A' and it is known that Vitamin 'A' stimulates the cells that we have mentioned.

Once night vision is obtained, it is easy to lose it again by looking at bright lights or through night vision scopes. It also takes much longer to regain your night vision when lost, therefore when observing at night consider the following:

• Scan areas of observation slowly

• Do not look directly at the object, the eye has a 'blind spot' so look slightly to one side

• Do not stare at an object, your eyes will play tricks on you

• Avoid looking at bright lights, this will ruin your night vision

• Keep your eyes closed when exposed to light such as car headlamp. If necessary, keep one eye open

• Rest your eyes frequently

• Looking through a night vision scope can ruin your night vision

Soldiers preparing to carry out night time operations (such as going into a night assault by helicopter) will often sit for 40 minutes in darkness to enable their eyes to become accustomed to the dark. The troops may wait in a special area or all the lights inside the aircraft may be switched off.

Red light does not affect night vision so some illumination in these areas helps you to see.

During the Falklands Campaign I served in a small reconnaissance unit tasked with carrying out forward recce patrols and OPs ahead of the main fighting units. When the patrol moved at night, I was one of two scouts whose responsibility up ahead, was to stop, listen and look to our front for enemy positions or patrols using image intensifying scopes. This was extremely hard work, once I had 'cleared' to my front, my partner Jan would move forward to clear his front and then I would come through and so on with the patrol following not far behind us. What made the job even more difficult for us was the fact that we would stop every 50 paces or so and scan through the night sight, in doing so we would lose our night vision in that eye. When we patrolled forward, visibility was difficult as we were effectively now blind in one eye having lost the night vision.

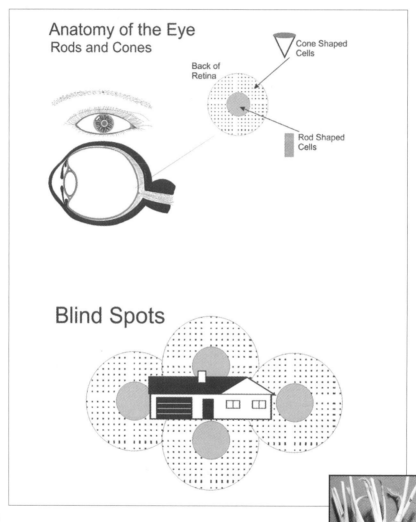

PETE'S TIP: *Go to your local grocer and order a bunch of carrots!*

Memory and Perception

Try to educate your memory. There are three different ways in which we memorise detail. On surveillance courses we show a number of items to the students which they have one minute to look at them and remember them. After which they have to write down and describe what they could remember. A number of tests carried out over a few days certainly improves their memory and their attention to detail.

Study the photo below for one minute, then close the book and attempt to write down the list of objects. Try to pay attention to detail and count how many there are as this helps

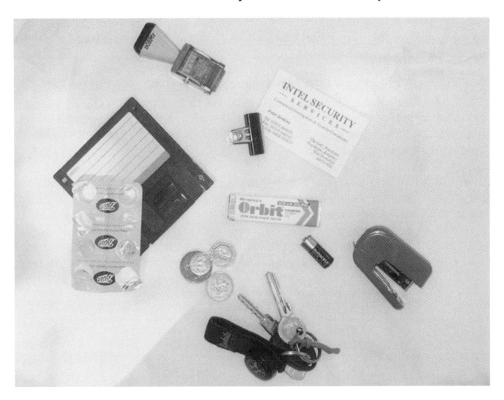

People have different ways of remembering the objects, some use 'association' where the set of cars keys would be linked to a petrol receipt or the packet of sweets would be linked to a toothbrush. Others think to themselves a bizarre story in which they link the objects together such as: *I left the house with my CAR KEYS in my hand, I looked at my WATCH because I was late, I had to fill up with PETROL and I bought some headache TABLETS at the same time.*

Others may group the objects into rows or clusters, such as the top row, the middle row and the bottom row. Everyone has their own personal way of remembering details, so use whatever system suits you.

List of Objects (answers)

Key fob with three keys, three silver coins, one bronze coin, packet of pills, Duracell battery, stapler, chewing gum, bulldog paper clip, business card, rubber date stamp, 3.5 inches floppy disc.

Perception

Noticing detail is very important but our minds can often play tricks on us without us being aware of it. For example, read the following sentence and then write down how many times the letter F is used:

**THE FLOPPY, FLUFFY BUNNY OF LITTLE SELF-WORTH
HAD NO IDEA OF THE NEED FOR SAFETY IN THE WOODS.**

The first time I read this I counted six, when there are actually nine! If you think I am mistaken, then count again....

This is a common mistake as your brains play tricks on us all the time. We discard the word 'of' because it does not require much thought and is not one of the main words we are looking at.

Here's another one, have a look at the picture below and count the black dots. How many did you count? eight, nine, in fact there are none!

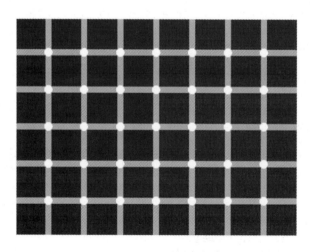

SURVEILLANCE LOGS AND REPORTS

As a member of a surveillance team, you should keep a brief log of exactly what occurs and what action is taken. The team leader may keep a more detailed log of team events (Master Log). It is important that all team members synchronise their watches and timers on photographic equipment so that the surveillance logs coincide with each other and there are no discrepancies. Remember all oddities may be brought to the attention of a court and could quite possibly discredit your evidence.

Should you be in a static observation position, you may be able to write down a fair amount of detail about the target area and the events taking place.

Depending on the nature of the enquiry, it will effect how you log and produce your written reports. It is recommended to have the surveillance logs typed up and submitted with accompanying photographs or video tape. Reports in this format include all details and log events in a chronological order.

Surveillance Logs

All timings, incidents and information should be recorded in a chronological order and preferably written down in note form. The notes that you take will be regarded as contemporaneous and will possibly be used as evidence and would have to be produced in court. Your notes may be written on anything at the time of the incident; pocket book, log sheets or even the back of a cigarette packet, but once written they should be preserved as evidence, more importantly so if you are investigating a criminal activity.

It is not always necessary to use prepared log sheets but they are simple, easy to read and make life easier when they have to be typed.

It is not always practical to handwrite a log, and so a running commentary, or details of an event may have to be kept on dictaphone tape. The details

Section of a log sheet

on the tape should be written up as soon as practically possible. On occasions (such as Criminal Investigations) the dictaphone tape will also have to be re-tained and preserved as evidence.

No ELBOWS!

When compiling our surveillance log sheets, there are certain guidelines that can help preserve the integrity of the log and its content and we use the pneumonic 'No ELBOWS' to remind us. There should be no:

E   Erasures

If you make a mistake, you should not obliterate the mistake with pen, rub it out or use correction fluids. If you make an error, draw a single line through it (so that the error can be read) and write the correction afterwards.

L   Loose Leafs

Ideally the sheets of a logbook should be bound with glue and each page serial numbered (as are the Enforcement Agency Logs). This way it cannot be open to suggestion that extra pages were added at a later time and also any removed pages will be identified.

B   Blank Spaces

Some people leave a blank line in between log entries in order to make it clearer that it is a separate event. This is in fact bad practise as it could be suggested that you have left the line clear in order to add an entry at a later time.

O   Overwriting

As mentioned above, if you make a mistake, do not write over the top of the error or cram the correction into the text. Use a fresh line.

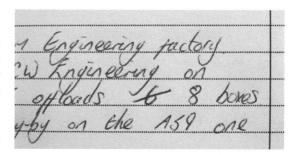

W   Writing Between the Lines

Do not cram words in between the lines of text if you realise that there is an addition you need to make to your log. If you realise that you have made an error or there is something that you wish to include in the log, then add it to the end of the log.

S   Separate Pieces of Paper

If at all possible, use bound surveillance logs. Separate log sheets are acceptable but can be left open to abuse and the suggestion that they were not the originals. If you use separate log sheets, ensure that you number the pages 2 of 2, for example. If for some reason you record your observations on a scrap piece of paper as it was the only thing to hand, then this must be preserved and retained with the log sheets. An entry should also be made in the log referring to it.

Eye Witness Testimony as Evidence

If you find yourself in court giving evidence, it is possible that the Defence barrister will attempt to discredit your evidence or put your 'witness testimony' to some doubt in order to confuse a jury. In a famous case (Regina -v- Turnbull and Others 1976), certain witnesses to an armed robbery were called to give evidence at the robbers trial, Turnbull was the getaway driver in the robbery.

These witnesses saw the robbery take place but their testimony was put to question by the Defence. Many questions were asked:

> *How far away from the Defendant were you when you saw him?*
> *If you were across the street was the road busy at that time of the day?*
> *Could passing buses obscure your view?*
> *How long did you have him in sight for?*
> *Are your sure it was him?*
> *How can you be certain?*

In summing up, the judge Lord Widgery, informed the jury that there should be a special need for caution when considering eye witness evidence and said that a single witness can make mistakes, several witnesses are likely to paint a more realistic picture of events but they can also still be mistaken. This case set a precedent and barristers now use this case as a guide when cross examining eye witnesses when identification is in doubt. Lord Widgery speaking for the English Court of Appeal in R-v-Turnbull referred to four guideline matters which a trial judge, when instructing a jury or himself, if sitting alone, must consider.

1.   ... whenever the case against an accused depends wholly or substantially on the correctness of one or more identifications of an accused which the defence alleges to be mistaken, the judge must warn the jury of the special needs for caution before convicting the accused in reliance on the correctness of the identification or identifications...

2. ... he should instruct them as to the reason for the need for such a warning and should make some reference to the possibility that a mistaken witness can be a convincing one and that a number of such witnesses can all be mistaken...

3. ... direct the jury to examine closely the circumstances in which the identification by each witness came to be made...

His Lordship then set out a number of factors one might consider when deciding whether or not there is evidence before the Court which would impact positively or negatively upon the correctness of the testimony, and continued:

4. ... remind the jury of any specific weaknesses which had appeared in the identification evidence. Recognition may be more reliable than identification of a stranger; but, even when the witness is purporting to recognise someone whom he knows, the jury should be reminded that mistakes in recognition of close relatives and friends are sometimes made...

His Lordship went on to state:

... If the quality is good and remains good at the close of the accused's case, the danger of a mistaken identification is lessened; but the poorer the quality, the greater the danger. In our judgment, when the quality is good, as for example when the identification is made after a long period of observation, or in satisfactory conditions by a relative, a neighbour, a close friend, a work mate or the like, the jury can safely be left to assess the value of the identifying evidence even though there is no other evidence to support it; provided always, however that an adequate warning has been given about the special need for caution....

If we take the case of **R-v-Turnbull and Others**, and can give answers to the points raised, we can be confident in our evidence. Using the pneumonic ADVOKATE we remember the points of which to provide detail in our surveillance logs, which you may be questioned about.

> *PETE'S TIP: If you are determined to commit an offence - ensure that there are no witnesses or a watching police officer!*

ADVOKATE

A   **Amount of Time**

How long was the target actually in view for?

D   **Distance**

How far away was the target from you?
Were you using optics such as binoculars or telephoto lenses?
Was the target so close that you had to avert you eyes?

V   **Visibility**

What was the weather like? Was it foggy? Was the sun in your eyes?
Were you having to look in your rear view mirror, was it a back to front image?
Do you wear glasses? Were you wearing them at the time?

O   **Obstructions**

Were you looking across a busy street, heavy with passing traffic?
Were you having to peer through heavy foliage?
Was there a lot of pedestrian activity?
Did the target go out of sight at any time?

K   **Known or Seen Before**

Had you seen the target before?
Was he known to you?
Did you have a photograph to recognise him from?
Had you carried out surveillance on him before?

A   **Any Reason to Remember**

I had reason to remember because that day in question was my birthday.
I remember the jumper he wore because I have one exactly like it.
I remember him because he had a likeness to.....

T   **Time Lapse**

Could your memory fail you?
What was the time span between seeing the incident and making your notes?
What was the time span between seeing the incident and making a statement?
What was the time span between seeing the incident and the identity parade?

E   **Errors or Discrepancies**

Is it possible.........?
Is it possible that you are mistaken?
You have stated this, another witness has stated that, could you be wrong?

I have given evidence in Court when the Defence barrister went systematically through the list above. At the time I was still a 'young investigator' and had no knowledge of R-v-Turnbull or ADVOKATE but I was able to provide the correct answers to his cross examination. This was only due to correct log keeping at the time, quick thinking and having the confidence in my own evidence.

A number of years ago in the United Kingdom, the TV presenter Jill Dando was murdered outside her home. Although there were no actual witnesses to the act, many witnesses gave evidence relating to a man that they saw loitering in the area before the murder. These witnesses gave very conflicting descriptions of the person they saw, 'He was white, clean shaven wearing a raincoat', 'He had a few days beard, Mediterranean appearance and wore a Barbour jacket'. The Defence barristers would have gone to town during their cross examination in order to discredit these witnesses and highlight the conflicting descriptions, I am certain they would have used the Advocate pneumonic as an aide.

PETE'S EXERCISE: Take a recent surveillance log that you have prepared and ask yourself whether you can answer all those questions listed above about a particular important incident.

Remember a defence barrister will want to:

- Shorten the time span that the target was in your sight

- Extend the distance between you and the target

- Cloud your view

- Prove that the view was fully or partially obstructed for a short period of time

- Intimate a wrong identity

- Question your judgement and memory

- Put to you any discrepancies, such as errors in your logs

- Put doubt in the minds of a jury

PRESERVATION OF PHOTOGRAPHIC EVIDENCE

The aim of the majority of surveillance tasks is to gain photographic evidence of an event taking place or to prove that a person was in a particular location at a certain date and time.

Should these photographs be used in legal proceedings (especially criminal) then they should be handled, preserved and exhibited as any other evidence would be. There should be a documented record of the evidence when it is transferred from one person to another for reasons of continuation. This is essential when handling evidence to be used in criminal proceedings.

Do not use the same film for multiple jobs in order to save money. Whether it is videotape or still film that you are using, always load a fresh film at the start of the job, add the cost to your invoice.

Having taken the photographs, the film should remain in your control until the photos are handed over to a legal authority such as a solicitor or the Police when they should be exhibited with your statements or surveillance logs.

Should the whereabouts of the evidence be unknown at any time, it could be used by the opposition in court to discredit that evidence, claiming that it had been tampered with and altered.

The most vulnerable time when the film is out of your control is when it is being processed and it is during this process when the evidence could be altered to provide an untrue image (although unlikely). To preserve the continuance of evidence it may be wise to have your photo processor sign a declaration stating that the film was processed by him/her and that it had not been altered and that it was handed directly back to you.

PETE'S TIP: Do not forget to reset your camera's timer when British Summer Time starts and finishes or travel between time zones.

We have used this system in the past, with the document stating:

> I, Karen Bloggs of Print It Photo Processors, Anytown, have received, one roll of 24 exposure Kodak film from Mr. Paul King on 21st March 2003 at 12.00hrs.
>
> The film was developed and printed on the premises by me and has not left the premises at any time. The photographs have not been altered or interfered with so as to make them false.
>
> At 16.30hrs on 21st March 2003 I handed the processed negatives and prints over to Mr Paul King.
>
> Signed: **K Bloggs**
>
> Dated: **21 March 2003**

This procedure may seem extreme or over the top, but if the photographs recorded a criminal event such as a theft, the defence barrister will ask you, "Were the photographs and negatives ever out of your control?", "Is it possible, that they could have been tampered with?". If the answer to those questions is 'Yes', then this destroys the chain of evidence and casts doubt as to the credibility of that evidence.

In the matter of video taped evidence, your original recording should be copied to be used as a 'working' copy to make further copies or make edited versions. The original tape should be labelled, secured and retained as evidence.

Camera Data Backs and Date / Time Generators

Many investigators make use of a 'data back' fitted to their camera. This device prints the date and time onto the photograph as it is taken. From an evidential point of view the date and time printed on the photo could be questioned in court, as it is possible to set an incorrect date and time on the device. Just because the photo has printed on it 12-6-03 it does not necessarily mean that it was taken on that date.

This does not mean that using a databack is a waste of time. Having the date/time assists in the compilation of reports and logs and provides documented corroboration. It makes the pictures look more professional and would only likely be challenged in court if there were discrepancies in other parts of that evidence.

Should you make use of a data back, ensure that the timer is synchronised to your watch or the time-piece that you refer to when writing a surveillance log. Should you realise after the pictures have been taken that the timer is not synchronised with your watch, make a note on the surveillance log to this effect.

Chapter Four
Communications

Communication is probably the most important factor when there is more than one investigator working on the same task. Team tasks can succeed or fail depending on whether good communication is maintained between team members, and that those members are well exercised in voice procedure and the giving of a radio commentary.

**Surveillance is all about teamwork,
without communications you will have no team to work with**

Communication is about being able to speak or indicate to another, in a manner that is clear, precise, detailed and understandable to the receiving party. In this instance, the sender will be passing information about a particular targets actions and intentions, or be issuing instructions to the remainder of the surveillance team.

Communication (or Comms) can be passed in any of the following ways:

- The telephone, including mobile phones

- Radio transmissions

- Radio telephones

- Hand signals

The Telephone

Mobile telephones are not recommended as a substitute for hand held radios. The cost of operating a mobile phone is probably one of the first disadvantages that springs to mind, but mobile networks can be very temperamental and calls have a habit of suddenly being cut off. If you are operating in a hilly or 'bad area' you will have no Comms at all.

With radios, you will be able to call and speak to an unlimited number of people at the same time, with a mobile, you can only speak to one person.

The main advantage is that mobiles have an unlimited range of transmission where you can get in touch with anyone throughout the country. Each member of the surveillance team **must** be in possession of a mobile phone. Operators often find themselves out of radio range, especially after a loss and the only means of communication is the mobile telephone.

Radio Telephone

A recent communications advancement is the mobile radiophone. One such system in the United Kingdom is called the TETRA or 'Dolphin' system designed by Motorola, which in effect is a mobile phone. At the press of a button you can set the phone to be used just like your hand held radio, where you have to press a PTT button to talk and then release it to listen. The advantages of this system are that it is 'secure' as the transmissions are digitised and no one can intercept them and that they have an unlimited transmission range. On the downside, everyone in the team needs to have one but if you are in an area where there is a poor mobile signal, you will not get through to anyone.

RADIOS

Communications are a very important factor in surveillance work where investigators have to work as a team. Therefore radio equipment is paramount and has to be:

- Reliable and robust
- Have sufficient transmit/receiving range
- Portable
- Secure
- Simple to operate

PETE'S TIP: Be cautious when using mobile telephones and video cameras at the same time. The transmissions from the phone interfere with the camera's picture and can cause extensive electronic damage to it.

Radio Frequencies

Two different wave lengths are available to the commercial investigator in the UK and the correct one should be selected to obtain maximum performance for the type of area that you are normally working in.

> • UHF or Ultra High Frequency should be used in very built up towns and cities or if you are constantly working in buildings. In the UHF range this is normally between 430 - 472MHz.

> • VHF or Very High Frequency is the most commonly used and is ideal for most situations, it is adequate for both built up areas and out in the open. In the VHF range, the frequency is normally between approximately 162 - 175 MHz.

It is preferable to have a power output of at least five watts to provide you with sufficient power and transmitting range, the majority of hand held radios can be set to five watts. Any less and you may not have a sufficient range.

If you purchase your own VHF/UHF sets, an operator's licence has to be obtained from the Radio Communications Agency (RCA). This is usually organised by the radio dealer, and the licence costs approximately £140.00 per year and can cover up to ten radio sets. When the licence is issued you receive an operating frequency onto which the radios are set.

Modified Kenwood TH-22E

Due to over-crowding of the airwaves within these frequency ranges, it is possible that you will hear other people on the air who are using the same frequency and likewise, they would be able to hear you. This 'sharing' of frequencies could create a problem during surveillance as your commentary could be interrupted and third parties will be able to hear your commentary.

Many modern radio systems utilise a system called CTCSS coding. This system enables the radio set to automatically transmit a coded signal to your other sets and 'opens them up' to receive your messages only. Radios using the same frequency without the compatible CTCSS coding will not be able to be listen in to your commentary nor will you be able to receive the others transmissions.

Types of Radio Sets

Radios come in various forms, the main two types being **hand held transceivers** (the walkie-talkie) or **vehicle mounted sets**. Both sets have their advantages and disadvantages:

Vehicle Mounted Sets

Vehicle mounted sets (as their name suggests) are normally mounted and concealed in a surveillance vehicle and will give you a high transmitting range, drawing its power from the vehicles battery. An output of five watts or more with an external magnetic mounted antenna (mag mount) will provide a range over seven to twelve miles.

It will not be practical to have a mag mount antenna located in the centre of your car roof, as it would look too conspicuous. Therefore it should be located on the rear bumper area or put inside the car itself. If it is put inside, ensure that the antenna is upright and that the base is on something solid such a metal plate or even a biscuit tin lid in order to provide what is termed a 'ground plane' and to reflect the radio radiation. A purpose built antenna fitted into the roof or wing of the car, made to look like an ordinary radio aerial is much preferred and is much more covert.

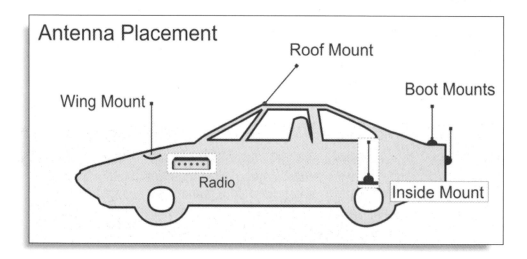

A vehicle mounted set requires approximately 12 volts DC to operate it and this can be obtained from the vehicle's own power supply via the cigarette lighter socket for a temporary measure or alternatively and much preferred, have it connected to the cars power system or from the battery.

These large sets can also be used as a base station or used in a static O.P. when greater transmission distances are required. The radio set can draw its power from the mains supply transformed down to 12 volts or run from a stand alone car battery.

Hand Held Radio Sets

Radio handsets offer more flexibility, as they can be carried about your person during foot surveillance, be located in your car or used in an OP as they have their own power supply. They can be fitted with accessories that will enable you to use the radio covertly such as an ear piece and a concealed microphone, they also utilise their own short antenna.

PETE'S TIP: Should you ever have to operate a hand held set whilst in the street or out in the open without any covert ancillaries, hold the set upside down (with the volume low) so that the antenna is not visible. It would then appear that you are talking on a mobile phone.

When used in a vehicle, the transmission range may only be up to one kilometre but this can be greatly increased by connecting the hand set to a mag mount antenna or a purpose fitted antenna as described above. This is a preferred method by many surveillance operators and in the past I have had some 20 kilometres range (across open ground) with a hand held set.

When using a hand held set in a vehicle, ensure that you keep it below the level of the dashboard, you do not want the target to see you using it in his mirrors. In the same vein, when using the radio, do not keep bobbing your head up and down as you speak each time into the microphone, act naturally. Try not to let your fingers or thumb curl over the microphone, as you will muffle out your commentary.

Different Types of Radio Sets

The Motorola GP300 or GP340 is a popular radio, it is robust and will take a knock or two. However, the ancillaries can be expensive and any changes to the radio settings such as adding new frequencies have to be carried out by an author-ised dealer, which incurs more costs.

The set preferred on the security circuit is the Kenwood TH-22E which operates in the VHF waveband or the Kenwood TH-G71E which is 'dual band'. This means that it operates in the VHF as well as the UHF wavebands.

Strictly speaking these two radios are not built or designed to operate within the commercial frequency bands but are set to the frequencies allocated for the amateur radio ham. We would not want to carry out a surveil-lance on these frequencies as all and sundry will be able to hear our transmis-sions but more importantly, it would also be illegal to do so.

To get around this problem, a quick modification is carried out inside the radio, which broadens the waveband to cover the commercial frequencies. You can then enter the frequency that you have been allocated. If you are operating with a team that uses their own different frequency, you can easily tap theirs into the set and away you go. If you obtain one of these sets, you will also need to change the supplied antenna for one which matches your operating frequency, in order to get the best results.

The Kenwood sets are very durable, very slim and easily concealable when using covertly. The batteries will last a full day and they will transmit with an output of five watts with a high power battery fitted.

Antennas

Whether you are using a hand held radio or a vehicle set, it is very important that you have the correct antenna (aerial) fitted otherwise you will have problems when transmitting and receiving. The antenna is probably one of the most important parts of your radio. It has to be the correct type and length and it cannot be any old piece of wire plugged into the set.

Kenwood UHF/VHF Dual Band Radio

The antenna should ideally be vertical and has to be the correct length to correspond with the frequency used and this can be done by a simple calculation. For example, a radio using a frequency of 174Mhz requires an antenna that is .43 of a metre long (or 43cms or 17 inches). When you buy a mag mount antenna or those for vehicle mounting, they are slightly longer than necessary so that they can be cut down to size for this reason. A pair of pliers or a hacksaw normally does the job.

This length of antenna is calculated by dividing the number 300 (a constant) by the frequency. We then divide the answer by 4 to give the length in metres.

So if we take 300 and divide it by our frequency of 174Mhz, this equals 1.724 (our wavelength). Divide this by 4, which equals 0.43 (our quarter wavelength) or 43 centimetres.

E.g. $\dfrac{300.00}{174.00} = 1.724$ then $\dfrac{1.724}{4} = 0.43$

I would agree with you if you said that it would look a bit odd to have a hand held radio with nearly half a metre of black wire sticking out of the top and you have probably already noticed that the antennae on these sets are fairly short. These are called 'helical' antennae and are in fact cut to the correct length; it is just that the wire is coiled up like a spring inside the covering. Some of our covert antennae are extended to a quarter wave length but are worn in a harness where the antennae runs across the shoulder for better reception.

If the radio has 'line of sight' to another set, you should achieve maximum transmitting range. When objects such as buildings, trees or hills become between them, the range will be drastically reduced. Radio waves find it difficult to pass through water which essentially is what your body is made up of. Therefore if your covert set is stuffed tight under your armpit, you may experience problems with range. Clipped to the belt in the small of your back or on your hip is preferable.

If you are in an OP where you are lying down, be aware of the transmission range reducing as you are close to the ground. The higher up you are the better the range therefore it would be advisable to use an elevated mag-mount by attaching it to a fence post or up a tree.

Dipole Antennas

This is a very simple and effective way of increasing your transmission range without an external antenna. A team of American Special Forces operators first showed it to me and I have not been without one since.

It is fairly simple to make your own 'dipole' antenna, which is very effective for use in vehicles, or OPs when it is not practical to use a mag mount. A dipole can be made by taking an old mag mount antenna and cutting off the magnetic base. Looking into the cut end of the cable (or coax

as it is called) you will note that the section is made up of four elements; the outer protective sheath, a fine wire mesh sleeve (called shielding), a strong plastic core with a copper wire running through it.

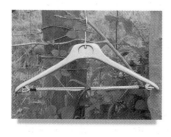

Firstly you need to calculate the length of your antenna, let's say it is 43cms. Now you need to cut away about 44cms of the outer sheath and throw it away so that you now have exposed the bare shielding surrounding the inner core. Next, very carefully make a small hole in the shielding where it emerges from the outer sheath and pull the inner core back through it being careful not to sever the shielding. You should end up with a hollow shield branching off in one direction and the inner core branching off in another, so that when laid flat out your cable should be in the shape of a 'T'.

All you have to do now is to wrap electrical tape around the 'T' in order to stop the wires from fraying and breaking loose. Measure and cut the length of the antenna (the inner core) and the shielding (ground plane) so that each is 43cms long.

With a BNC connector at the other end, plug it in to your radio and you are ready to transmit. Ideally the two elements (wires) should be set in the shape of a 'V'. I have one taped to a coat hanger, which is very effective when hung up in a vehicle with a jacket over it. It can also be used to good effect in a static observation post by hanging it up in a tree or foliage.

Covert Radio Systems

A semi-covert set of wires can be purchased for about £40.00. This comprises of a 'Walkman' style earpiece and a lapel microphone. The earpiece is not 100% covert as it can be seen but it is very effective if you are operating on a budget. We see many people about these days with earpieces in; mobile phones, hands free kits and Sony Walkmans so you will get away with this type of equipment to a certain extent. The microphone is worn just under the collar and operated with a PTT switch to transmit, you do not necessarily need a carry harness as the radio can be clipped to your belt in the small of your back. One company in the UK (Niton Products Ltd) supply good quality harnesses for just over £25.00

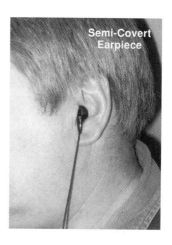
Semi-Covert Earpiece

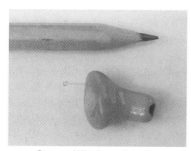
Covert Wireless Earpiece

The more professional accessories comprise of a carry harness similar to that of a pistol shoulder holster, which carries the radio. Built into the harness is the antenna, microphone and an induction device which 'transmits' voice to a small ear piece placed in the ear. There are no tell - tale wires to the ear piece which appears very similar to a hearing aid. This equipment is very effective and was once described as being 'the closest you would ever get to being telepathic'.

For women operators, the set can either be body worn or concealed in a handbag. In this instance the microphone, inductor and PTT switch are all contained within the shoulder strap. These handbags are in common use by store detectives.

COVERT RADIO SYSTEMS

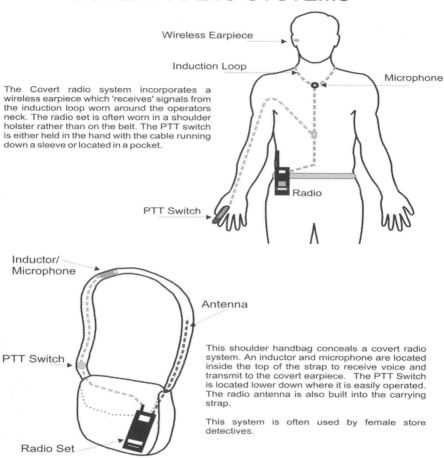

Wireless Earpiece

Induction Loop

Microphone

The Covert radio system incorporates a wireless earpiece which 'receives' signals from the induction loop worn around the operators neck. The radio set is often worn in a shoulder holster rather than on the belt. The PTT switch is either held in the hand with the cable running down a sleeve or located in a pocket.

Radio

PTT Switch

Inductor/ Microphone

Antenna

PTT Switch

This shoulder handbag conceals a covert radio system. An inductor and microphone are located inside the top of the strap to receive voice and transmit to the covert earpiece. The PTT Switch is located lower down where it is easily operated. The radio antenna is also built into the carrying strap.

This system is often used by female store detectives.

Radio Set

There are two types of covert fit, the Inductor and the Loop. The inductor is a small plastic tab about 5cms long which is pinned to clothing in the area of your collar bone. This inductor transmits signals to your earpiece (which has to be fitted in the ear on the same side as the inductor) and also has a built-in microphone.

The induction loop is what it says it is, a loop of wire (coloured pink) that is worn over the head like a necklace and is also fitted with a microphone. With the loop, it does not matter in which ear you wear your earpiece.

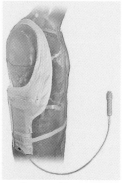

Covert Harness

Walk and Talk

Surveillance students often find it very difficult to use covert radios in a natural manner until they have gained confidence after a few hours of use. Remember that we have to act naturally in everything we do and it is not always easy when you have a lump of equipment strapped to your body and you are required to walk down the street whilst talking to yourself.

Have confidence in the equipment and this only comes with constant practice.

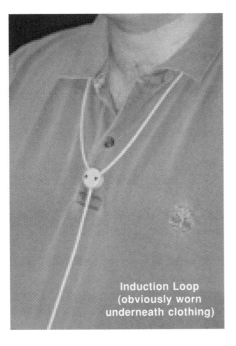

Induction Loop
(obviously worn
underneath clothing)

• Speak at a normal level and do not talk directly into the collar or microphone. It looks odd to see a person walking down the street with his chin glued to his collar bone.

• Do not worry about talking to yourself there are many people that do it! Obviously if you are in close proximity to someone (especially children) be that extra cautious. If you have to talk and the situation is difficult (you may be next to someone on a bench), then pretend to be using your mobile phone but remember to switch off the ringer or you would look daft if it suddenly goes off.

• You may have your PTT switch running down the inside of your sleeve, so keep your arm relaxed. Do not walk with your arm outstretched and appear as if you are carrying a bag with a bomb in it. In a similar manner, if you have your hands in your jacket pockets, do not let your elbows stick out like the proverbial teapot.

Inductor Tab

• Refrain from constantly touching the earpiece, an aware target may notice this. If you are not hearing very well you can do one of the following; adjust the volume, move the inductor closer to the earpiece or wash out your ears!

• Act naturally when you are having to listen in to the commentary and avoid stopping in mid street with a vague distant look on your face. You will look unnatural and anyone who is aware, may notice you.

A covert system is a must for any foot surveillance work. Most professional surveillance operators carry a handheld set in a covert fashion in addition to their main car sets.

Radio Security

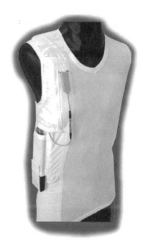

The Delta Vest by Sonic Communications

Leg Harness

Radio transmissions are open to interception and so security is an important factor when transmitting a message. There is little you can do to avoid interception, except from use 'secure' radios which encrypt all messages or use veiled speech and codes.

There are a number of people that may wish to listen in to your radio transmissions:

• The radio enthusiast or radio ham

• The person that unintentionally listens in to you by chance finding

• The person who intentionally listens in

The Radio Ham

These people may spend thousands of pounds on radio receiving and scanning equipment in order to enjoy their hobby. They are able to pick up transmissions and talk to other enthusiasts from all over the world. If they pick up your transmissions, they may be listening for a short while in order to satisfy their curiosity but they may make a note of your operating frequency and return to it at a later date to see what you are up to. Radio hams are 'proud' of what they do and are likely to report to the authorities any misuse of radios, voice procedure or bad language.

The Unintentional Intercept

This could be anyone scanning the airwaves just listening out for anything of interest. They may not be purposefully looking for surveillance operators but if they hear transmissions relating to 'target' or places that sound familiar to them, their interest will be aroused even more.

The Intentional Intercept

Some of the criminal fraternity make use of 'scanners' that are freely obtained from electrical stores and radio shops for as little as £75.00. They will tend to listen into Police broadcasts but they will also lock onto your frequency if you are nearby. These scanners usually lock onto the most powerful and nearest radio signal; they are small and can be carried about the person, used in a house or even in the car. These  people may react to transmissions, if you are overheard stating that you are 'plotted up on the junction of Haworth Road and Gate Lane do not be surprised if you are paid a visit!

There is not much you can do to minimise the risk of interception by eavesdroppers except to use secure radios, therefore the following should be considered:

- Use mobile telephones to send sensitive information

- Keep transmissions to a bare minimum

- Change frequency regularly

- Refrain from sending 'identifiers' such as street names and place names

- Use pre-arranged code words and phrases

- Use Spot codes

Encrypted Radio Sets

Radios that transmit encrypted (or Scrambled) signals are available to the investigator and are essential if you are sending very sensitive information but they are much more expensive to purchase. Law enforcement agencies tend to use encrypted sets manufactured by Racal such as the 'Cougar' PRM 4515 or the latest PRM 5120. Also available is the very latest 'Vector' radio by Thales Communications but this is probably only available to Enforcement Agencies.

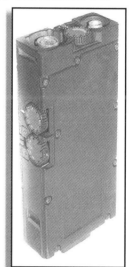

RADIO CALL-SIGNS AND NETWORKS

The Police, Military and other Enforcement Agencies use specialist call signs as a matter of course. Call-signs not only identify the individual operator but also give an indication to what unit, sub-unit or team he belongs to. Complex call-signs and networks are only necessary when there are many operators on the ground with varying tasks.

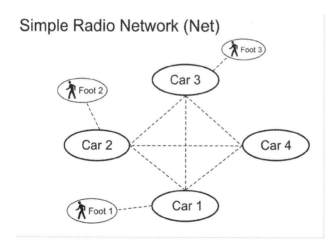

Simple Radio Network (Net)

As a simple network the following diagram shows how the team are labelled, remember, all call-signs can transmit and receive each other. You will note that the team comprises of four cars; Car 1, Car 2, Car 3 and Car 4. These are the call-signs that they will use throughout the surveillance irrespective of where they are in the surveillance convoy.

Car 2 and Car 3 may have a passenger who would be expected to deploy on foot when the need arises. These operators respective call-signs become Foot 1 and Foot 2 in relation to their own vehicle. Should Car 3 pick up Foot 2 for some reason, that person still retains the call-sign of Foot 2.

Advanced Radio Net

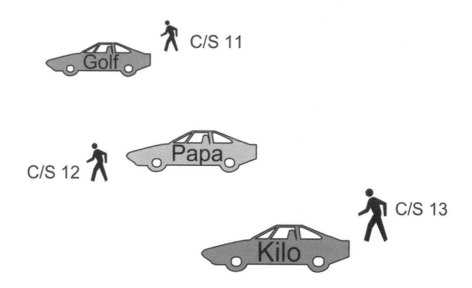

Should the team be on the ground and a base is used as a control point such as an operations room they could use call-sign 'Zero' or 'control'.

On the commercial surveillance circuit it is rare that we go out with two operators in one vehicle (two up) mainly due to the cost implications. When operating 'one up', we tend to keep to a personal call-sign, for example, Peter (PAPA) and Robert (ROMEO).

Another effective call-sign system especially when you are using large teams that are operating on foot as well as mobile is shown in the picture above. Each car has its own individual call-sign such as Golf, Papa or Kilo. When you are 'complete' your vehicle or mobile you use this call sign. However, if you deploy on foot, you then use your foot call-sign such as 11 (one one). This enables other operators to identify whether you are in your car or out on foot.

Establishing Communications

Prior to starting the task, make sure that all radios are working properly and carry out a radio check to ensure that everyone can transmit to and receive each other. If there is a problem, sort it out there and then before getting out on the ground. Ensure that the batteries are charged and that antennas are fitted correctly and tightly. Fresh batteries should be placed in covert earpieces, ready for use.

Radio procedures differ from organisation to organisation such as military or police. The military way of calling a station always states the other persons call sign first and then state your own. So that PAPA wanting to speak to ROMEO would be:

Voice Procedure	Meaning
"ROMEO, PAPA	(Romeo this is Papa)
"ROMEO, send"	(This is Romeo, send your message)

The police way of doing it is the opposite way round:

Voice Procedure	Meaning
"PAPA to ROMEO receiving?	(Papa is calling Romeo)
"ROMEO, go ahead"	(This is Romeo, send your message)

Both differ and neither way is any better than the other, so use the procedure that you are used to.

Radio Check!

As mentioned, you must establish Comms and carry out a radio check before going out on the ground and also when in position on the ground. If Comms is poor due to distance for example, you cannot receive the trigger person, it is you that will have to move to a better position (higher up, move closer or transmit over flat ground) because the trigger is the person who is static and cannot move anywhere.

The sequence of a radio check between call-signs PAPA and ROMEO (with PAPA sending) would be:

> **"ROMEO, PAPA, radio check"**

"PAPA, okay over"   ('difficult' if barely audible, or 'unworkable' if message is not understandable).

"ROMEO, okay out"

If you do not get a reply, send another radio check, if you still do not get a reply then check:

- Your set is switched on!
- Your volume is turned up
- You are on the correct channel or frequency
- The battery is secure and charged
- The antenna is securely in place
- Any ancillary equipment is plugged in properly

If this still does not get a reply transmit send over the air "Nothing Heard". If the other station is able to hear you, they will know that you are unable to receive them. In addition any other team members will know then that there is a communication problem and they would then be able to offer to relay any messages. As a last resort, use your mobile phone to call the other team member in order to establish what the problem is. More often than not, if a radio fails to operate or work it is due to operator error, so check and check again.

If we have a four car team using the call-signs as illustrated above (Car 1, Car 2, Car 3, Car 4), the response should always be in numerical order. For example:

'All call-signs this is Car 1, radio check...'

The response should be:

'Car 2, Okay'
'Car 3, Okay,
'Car 4, Okay'

Followed by:

'Car 1, Roger that, all cars received'

If Car 2 responds and then there is a pause (possibly because Car 3 has a problem). Car 4 should normally wait for about five seconds before he acknowledges, allowing Car 3 time to respond.

Many people from various organisations use the voice procedure that is best suited to them. In surveillance, the radio commentary has to be fast, accurate and to the point, to this end it is greatly abbreviated and pro-words such as OVER or OUT are normally dropped altogether. Many people incorrectly use the word OVER to finish a transmission, this word actually demands a response.

VOICE PROCEDURE

There are various common phrases or words used when transmitting over a network called 'pro-words' and mean the following:

Pro-word	Meaning
OVER	I have finished transmitting and wish you to answer
OUT	End of message and transmission
ROGER	Message received
WAIT	Used as a temporary break in transmission, no one should interrupt
SAY AGAIN	Repeat your last message
RADIO CHECK	An offer to test comms which requires a reply such as Okay
I SPELL	Used prior to spelling out a name in Phonetic Alphabet
NOTHING HEARD	When no acknowledgement is received when calling another station, the phrase "Nothing Heard, Out!" is used. This lets the recipient know that you cannot hear him even when he may be able to hear you
RELAY TO	Used when asking to relay (or pass on) a message to a station that is having difficulty receiving the calling station
PERMISSION	When operating in a large team and a member wishes to say something, he should call the team leader or eyeball and ask for PERMISSION to speak. This avoids the interruption of important commentary
STANDBY!	Used to put the team on alert. This is never to be used in replace of 'WAIT'

At the rear of the book there is a Glossary of Terms, which details further pro-words and phrases commonly used in surveillance voice procedure.

Relay To...

Relaying Messages

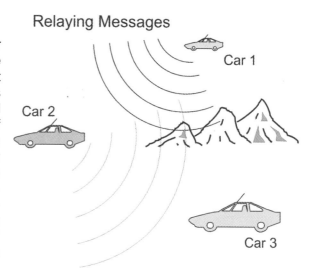

Quite often, one operator may not be able to receive another due to the fact that he is out of range or there is an obstruction such as a hill blocking transmissions. If this is the case, then another operator (who may be located in between the two operators having diffi-culty) can pass on a mes-sage or 'relay' it between them by saying, 'Relaying' and then pass the message on.

A relay car is better located on high ground as it will receive and transmit signals over a wider range. In town centres, the top floor of a multi-storey car park is an ideal location.

Eyeball Permission?

Some enforcement agencies, especially the Police, use a strict method of con-trol over the radio network. When the Eyeball is giving a radio commentary, he is in total control of the radio net and no one should interrupt the commentary for any reason.

Within these particular teams, if another member of the team wishes to speak, they firstly have to ask permission from the eyeball, for example:

> **'Car 1 has the Eyeball, that's the target still inside the premises, no change'.**
> **'Car 2 to Car 1, Permission?'**
> **'Car 1, go ahead'..**
> **'Car 2, can you tell me what the target is wearing?'**
> **'Car 1, yes, blue jeans and black T-shirt'.**
> **'Car 2 received, back over to you'.**

This system has its advantages and disadvantages, for the people that use it regularly, it is a disciplined system and works for them. It could be argued that that this system is rather long-winded and unnecessary. If you need to say something, why not wait for **suitable** break in the commentary and quickly say it. Experience will tell you when you should not interrupt at an important time. The following commentary would be much shorter and quicker:

'Car 2 to Car 1, what's he wearing?'
'Blue jeans and black T-shirt'.
'Car 2 Roger'.

Done, dusted and history...

Phonetic Alphabet

When words or car registrations have to be spelt out over the air the 'Phonetic Alphabet' is often used and is internationally recognised as a means of doing so. This is so that the letters of the words cannot be mistaken for any other and thus avoids confusion.

A	ALPHA	N	NOVEMBER
B	BRAVO	O	OSCAR
C	CHARLIE	P	PAPA
D	DELTA	Q	QUEBEC
E	ECHO	R	ROMEO
F	FOXTROT	S	SIERRA
G	GOLF	T	TANGO
H	HOTEL	U	UNIFORM
I	INDIA	V	VICTOR
J	JULIET	W	WHISKY
K	KILO	X	X RAY
L	LIMA	Y	YANKEE
M	MIKE	Z	ZULU

Target Identity Codes (I.C. Codes)

A number of Enforcement Agencies for many years have used a system of codes in order to describe a person's ethnic origin. This code in recent times has been the subject of debate as it has been suggested that it is not politically correct to use it. However, the code has been in place for many years and is still used today in some circles.

I.C. Code	Ethnic Origin
IC 1	White European
IC 2	Dark European
IC 3	Afro/Caribbean
IC 4	Asian
IC 5	Oriental
IC 6	Arabic
IC 7	Pacific Islander
IC 8	South American Indian

Commentary During a Surveillance

During a mobile surveillance, a running commentary should be given by the lead vehicle (Eyeball) to the remainder of the team to inform them of the targets movements and intentions. It is possible that 'Tail End Charlie' is some 600 metres behind and 'driving blind' and so he will be relying on the commentary in order to put him in the right direction. Commentary during a mobile surveillance is described fully in Chapter Seven on mobile surveillance.

During a surveillance the targets direction of travel (whether on foot or mobile) must always be given as 'Left', 'Right', 'Straight' or 'Reciprocal'.

These directions are always in relation to the **target's** 'Left' or 'Right' and not yours as you look at him.

Spot Codes

Spot codes are used to designate road names and junctions by means of allocating them a colour and a number. This provides two things, security on the net (by not having to give specific road names over the air) and also to quickly communicate to the rest of the team, the targets location and intentions.

Just by stating, "Targets Blue One to Red One" tells a picture of what direction the target is travelling and also his approximate location. When a team is

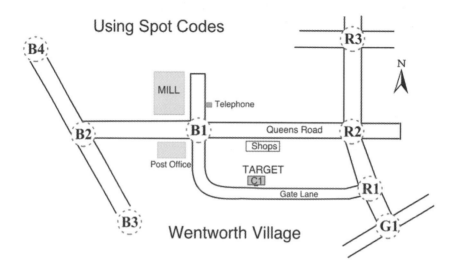

Using Spot Codes

Wentworth Village

deployed on the ground a mobile operator will be assigned an area to 'plot up' on and cover an area such as the Blues, Reds, or Greens.

Depending on the locality, a small number of streets in the vicinity can be spotted, alternately a small village could have all its major junctions spotted as shown in the diagrams.

Hand Signals

Hand signals are to be used when there is no other means of communication or when silence has to be maintained in a situation such as an O.P. Should you be out on foot and communications is lost, you may have to resort to subtle hand signals and 'nods' of the head in order to communicate.

Identity Systems

As previously mentioned, the security of information given out over a radio is very important. Without encrypted radios it would not be practical give sensitive information such as names, addresses, telephone numbers and vehicle details over the air. Anyone being able to monitor your frequency and channel will soon know about the subject of your enquiry and your operation.

In addition, unidentified people or premises should be given an identity if they cannot be named and are unknown to you. It is possible that the subject of a surveillance will meet up with others who are unknown to you and they will require to be identified or given a name/nickname.

There is a simple system, which lets us assign identifier codes to our target, and anyone that he/she has contact with.

For example:

- A male is referred to as an ALPHA
- A vehicle is referred to as a BRAVO
- A property, such as a house or building is a CHARLIE
- A female is referred to as an ECHO
- An unknown is referred to as a UK

OPERATORS BRIEF

A1:   Alan Morris
          35yrs, 5'10"tall, slim build, short fair hair

B1:   Red Ford Focus, Reg: FH52 FGD

C1:   25 Redmond Street, Haworth, West Yorkshire, BD23 9GH
          Tel: 01535 837365

C2:   Novatech Ltd, Gibraltar Ind' Est', Bradford, BD4 6TT

• Individuals

When used in context, the primary target (if it is a male) would be known as 'Alpha 1'. Should he meet up with another male, that male would then become 'Alpha 2' and so on.

If an unknown male arrives at the target's address, he would initially be referred to as a 'UK Alpha'.

In a similar fashion, the primary female target would be known as 'Echo 1'. Or if 'Alpha 1' is your Target, his wife or partner may be assigned as 'Echo 1'.

By assigning individuals I.D. codes it creates less confusion when giving a radio commentary. During a surveillance, the Target may meet up with an unknown male (who could be described as: male, white, thick black hair wearing a blue jumper with a white stripe across). Rather than use this awkward description every time you want to mention him, it is easier to refer to him as 'Alpha 2'.

• Vehicles

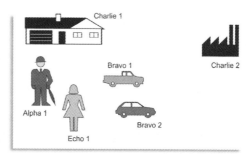

The primary vehicle used by 'Alpha 1' would be 'Bravo 1'. Should you arrive at 'Alpha 1's' home address to commence a surveillance and find two vehicles in the driveway they could be designated 'Bravo 1' and 'Bravo 2'. Any subsequent vehicle related to the task would be further assigned 'Bravos 3, 4 and 5'.

• Premises

In a similar fashion any property or building is referred to as a 'Charlie'. The primary building such as 'Alpha 1's' home address would be referred to as 'Charlie 1', his place of work as 'Charlie 2' and so on. This system or variants of it, are generally used on the security circuit.

Procedure

Radio commentary has to be clear, precise and quick. The terms listed above assist in the speed of transmissions, making them understandable by all. For example, the following message given by a 'trigger' would be long winded and insecure:

> **"STANDBY STANDBY, That's Mr. Jones and his wife leaving the house, walking past the blue Escort and getting into the red Peugeot".**

and could be given as:

> **"STANDBY STANDBY, Alpha 1, Echo 1, exit Charlie 1 going complete Bravo 2".**

or another example:

> **"That's Jones and the male with the long grey coat and beard walking from the blue Escort back into the office building".**

could be given as:

> **"That's Alpha 1, Alpha 2, foxtrot from Bravo 1 to Charlie 2".**

You will note that the messages are shorter, to the point and to some extent, encrypted. The system is simple and effective when used properly and eliminates the need to mention any names that should otherwise be given in 'clear'.

It is the task of the team leader to designate all initial identity codes on a briefing sheet prior to any surveillance task which each operator will be given or nominated during the surveillance.

Encryption of Numerical Information

When other sensitive information such as telephone numbers, house numbers or vehicle registrations have to be transmitted by radio they should be encrypted in the event that they are intercepted by an unauthorised listener.

A simple system we call 'LUDO' can be used to transmit numerical figures. The pro-word 'LUDO' should always be given prior to the numbers being sent, so that the recipient knows that they are encrypted.

Should you want to transmit the telephone number: 750259, add a 1 to each figure, so that it becomes: 861360. Note that a 0 becomes a 1 and that a 9 becomes a 0.

When you transmit your message, it would be in the form of:

"Telephone number, LUDO 861360".

The recipient having heard the pro-word LUDO, then subtracts 1 from each figure to obtain the original number.

In the same manner, house numbers or vehicle registrations can be given so that A123 ABC becomes LUDO A234 ABC, or house number 169 becomes LUDO 270.

The LUDO 'factor' used here has a value of 1 (the numbers alter by 1). This can be altered to 2, 3 or even 4 on a daily basis if your security demands it.

There are many systems of encoding numerical information, one other simple method is to double the original number before it is transmitted or another is to reverse the whole number. It does not matter which system you use, so long as the recipient knows what to do with the information in order to make sense of it. Rather than use exact map grid references, it may be easier to letter and number the grid squares as shown in the picture, in order provide some security

If in doubt, transmit sensitive information by cell phone.

The Click System

When it is not practical to speak, for instance you may be inside a shop or café or when it is difficult to use the radio, a procedure known as the 'Click System' may be adopted.

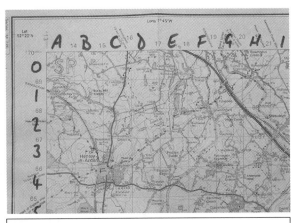

A 'Gridded' Ordnance Survey Map

This system enables you to communicate by pressing the pressel switch (PTT) a given number of times, in answer to direct questions received. The receiving radio receives and hears these presses as 'clicks'.

There are a number of variations to this system depending on the organisation using it. The military tend to use two clicks as YES (double click) whereas Enforcement Agencies would interpret two clicks as NO.

The Enforcement Agency system is as follows:

4 clicks on PTT = Ask Me A Question (AMAQ)
3 clicks on PTT = Yes
2 clicks on PTT = No
5+ rapid clicks = Standby, Standby

In practical terms, the target may get onto a bus and hopefully a foot person will get onto the bus also. Prior to getting on, you have told the remainder of the team of what you are doing. The team realise that you are getting on the bus and therefore they would not expect you to start transmitting, as you may be in close proximity of others.

Hopefully you will have another member of the team following the bus in a car to act as your back up. From the bus you want to communicate with your back up so you will instigate the conversation by giving four clicks (ask me a question). Your back up should hear the clicks and respond.

'Four clicks received, do you want a question?'

To which you respond with three clicks (Yes)

'Three clicks received, do you have control of the Target?'

Click, Click, Click (Yes)

'Is the target with anyone?'

Click, Click (No)

'Roger that, two clicks received. Can you give a standby when the target gets off the bus?'

Click, Click, Click (Yes)

'Three clicks received, roger that'.

When the target makes a move to get off the bus, you need to give a standby and give a series of rapid clicks to which your back up should acknowledge with,

'Roger that rapid clicks, Standby Standby.'

Be careful not to bombard the eyeball with unnecessary questions. The eyeball may be in a position where he is trying to overhear conversation or remember certain facts. The last thing he wants is someone gibbering over the net into his earpiece at the wrong time.

Remember, you can only ask direct questions which require a Yes or No answer.

Care of Your Radios

Your radios are the backbone to your surveillance and so you have to take care of them to ensure that you get the most out of them and that you can rely on them at all times.

- Always keep them clean and dry. If you are working in dry and dusty environment, consider wrapping it up in Clingfilm but let it 'breath' or moisture will damage the set

- Do not let them get wet

- Never switch the set on unless there is an antenna fitted, you will damage it

- Fully discharge the battery before recharging

- Switch the set off when changing batteries

- Be careful when removing ancillaries, you may damage connections and sockets

- Try not to bend or crease the wires in your covert loops and inductors

- Regularly check antenna cables that may have become 'pinched' after being trapped in car doors

Check and test all radio equipment on a regular basis

Chapter Five
Specialist Equipment

5

The investigator will make use of his knowledge and experience to assess a situation and decide how best to tackle the problem to achieve a result. To do this he will have to make maximum use of available equipment.

The equipment he chooses has to be cost effective, long lasting, efficient and most importantly, reliable. It is not always the best policy to buy a cheap alternative if the success of the investigation relies upon it.

The list for equipment is endless, but listed below are items that are frequently used in surveillance tasks. Most surveillance operators make use of a small 'car bag' which is easily portable and carried to and from vehicles, hotels and the office.

The minimum equipment an operator should carry on his person or in his vehicle are:

- **Radio**
- **Dictaphone**
- **Log Sheets**
- **Camera**
- **Binoculars**
- **Mobile Phone**
- **Money**
- **Penlight Torch**
- **Maps & GPS**
- **Identification or Driving Licence**

Identification Cards

Most people carry some form of identification but it may be wise to carry your driving licence with you during surveillance. Inevitably, you will be stopped by the Police from time to time who will ask for some form of identification. If you have your licence with you, not only are you able to show who you are but you also minimise the risk of being asked to produce your licence and any other documents at a later time at a Police station. If you belong to a trade association such as the 'Association of British Investigators' or the 'Professional Surveillance Association', then carry these with you also.

Surveillance Vans

An important piece of equipment is the surveillance van, the majority of surveillances that I take part in, will have a van on the team. Primarily the van can be used to provide the 'trigger' for a mobile surveillance. As a static observation post the operator can observe, record and report events taking place outside for many hours. If I am using a van on a surveillance (but not acting as the trigger), I will often get into the back whilst waiting for a 'standby' in order to hide and get away from prying third party attention.

The type of van is very much up to personal preference, the Ford Escort and Fiesta models are ideal. The Escort is a popular van and is roomy, the Fiesta, although small, is roomy enough and comfortable and is small enough to park almost anywhere. It is not a high vehicle and will therefore not stand out in a line of traffic. From the front and rear it looks like a car and therefore can also be used for mobile surveillance. In the past we have also used a Vauxhall Nova, Renault Clio and a Fiat Punto.

You will be required to make certain alterations to the vehicle, some of which will be essential.

Colour

Which colour should your van be? If it is white will it stand out, or should it be a dark colour? The choice is yours, where dark vans will not stand out as much, a white van can be used just as well as there are many of them about. The van can be left plain or magnetic removable signs can be used to change its appearance.

If you decide to use magnetic advertising signs (Jim's Electrical for example) consider adding a mobile telephone number to it. If any curious third party decides to ring the number to enquire about the suspicious van in the street, you will be called and alerted and be able to provide them with a suitable excuse.

Observation

Obviously you will need to be able to observe your target without them being able to see you. The rear windows of the van could be covered with a film that gives you the ability to look out without anyone being able to see in. Many different types are available and come in roll form from car accessory dealers.

This 'Mirror Tint', comes in differing colours of silver, gold and blue. When applied, visibility out is near perfect whilst from the outside it is almost impossible to see in unless pressed against the glass or in certain light conditions. Many tradesmen's vans have this film fitted and so it does not always stand out or appear odd.

Another film similar to mirror tint is the Smoke Tint. This is black in colour and is just as effective when the inside of the van is made light proof from the front. The smoke tint is more preferable as it does not tend to stand out as much as the reflective mirror. Another alternative is to have a false wall built at the rear doors through which you will be able to observe.

The rear of the van also has to be made light proof from the front for the windows to be effective. Plywood or a curtain suspended from a rail behind the drivers seat is sufficient. This also gives you the ability to view through the front and side windows, when necessary.

Windows and Vision

Your surveillance van needs to be operational in all weathers. A rear windscreen wiper is essential in the event of rain. You should be able to operate it from within and without the ignition being switched on. Likewise in cold or damp weather the inside of the window is likely to mist up, therefore the screen de-mister should be rewired to enable it to be operated in the same way. If your vehicle is going to be adapted it would be recommended to use a secondary battery rather than the vehicles primary battery so as not to run the vehicle battery flat.

Some van operators use a 12 volt hairdryer obtained from camping shops, attached to a spare battery. This gets rid of condensation after a minutes blast of

PETE'S TIP: A tiny amount of washing up liquid on a cloth and lightly smeared over the window will prevent it from misting up. Do not over do it or you will leave streaks and marks which will show up on photographs or video.

warm air. Alternately, you can buy a special fluid from motorcycle shops that prevents helmet visors from misting up and apply this to the window.

Interior

The inside of the van should be panelled with plywood and painted black. This provides you with insulation from the cold, makes the vehicle more sound proof and enables you to attach any fittings such as a shelf or radio.

This American van is a bit too luxurious

Something comfortable to sit on should be provided such as a bean bag. There is nothing worse than being uncomfortable and cramped for long periods of time, always try to sit facing the target rather than having to crane one's neck, it becomes uncomfortable after a short period.

Some form of ventilation should be provided by means of a proper ventilator or by just opening the front windows half an inch or so. In hot weather fresh air is required, in colder weather a flow of air is required to prevent windows misting.

It may not always be viable to observe through the rear window and so the vehicle should be parked in such a manner that viewing is done through the front windscreen or through the side windows whilst sitting in the back. If the weather is extremely cold it may be wise to put some form of hot water bottle on the dashboard under a cloth to prevent the glass from misting and freezing. The rear view mirror should be detachable to enable a clear view and prevent an obstruction for taking photographs.

Alarms

In addition to a standard vehicle alarm a second alarm horn could also be installed, to be operated from within by means of a switch. On occasions, third party curiosity may invite them to take a closer look at the unfamiliar vehicle nearby, a quick burst of high decibel alarm as they touch the vehicle would possibly keep them at bay! In addition it would deter car thieves from stealing the vehicle whilst you are still in the back.

Food & Drinks

Take adequate food and drinks for the duration of your stay. Avoid messy foods and a flask is indispensable. Ensure that you take plenty of water in hot weather to avoid dehydration, some vans can soon become like baking ovens.

Be aware of hot drinks from a flask in cold weather, they will mist up your windows.

Hygiene Provisions

You may be in situ for many hours where it may not be possible to leave to use the toilet. Therefore adequate provision has to be made for urinating or defecating.

Keys

Once in position the keys should be removed from the ignition and placed in a handy spot by the dashboard for easy access. A member of the team should also carry a spare set to be used when the van is being inserted and extracted.

Radio Equipment

Communications are a very important factor in surveillance work where investigators have to work as a team. Therefore the correct equipment is essential.

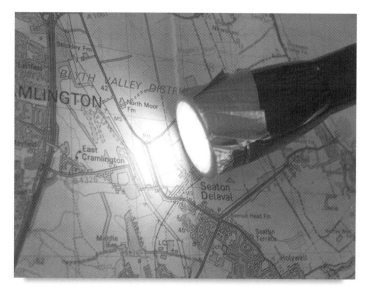

Torch

A small penlight torch is useful for map reading or note taking at night, and will save you from putting on the interior light. Not only will it alert to your presence but also ruin your night vision. If the beam is too bright, cover it with a piece of sticky tape to diffuse the beam.

A large 'Maglite' type torch is strong and durable and can also double up as a means of protection if the need arises.

Optics

As an aid to your vision and to bring your subject 'closer', various optical instruments are available, they should be handled with care and the lenses protected at all times.

Binoculars

There are many different types available and a pair should be selected for their cost, robustness, size and magnification. It is not always the best thing to opt for the most powerful pair you can lay your hands on, nor the smallest pair that will fit into the smallest of pockets. Many people think that the smaller they are, the more covert they will be but at the end of the day, you still have to lift your hands up to your face in order to use them whichever size they are.

Magnification

The power of a pair of binoculars refers to the number of times the subject in view is magnified. Lenses with a power of 'times 8' (8x) magnify the subject 8 times. This has the effect of making an object which is 400 metres away appear to be only 50 metres away.

Binoculars are commonly quoted with a magnification number such as 8 x 25. As mentioned the 8x refers to the lens magnification, the 25 relates to the diameter in millimetres of the objective lens (the larger lens at the front). This is important as the larger the objective lens is, the more effective they will be in low light. If you intend to use your binoculars mostly in the dark hours such as dusk and dawn, then the larger the objective lens the better.

A magnification of about 10 times is suitable for most purposes. Any higher could result in sore eyes and headaches if used for long periods of time.

Field of View

The field of view may be referred to in an instruction booklet and this is the extent of the view to the left and right as you look straight ahead. It is expressed in either degrees or in meters at a range of 1000 metres. That is to say that a field of view of 75° will show you 75 metres of landscape at 1000 metres distant. The greater the magnification the less is the field of view.

Telescopes or Spotting Scopes

Telescopes are ideal when in a static location and you require more viewing power than binoculars. The magnification/lens size guides are the same as for binoculars. However, with a more powerful scope the field of view may be quite narrow. In this case it would be useful to have it mounted on a tripod as hand holding the scope may not be steady enough especially when in an OP for a long period of time.

Many telescopes utilise a zoom facility which enables you to range the power from 8x through to 25x and upwards. If using a zoom lens always initially focus at is closest point and then pull out of the zoom to the required setting.

Lens Hoods

When viewing a subject always be aware of the position of the sun. If it's to your front, remember that any direct sunlight entering the optics will also be magnified and may cause eye damage and blindness. The light may also be reflected off the lens and be seen to glint by your target. To remedy this, use a piece of fine dark netting (or stocking) held over the lens with an elastic band should suffice, without distorting your image. This will cut down reflection and protect your eyes. In addition a purpose made 'lens hood' will prevent stray light from reflecting off the lens.

Night Vision Optics

Night vision equipment is divided into two categories:

- **Passive**

- **Active**

Active devices are always operated in conjunction with an Infra Red light source. The viewing device allows observation in total darkness, without the observer being seen. On looking through the scope nothing will be seen unless there is an amount of infra red light present to illuminate the subject.

Dark Invader
**Image
Intensifier**

Infra red light can be provided by means of a special filter which is placed over the front of torches, vehicle headlights and lamps. On viewing through the device and illuminating the area with an invisible infra red light source, the subject can be observed clearly in the darkest of conditions.

Infra red equipment is cheaper than image intensifiers but has the disadvantage of having to use an active additional light source. The 'Night Shot' facility that you get on modern Camcorders works in this way. Active night vision equipment is not used that often today.

Passive night vision devices are called Image Intensifiers. They do not rely on an additional light source such as infra red to provide a clear view in darkness but they rely on the available light in the sky (which the eye cannot see in darkness) which comes from stars, moonlight and glow. The intensifier magnifies the available light by millions of times to produce an image. This image (as with Infra Red) viewed on a screen within the device and is seen as shades of contrasting green, white and black.

Infra Red Torch Filter

Image intensifiers can also 'see' infra red light and can be used in conjunction with an infra red light source. This enables viewing in shadows and areas of low light.

Many devices are on the market, some are ex Soviet military and can be bought fairly cheaply for a couple of hundred pounds but the quality is very poor and they cannot be adapted to be used with cameras. At present there are four generations of devices. The first being rather bulky and heavy, the fourth generation being lightweight, compact and visually very clear. A good affordable device can be bought for as little as £140.00

Never switch on or use these devices in daylight, unless they are fitted with the correct filters as the internal components can be damaged.

Night Vision Photography

Some of the latest light intensifying scopes can be attached to SLR cameras and Camcorders using specially designed fittings. This provides very good quality low light photographs. High Speed film should be used to enable fast shutter speeds (the scope adds length to the lens and so creates camera shake), the camera should be operated manually and tested to check if the cameras metering system functions correctly. If not, experiment by bracketing exposures to give you the correct and best settings to use.

Using digital video cameras for night work is preferable as the images are immediately available on the viewfinder or monitor, therefore focusing and aperture settings can be adjusted as required. Many camcorders have a system called 'Nightshot'. This camera is able to be used in complete darkness and has its own built in infra-red lamp.

Infra Red Light Source Devices

As already mentioned, infra red light from a torch fitted with a special IR filter enhances the performance of image intensifiers. Other devices are available which can be used for covert applications such as:

• IR Beacon

This small device, the size of a match box emits infra red light from a series of diodes. This beacon is battery powered and can last for four days, providing enough IR light to illuminate a small sized area such as a doorway or a small room. This beacon can be concealed in a target area to be viewed and then observed from a distance.

• Chemical Lightsticks

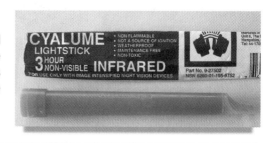

Chemical Lightsticks (manufactured by Cyalume) provide a disposable invisible light source. These lightsticks are in the form of a sealed plastic tube containing chemicals.

When activated (by bending) they produce an intense light source (obtainable in many different colours) and lasts for eight hours. An infra red light stick is available and when activated no emitted light is seen by the eye. But when viewed through IR goggles or an image intensifier it will illuminate a small area with invisible light. These are particularly useful illuminating dark doorways or marking access routes when retrieval is not paramount. In addition they can be attached to a 'trip wire' device which will activate the lightstick when a gate is opened or someone walks across the wire.

Dictaphones

Dictaphones or hand held cassette recorders are a must and are ideal for recording events as they happen, especially when you do not have time to write down any notes such as during a mobile surveillance. You should transfer your recorded notes as soon as practically possible to a hand written log. Tape recorders have a habit of malfunctioning, running out of tape or the batteries running flat at the most critical time.

Tracking Equipment

In surveillance, you cannot have anything better than having actual 'eyes on' of the target. A good surveillance team will be able to keep control of the target by always having him in view.

This is not always possible especially with a very aware target and so technical means may have to be deployed in order to track their movements and there are various means available to us.

Vehicle Tracking

Up until a few years ago, the only way to track a vehicles movements was by using Direction Finding (DF) trans-mitters and receivers. These transmitters were concealed in or under a vehicle that emits a 'bleep' signal every couple of seconds over a fairly wide distance.

Vehicle Tracking Using GPS Satellites

Those that are doing the tracking have a special receiving unit in their vehicle, which gives them a general direction of where the transmitter is. In addition, the audio level of the 'bleep' will let the tracker know how far away the target is.

A second vehicle fitted with the same equipment would also have to be deployed, this way a more accurate location of the target will be obtained as both tracking vehicles can provide a compass bearing which can be plotted on a map and thus pin point an accurate location. This method was fairly accurate when used by experienced operators, however technology moved forward and now similar devices are still available but only one tracking vehicle is needed which uses an array of antennas on its roof. The device will give you a direction and a rough distance and your map reading has to be on the ball to use it.

Satellite Technology

Technology has moved forward in relation to tracking equipment. Like the majority of most surveillance equipment, much of it started life having a commercial use but has now been adapted to suit the surveillance operator.

You my be familiar with Global Positioning Systems (GPS), originally designed as a navigational instrument for aircraft and maritime vessels to show exactly where they were, they have now been made more available to the general public for use in outdoor sports as a portable navigational aid.

These small hand held units have the appearance of a mobile phone and rely on three navigational satellites to pin point their location anywhere on the planet. They are simple to operate, switch in on and it will instantly provide you with a map grid reference or a latitude / longitude co-ordinate of where you are, to an accuracy of 10 metres.

Many of these GPS devices have an internal memory and can automatically store 'waypoints' over a particular time period. What this means is that you can programme the GPS via the menu to store a grid reference of its location every five minutes (or whatever applicable). If one of these devices were to be concealed in a vehicle and programmed to store a waypoint every five minutes you can use it as a tracking device albeit historical. As the vehicle goes about its business all day, it automatically stores these waypoints or grid references in its memory. At the end of the day, the GPS can be removed and the grid references read from the device and plotted on a map showing the route that vehicle has taken. The majority of GPS have the ability to be connected to a laptop computer using digital mapping software and so the data can be plotted on a map automatically, and all this can be done for as little as £200.00.

Garmin 12 GPS

Covert Remote Monitoring

There are many companies world-wide producing GPS systems specifically to track the movements of vehicles, more as a fleet management tool rather than a surveillance device, but there are also companies producing these specifically as surveillance devices.

The device can be installed in a vehicle or be attached by magnets to the underside. Simply explained, a GPS receiver as mentioned above, is interfaced with a GSM mobile phone. The GPS receives data transmitted from navigation satellites and plots its location on the ground. The device can then be interrogated by dialling into the mobile phone interface by telephone or computer and you will obtain a grid reference or a Latitude/Longitude of its position. If you are interrogating the device via a laptop computer, you will be able to locate the vehicle using digital mapping to a very high degree of accuracy and so keep it under surveillance from a comfortable location, or be in a vehicle in the vicinity following from a distance without being in view of the target.

This equipment is available on the open market for as little of £1,500. Getting a bit more technical, these devices can also be fitted with microphones so that you can actually listen in to conversations taking place in the target vehicle.

Other Tracking Systems

GPS tracking systems can be fairly bulky (about the size of two cigarette packets), this may not pose a problem when concealed in a vehicle but at times we may need to keep track of certain objects that do not offer much space for concealment. As with most electronic devices, they all need a power supply and this can often be larger than the device itself, especially when long term monitoring is needed.

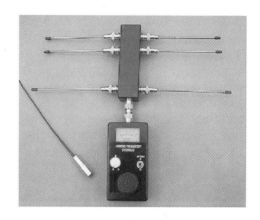

An alternative system to tracking can be carried out with miniature direction finding transmitters similar to those mentioned above. These devices can be concealed in any item or product and be activated when it is moved and then tracked to where it goes and rests.

There are many crude devices like this on the market but the best and probably the most reliable transmitters for this application are designed and used by Falconers in order to track their birds of prey. The transmitter is about the size of a paper clip, they have their own small power supply and are totally weather-proof. When activated, (by switch, motion or light) it will emit a 'bleep' and will operate over long distances. A special hand-held receiving antenna (called a Yagi antenna) is used in order to find the direction that the signal is coming from and is fairly accurate.

Technical Triggering Device

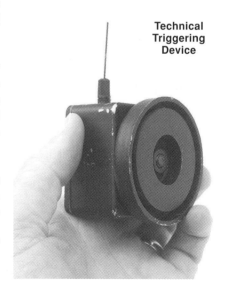

Using two receivers, or more accurately three, it is possible to provide an accurate location of where the device actually is. The batteries can last a number of weeks and have a transmitting range of up to 25 kilometres line of sight.

Tracking equipment, like any other electronic surveillance device is open to failure and so it would only be used as an aid or to back up a physical surveillance. What is frightening about satellite tracking is the high degree of accuracy that it can place a vehicle anywhere on the planet.

Technical Triggers

When it is not possible to observe and trigger a target (for one of many reasons) it would be advantageous to have a system that gives prior warning of the vehicle going mobile. The surveillance team could then be put on 'Standby' and be observing their 'areas' in order to pick up the vehicle for a follow.

A device marketed as the 'Go Tag' can be covertly attached to the underside of a vehicle by magnets or can be wired into the vehicle itself. Approximately two inches square, the device remains dormant until the vibration of the starting engine activates a transmitter, which can be received from some 500 metres away.

The transmitted signal is received on a unit such as a scanner (held by an operator) which gives a bleeping tone when activated. The operator can then put the surveillance team on 'standby' and await the target going 'mobile'.

The equipment list for an operator is virtually endless, as there is so much that can be used to assist in an investigation. You should remember that the equipment is only to be used as an aid and will not carry out the investigation for you. To this end the equipment is only as good as the person operating it. You should be familiar with the equipment, know how to use it proficiently in the daylight as well as in darkness and know its full limitations.

Chapter Six
Foot Surveillance

As a surveillance operator you will obtain more information whilst out on foot. The exposure risk is high and confidence is an important factor. A foot surveillance carried out single-handed can be risky and so a minimum of two operators is recommended. A good standard of foot surveillance by an operator or team, can only be acquired by constant practice and experience.

Difficulties will most certainly occur when carrying out foot surveillance if there is a lack of communication between the team. Without radios, confusion arises and the likelihood of a loss of contact or actually 'showing out' is very high. Covert radio equipment is essential and communication with each other is essential as described in Chapter Four.

The Surveillance Operator

As previously mentioned, the ideal operator could be described as being the 'Grey Person' or

> **Mr 'Nobody' but a Mr 'Everybody' who looks like Mr 'Average'**

During surveillance, there are two things that will always get you noticed, especially whilst on foot:

- **Multiple Sightings**

- **Unusual Behaviour**

• **Multiple Sightings**

It is obvious that the more times a target sees you, the more chance of him remembering you. He will remember you if he is 'surveillance aware' or by the way that you dress and act whilst out on the street.

Wherever we are, we attempt to stay out of the '10 to 2' arc of vision, especially whilst on foot. You should remain to the side or behind the target at all times. If you find yourself in a situation where you do get in front of the target, get out of the way as soon as possible; get into a shop, a doorway or side street but do not linger in his '10 to 2'.

> Remember: If you can see him, he can see you

• **Unusual Behaviour**

In everything that we do, we have to act naturally and give a reason for being there, but this is easier said than done. On training courses we find that students realise that this is one of the hardest things to do in surveillance. Anyone can walk down a street or stand in a shop doorway but give them a radio and a mission (for example, watch that shop front) and they turn into a different person. They talk noticeably into their collars, constantly touch their earpiece, shift about and 'balloon' around the high street as if trying to dodge a swarm of bees. This is expected in a beginner but as training, practice and most importantly confidence builds up they eventually become effective covert operators.

Foot Surveillance Tactics

If we look at the diagram, this provides us with a basic street layout as you would expect to find in a town centre. Our scenario is where we wish to put a member of the Burger Bar staff under surveillance in his lunch hour, in order to see where he goes during that time. We need to 'plot up' in the area using a three-man team.

Remember our three phases of a surveillance; the **Pick Up**, the **Follow** and the **Housing**, so we will commence with the Pick Up phase.

The Pick Up Phase

We have already discussed various trigger positions in Chapter Two so we have decided to put your trigger man in the telephone box outside the Chemist.

The trigger should be in a position close enough to identify the target but far enough away not to be seen and out of the '10 to 2'. He needs to carry out a

Foot Trigger Positions

Bus Shelter 1				Post Office		Cafe'
K	Clothes Shop	Burger Bar A	News	Jewellers	Estate Agent	
	D	F				
Pay Phone B	E	Benches	C			J Bus Shelter 2
	Chemist	G Electrical Store	Cards	H Travel Agent	I Public House	Bank
				Pet Shop		

radio check with the other team members and ensure that they are in position, ready to take the follow. If nothing is happening (you may be in for a long wait), the trigger (or Eyeball) should come up on the radio and report, 'No change, No change'. This is for a number of reasons; it lets the team know that nothing has happened, it acts as a radio check and it gives confidence to the other members, as they know that you are in control and your radio is working okay.

There is nothing worse on a radio network than long periods of silence. If nothing is heard, operators start to lose confidence and think that something has gone wrong. They start to fiddle with the radio to see if it is working okay and possibly move position to see what is happening, so keep the team informed at regular intervals.

During surveillance training we have found that one of the hardest things for the students to do was to stand still. If the target had entered a store, one of the team has gone in with him, leaving the other two outside to cover the exits. The two acting as back up find it hard to keep still without feeling obvious. If there is a shop doorway, stand to one side of it as if you are waiting for someone and stay there rather than keep shifting about.

If there is a seating area or bench then sit on it, they are natural places for you to remain static. In addition, if there is an empty phone box nearby then get into it.

So we have callsign Foot 1 giving the trigger, located in the telephone box. From here he can cover the exit door, give a 'standby' when the target appears out in the open and also give a direction of travel.

Foot 2 and Foot 3 need to be located either side of the target and out of sight. Foot 2 has taken a position up in the bus shelter, left of the target outside the Bank, and Foot 3 has taken up a position in another bus shelter which is right of the target and around the corner on West Street.

Remember, only one person has to see the target (the eyeball), the other two team members have to be 'off the plot' and out of the way. You do not want the target to come out of the premises, turn left or right and have a 'head on' collision with you.

STANDBY STANDBY!

When the target appears, the eyeball should immediately call, 'Standby, Standby'. This is a wake up call to the team to say, 'let's go' and listen in to the commentary'. The eyeball should give a direction of travel and a brief description, for example:

> **'Standby, standby, that's Alpha 1 out and gone Left, Left, wearing blue jeans and a brown jacket, continuing up the high street passing the newsagent on his nearside'.**

As the target has come out and gone left, Foot 2 should not move anywhere, he can stay where he is for the time being. Foot 3, having heard on the radio that the target has gone left will realise that he is walking away from his position. That should be his cue to leave the bus shelter, come around the corner onto the high street and take the 'first follow'. He would come up on air and state, 'Foot 3 has the eyeball', and then takes up the commentary. We say that there are no rules in surveillance but a very important rule is the fact that the trigger person never moves on a standby (unless as a last resort) to take the first follow.

Remember it is a team effort, so the trigger person 'triggers' the target out and another member takes up the first follow. If the target were to be aware at anytime, it would be when he leaves the premises and so the trigger person (who can see the target, so the target can see him) should remain where he is until out of the targets view.

The Follow Phase

As soon as practically possible the surveillance team will filter themselves in a position as illustrated in the diagram below.

Foot 3 has the eyeball and positions himself behind the target at a safe distance depending on the area and the amount of people about. Foot 2 is the back-up and positions himself behind the eyeball, also at a safe distance. It is not necessary for the back-up to see the target. Tail end Charlie takes up a position on the other side of the street. The team is now positioned in what is called the classic A, B, C formation.

A.   Operator 'A' (Foot 3) is behind the target with a reasonable distance between them depending on cover, crowds and the area.

B.   Operator 'B' (Foot 2) is on the same side of the street and is 'backing' Operator 'A'. There is no need for him to see the target and he should be able to see Operator 'C'.

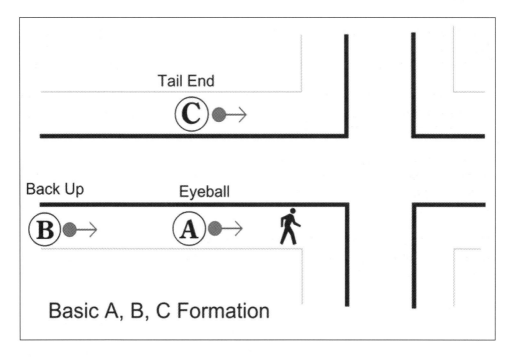

C.   Operator 'C' operator is positioned on the opposite side of the street from the target and is slightly behind him.

Three Man Team (A, B, C Method)

The foot surveillance team requires the mobility and the frequent changing of its operators in order to prevent compromise.

In diagrammatic form, the formations appear regimented and give the impression that the positions have to be strictly adhered to. This is not so, as once on the ground, the experienced operator will take up his position without thinking. The use of three men in a team permits greater variation in the position of operators and also allows for a member who may be getting 'warm' who can be replaced by another operator from the team. It reduces the risk of losing the target and affords greater security against showing out.

Impose Surveillance

Should the target cross from the nearside of the precinct to the offside (left to right), the eyeball and back-up should not follow him, this is why we 'impose' surveillance on a target, rather than 'follow' him.

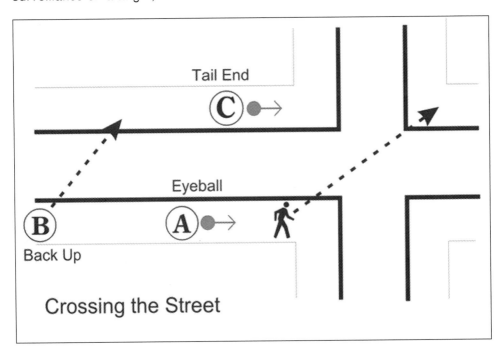

Crossing the Street

To recover from this situation, operator 'C' can take the eyeball, as he is already in a position on the other side of the street, and operator 'B' can then move to the other side of the precinct in order to 'back' the eyeball. Operator 'A' can stay where he is and cover the other side of the street.

Foot surveillance is about team work and communication. If you lose sight of the target, we use the term 'temporary unsighted' so that another team member can take control if need be. During the surveillance, remain out of the targets '10 to 2' at all times and use whatever is around you to act as temporary cover. By this, you should not be diving in and out of cover, but you need to momentarily have something between you and the target, so that if he turns around you will not be in direct view.

Remember: If you can see him, he can see you

Use what is termed as 'street furniture' to provide temporary cover, this could be:

- **Other pedestrians**
- **Telephone boxes**
- **Advertising boards**
- **Parked cars**
- **Bus shelters**
- **Trees**
- **Lamp posts**
- **Shop doorways**

On the street you have to make constant appraisals as to the targets intentions and always think to yourself, What If.

What if he crosses the road...
What if he enters a building...
What if he turns and walks towards me...

The A, B, C method in very crowded streets can be difficult to keep to, and at times it may be necessary for all three operators to be on the same side of the street. If you are close to the target, do not let him hear your radio commentary.

The A, B, C method on a street with little or no traffic such as a housing estate can create difficulties, and it may be that only one operator is on the same side of the street as the target with the other two operators on the opposite side. If a vehicle is used as back up, a footman can be picked up and re-deployed ahead of the target if need be.

TACTICS IN FOOT SURVEILLANCE

A surveillance operator is a member of a team and he must at all times be in communication with the others. In the event of radio failure, use simple hand signals which are unobtrusive and discreet and which have been pre-arranged with the other members of the team. Failing that, you will have to resort to using mobile phones.

The use of these signals and tactics must be automatic and apply to every team member.

When on the ground consider the following:

• Avoid eye to eye contact with the target. If you do have this eye to eye contact, you know and he knows that something is amiss and you will be compromised.

• If the target approaches you, never act surprised but act naturally. Have a good cover story ready in the event you are questioned. It is more realistic to dismiss the target as a 'nutter' rather than go into an elaborate and unrealistic excuse.

• Always remember that you may be seen but not necessarily noticed, therefore act naturally at all times and be aware of your dress sense.

• Always ask yourself, am I in the right position? If not, get into it.

• Do not dodge behind corners or into shop doorways if the target turns round, this only attracts attention to you. Do not forget that shop windows can reflect the activity of persons on the opposite side of the street. They can be of use to you but they can also be of use to the target.

• Always act naturally if the target turns round and retraces his steps, walk on and avoid eye contact. Remember, another team member should automatically take control. Whatever you do, do not look behind you, as sure as the sky is blue, if you look over your shoulder, the target will be doing the same.

• When in a confined area always endeavour to be doing 'something' but act naturally doing it, give yourself a reason for being there.

• In crowded areas, walk on the outside of the pavement. This gives better vision and less obstruction. The nearside of the pavement is good cover when the streets are less crowded.

• Do not take unnecessary risks.

• Ensure your mobile phone is in silent mode.

• Stay out of the '10 to 2'.

• Be third party aware at all times.

Change of Eyeball (Handover)

It must be realised that the closer the operator is to the target, the more likely he is to be seen and noticed, therefore he must be changed at regular intervals in order to prevent having a compromise. In some ways you could follow him all day on your own and not be noticed, so long as the target does not turn around. However, surveillance is not like that and so we have to act accordingly.

After having the eyeball for a period you may feel that you have had a bit of 'exposure' or you feel 'warm' and therefore could do with a change to let someone else take the eyeball.

There are four occasions when we would normally carry out a handover:

• **When you are 'warm', or you have had the eyeball for sometime**

• **When the target changes direction**

• **When the subject stops and then moves off again**

• **If you are compromised**

The larger the team, the more changes can be made, but do not make changes for changes sake and it is normally the eyeball that will decide when to handover.

Simple Handover

When walking down a street and require a handover, you should ask your back up if he is in a position to take the eyeball (this is what we call a 'planned handover'). If he replies 'Yes', then you can handover to him by turning in to a shop, a side street or moving to the other side of the street and letting the back-up come through to take the eyeball.

Tail end Charlie should then move in a position to act as back-up.

Cornering Drills

Should the target change direction by turning a corner, we need to maintain control over him. What we should never do is turn the corner and go around with him in the event that he suddenly stops. He may stop because he is suspicious of you, he may be browsing in a shop window, or he may be waiting to cross a road. For this reason, we do not want to go around a 'blind' corner or this 'zone of invisibility'.

As the eyeball does not want to go into this zone, one of the team members should 'clear the corner' and let the eyeball know if it is clear to come round or through.

You will note in the diagram below that the eyeball (operator 'A') gives advanced warning of a junction or a corner. This should be the cue for operator 'C' to move up to the corner on his side of the street to enable him to see and clear the corner. If the target has stopped, operator 'C' will state, 'It's a Stop Stop, hang back'. If the target has turned the corner and continues up the street, Operator 'C' can say, 'Corner clear, come through'.

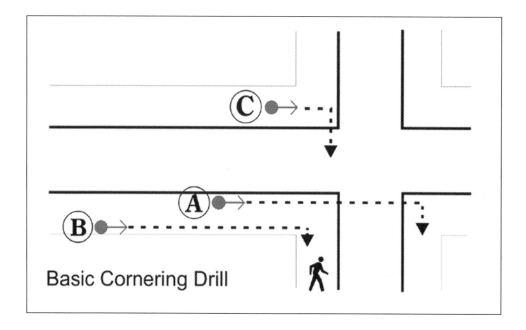

Basic Cornering Drill

As we are changing direction, it may be a good time to carry out a handover, in the event the target is changing direction in order to identify followers. To do this, once operator 'C' has cleared the corner, rather than the eyeball actually turn the corner and continue the commentary, he should cross directly over the road to take up a

'C' position. The back-up can then come around the corner and take over as eyeball, and the operator who has cleared the corner then acts as back up.

We have now carried out a basic cornering drill where we clear the corner and carry out a handover at the same time.

If you are on your own, there is no way that you would want to go around a blind corner. Therefore to recover this, you should consider moving to the other side of the street and effectively clear the corner for yourself and then move into a safe position to follow.

Housing Phase

We have picked up the target, we have followed him and now he suddenly stops. At this stop, we need to carry out a set drill so that the team can work effectively. If he goes into a shop, we must decide, if it is necessary that we go in with him.

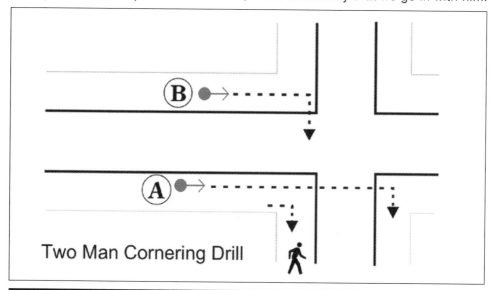

Two Man Cornering Drill

Think about your aims and objectives, if you are investigating a person suspected of copyright infringement of music CD's who enters a newsagent and then goes into a chemist, it may not be necessary to go in with him at a risk losing a life. If however, he goes into a record store then we need to get in close in order to gain some intelligence.

Action on a Stop

If we have the target under control walking down a street and he then enters a shop (newsagent) we have now entered our 'housing' phase of the surveillance and so we now have to re-plot and prepare for the 'pick-up' phase.

We have decided that we are not going to enter and so a set drill is put into action as per the diagram below.

a. The eyeball (**A**) should call, 'It's a Stop Stop at the newsagent'.

b. He should then carry on straight and overshoot, stating, 'I'm going to overshoot, back-up, can you?' (take the eyeball). Hopefully the reply would be, 'Yes Yes'.

c. The back-up (**B**) then takes the eyeball, moves into a safe position and takes control of the doorway and takes the trigger.

d. Now that the doorway is under control, operator '**A**' overshoots and takes up a position on the original route and operator '**C**' takes up a position on the reciprocal route.

e. We are now back to our pick-up phase and the process starts once again.

Multiple Exits From Buildings

If you suspect that the premises has another exit or is located on a corner, operator 'A' should not only overshoot, but also check the rear and side for possible exits. If there are any, he should notify the team and get a trigger on those exits also.

Get In Close

If you decide that an operator needs to enter the premises with him, try to let the back-up go in rather than the eyeball. Tell the team that you are going 'complete' (or in with him) so that the team can expect you to 'minimise' on the radio. If you need to communicate to the team, you can resort to the click system.

For the team members on the outside, consider that the eyeball may be trying to obtain information by listening into the targets conversation. Therefore, do not start talking unnecessarily on the net as the last thing the eyeball wants is a distraction by your voice coming in through his earpiece.

Communications

Communications can literally make or break a foot surveillance. A foot team should normally carry covert radio sets as mobile phones are not suitable and the team should know and be familiar with basic hand signals.

During surveillance training courses we carry out a foot exercise and allow the students to use covert radio sets. They appear to do reasonably well, except for dropping their heads into their chests in order to speak into the concealed microphone. This is not necessary as you can talk quite openly whilst acting normally.

As the eyeball, you should now be giving a commentary on the targets movements. Many surveillance operators prefer the back-up to acknowledge his transmissions now and again (after every three or four transmissions or on a change of direction). After the eyeballs transmission, all the back-up has to say, very briefly is, 'back-up roger'. This tells the eyeball that his messages are coming across and also gives him confidence, knowing that his back-up is in position.

Cross Contamination

Now and again, you may have a problem with your radios or there may be a need when you have to meet up with, and talk to, another team member. If you have to, ensure that you are out of sight from the target because if he is aware and is suspicious of a particular team member, who then comes over to you, you put yourself at risk of compromise if seen by the target.

Action on a Loss

Should the target go out of your view you must alert the team with the call, 'Temporary Unsighted' and give a reason, such as 'Temporary unsighted due to traffic'. If you regain sight, you can inform the team by calling, 'Eyeball Regained'.

PETE'S TIP: If you are in close proximity to members of the public (you may be sat on a bench) consider taking out your mobile phone and pretend to be speaking on it when you are actually transmitting. Remember to switch off the phone or have it in 'silent/vibrate' mode, the last thing you want is for it to start ringing in your ear.

Now and again the team will suffer a loss where the target has disappeared. This has to be acted upon very quickly as the longer the target is 'unsighted' the further he will be getting away from the team. A set drill should be carried out in the event of a loss and the eyeball should call, 'Total Loss, Total Loss' as soon as possible.

Search Procedure

• The eyeball should decide which is the most logical route or quickest escape route that the target could have taken and head for this, searching to his left and right as he goes along.

• The back-up should take the second most logical or quickest escape route.

• Tail end Charlie should hold the 'point of loss' in the event that the target returns through it.

• By holding the point of loss, that operator is also in a good position to act as back-up if contact is regained. He is also in a position to relay radio messages to the team who may be getting further apart.

• If contact is regained, the eyeball should call, 'Contact Contact, target (or Alpha 1) went Left Left at the point of loss and is continuing along East Street'.

Cafés & Public Houses

If the target goes into a café you must decide whether to follow him in or not, remember, he could be meeting someone. If you do decide to go in, consider the fact that you may have to 'lift off' after the target leaves, as you may not be able to re-join the team on the surveillance due to risk of compromise.

If you go into a café but it is not necessary that you get in close to the target, you need to position yourself where you can 'dominate' the room. By this we mean that from where you sit, you should be able to see the target and the exits, including toilet doors.

If it is necessary, get as close as possible to the target without being obvious. Consider sending two people in (preferably a man and woman) to make their presence appear more natural and sit opposite your partner. You can then talk on a radio giving the appearance that you are in conversation.

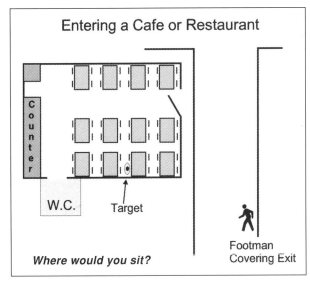

Entering a Cafe or Restaurant

Counter

W.C.   Target

Footman Covering Exit

Where would you sit?

• Do not feel awkward in public places, you have a right to be there, you are a member of the public.

• Always have cold drinks. If the target suddenly leaves, it may appear odd for you to leave a hot drink or meal on the table and walk out.

• Pay for your beverages as you receive them. If the target departs, you do not want to be left in a queue waiting to pay.

• Sit close if a meeting is in place, you do not necessarily have to face the target.

• Use the crossword page of a newspaper to write and make notes if necessary.

• Use the click system to communicate to the rest of the team. It is the trigger person outside who should respond to you.

• Switch you mobile phone onto 'silent' mode.

Buildings with Multiple Exits

Should the target enter a building with multiple exits such as a department store, be aware of both uniformed security guards and store detectives. They are trained to recognise anything out of the ordinary or suspicious and they will soon notice you if you do not act naturally. Many store detectives make use of covert radios and you will soon become the target under surveillance, in addition it is likely that you will be tracked by closed circuit TV.

Be extremely careful if you enter a store with a bag containing a covert camera such as a sports bag. Store detectives will naturally 'lock' onto anyone entering a shop carrying a bag, for obvious reasons.

When the target enters a building or a large department store with multiple exits, the team must deploy to cover all the exits out. Many large stores are used as a cut through for shoppers to make short cuts and so he should be kept under control visually until all the exits are covered. It may be necessary for the whole team to enter the store.

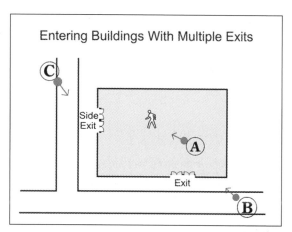

Entering Buildings With Multiple Exits

Indoor Shopping Malls

Treat indoor shopping malls as you would streets, and position yourself in the classic ABC formation. You should be aware of hazards such as security guards and CCTV cameras in operation, if you act unnaturally you will be tracked.

Some areas have multiple levels and so be prepared for using stairways inside shops, elevators and escalators. It may be wise to deploy an operator on a separate floor.

Telephone Kiosks

The target or yourself can use telephone kiosks at any time for various reasons:

• By the Target

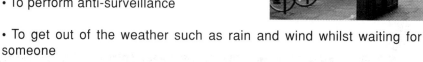

- The obvious, to make or receive a phone call

- To perform anti-surveillance

- To get out of the weather such as rain and wind whilst waiting for someone

You should always be wary of any stop at a telephone kiosk, the target, even if making a call, has a clear view to three sides and it is a natural tendency for him to look around outside whilst talking on the phone. Some public call boxes have advertising pictures stuck to the glass windows in them, these adverts enable you to see out of the box but observers cannot see into them. They are a good form of cover if you need to take photographs or video film.

• By Yourself

> • Use the box as natural cover from where to observe

> • Act natural, remember to pick up the phone and pretend to speak

> • If there are two boxes adjoining can you get into the second box and listen into the targets conversation? If you do, place your back towards him, don't let him see your face or earpiece

Buses

If the target makes for a bus stop, inform the team as soon as possible as you will probably have to get on with him. Do not get unnecessarily close whilst waiting for the bus to arrive and consider keeping away from the bus stop altogether especially if there is no one else around.

As the bus draws near, attempt to obtain the fleet number, registration number or other identifying feature and relay this to the team. You may have an operator in a car backing you and so he does not want to end up following the wrong bus, they can all look alike!

Inform the team that you are getting on the bus so that they will know that you will be unable to communicate. If you can over hear the targets destination, you can ask for the same. Keep a hold of your pressel switch whilst asking for the ticket, as this will be transmitted to your team.

You do not want to be sat in the targets '10 to 2', so attempt to sit behind him so that he does not have you in his view. If he goes upstairs on a double decker, remain downstairs at the rear and cover the stairs. Obviously, if there is a strong possibility that he may meet someone on the bus, then you need to get close.

PETE'S TIP: *Always clear the telephone box when vacated, the target may have left a scrap of paper or a note with important information on it. If you do this, ensure that you do so out of view of the target.*

If you have your back-up following in a car you will need to communicate with him and so instigate a communication by giving four clicks when you can. If the target shows intention of getting off (anxiously looking out of window, doing up jacket, picking up bags) then give the team a 'standby' as they can then prepare themselves for deploying on foot.

Trains

Should your target arrive at a train station, Panic! (No, not really). The team leader will decide whether to put an operator or two on the train with him. The size of the surveillance team will obviously dictate on what course of action to take. If it is envisaged that the target is likely to use a train, or that it is part of his routine to do so, you can be better prepared and deploy a larger surveillance team. A train journey can be broken down into three parts, the beginning, middle and the end, and it is at the end phase or destination when you are most vulnerable.

On entering the station and ticket office, the following should be adopted:

• The eyeball gets right behind the target at the ticket counter (if the destination is unknown). He is to establish the targets destination by overhearing the target or by 'blagging' it out of the counter assistant.

• The eyeball purchases return tickets for the team to the targets destination and informs the team of the details by radio. Obtain return tickets in the event the target returns; if he does not, at least the team can get back.

• Keep control of the target on the platform; if there are not many people about keep away and out of his sight until the last minute that the train arrives.

• The team leader should decide whether to put two or three operators on the train (recommended) and deploy a mobile unit to the trains destination (if practical).

• The eyeball should keep control at all times and not relax, the target may get off the train at an earlier halt than expected, especially if he is surveillance conscious.

• The remaining team should locate themselves in the carriages either side of the targets carriage and preferably facing the adjoining door. If the eyeball is unable to tell you that the target is moving carriages, you should at least be able to see it happen.

• Remember to put your mobile phone onto 'silent' mode. You do not want the whole train looking at you if it rings.

When on the train, you have to keep tight control of the target. Just because he bought a ticket to somewhere does not necessarily mean that he will get off there. You may consider deploying your other team members in different compartments in the event the target moves.

If you are the eyeball, you may find it difficult to communicate to the rest of the team, especially when the train arrives at a station. A click system could be used in a similar fashion as we have already described. If the target starts to get off the train, then rapid clicks can be given (standby). If the target stays where he is 'two clicks' could be given to let the team know that he is still on the train. This procedure can also be used on a bus.

Following a target on a train is fairly simple, as he has nowhere else to go. The difficult part of the surveillance is when he arrives at his destination, as so many options are open to him. He could:

- Get on another train
- Take the underground
- Continue on foot
- Get into a taxi
- Take a bus
- Be met by a car
- Have his own car parked nearby
- Cycle

Underground Railways

Tube trains should be covered in a similar manner to that described above. There are other hazards that work against you; you will not have any communications to those 'up top', it will be very crowded and so you will have to close in to the target as much as possible.

Taxis

At times your target may take a taxi. Treat this as you would a mobile surveillance but be aware of certain dangers:

- The driver will probably know all the short cuts and 'cut throughs' and so he will make many short left and right turns, therefore handovers should be carried out more frequently if you are in a following vehicle.

- Expect him to stop at short notice and stop anywhere.

- If you are also following in a taxi, be careful of what you say to the driver as you do not want your driver to alert the targets driver. Some taxi drivers can be very protective over their comrades.

- Make a note of the taxi firm if it is a private hire company. If you have a loss, you may be able to phone the company and 'blag' the destination from the controller.

On a recent surveillance, this happened to us, so we telephoned the cab company and said that the person who had been picked up from 'Smiths Offices' had forgotten their mobile phone. They told us where he was dropped off so that we could send someone round with it. It worked.

Lifts & Elevators

Should the target enter a large building with many floors, the team should expect the eyeball to minimise on his radio and possibly resort to 'clicks' to communicate. If the target makes for an elevator, you could follow him in but consider:

• Is it necessary and will we achieve anything? The operator, having been in close will have to pull off the surveillance afterwards as he has been exposed.

• Is it safe or wise to enter with him? The target could be a bit of a 'hard man' and have a go at you.

• Remove your covert earpiece, it may be seen or heard in close proximity.

• Avoid eye contact at all times.

• Take control of the button panel. If you do, you can ask the target which floor he wants (as any person would do), you then get off at the same floor or the one above or below.

• Be prepared for casual conversation with others or the target himself.

• Switch your mobile phone onto 'silent' mode.

• Relay the floor to other team members as soon as possible.

If the targets intended floor is unknown (as he had taken control of the button panel) your best option is to take the second to top floor if he is going up. This way you will be able to identify which floor he gets off at, and get off at the floor above. If he gets off at the same floor as you, 'Bingo!', if he remains in the lift he only has one other option open to him (the top floor).

After being in close proximity of the target, you have to consider that you have had much exposure (although not necessarily compromised) and so you may have to come off the task so that you do not become compromised.

Escalators

Many indoor shopping centres and underground train stations have escalators which should not cause too much of a problem. When on the escalator:

- Keep to the right side and use other pedestrians as cover

- Put only one member of the team on the escalator at any one time. If the target turns around, he may see all of you

- There may be a short period when the target is 'unsighted' as he disappears over of the apex of the top, so quickly take control or he will be lost

Deploying on Foot from a Car

When the target departs on foot or leaves his vehicle, the surveillance team has to act with urgency in order not to lose contact with him at this critical stage. Prior to the surveillance commencing, the team leader should have planned and briefed his team what to do, in the event that the target goes on foot.

If the team is involved in a three car follow and the target parks up and walks into a town centre, a foot operator should deploy straight away to take control of the target. The remainder of the team can then position their cars for the departure and then join and 'back' the eyeball on foot. Think ahead, if the target enters a car park, it is likely that he is going to park his car and go on foot, so you should be thinking of deploying the second he enters the car park.

Ideally, one operator should remain and cover the target's vehicle in the event the foot team have a loss

Reverse park to ensure a quick getaway

and the target returns to his car. At times the footman will have to 'dump' his car and risk parking fines and watch out for wheel clampers. If at all practical, another operator can move the footman's car to a safer location for him.

Deploying on Foot

When deploying on foot remember:

- Before you deploy. Ask yourself: 'Is it necessary, do I have to get out?'

- Never screech to a halt. Act naturally and never run or appear to rush

- Always reverse park your vehicle to enable you to manoeuvre away quickly

- Cover up any equipment, paperwork or maps

- Inform the Team Leader of your intention to go on foot

- Switch your main radio off and your covert set on

- Don't forget your mobile phone and wallet, you may end up on a train!

- Ensure your car is locked

- Carry out a radio check with your covert radio set

- Do not run

- Take control of the target

If you are 'two up' and the passenger gets out on foot. Remember where you were dropped off, as this should be the same spot where you get picked up again afterwards. If it is not practical to do so, ensure that you designate a place to get picked up from.

Vehicle Back Up (Shadow Car)

Once the team is deployed on foot and has control of the target, one of the operators should remain with his vehicle in order to act as back-up and 'shadow' the team. Not only can he pick up and re-deploy any footmen but if the target gets into another vehicle or onto public transport you will still have a mobile option.

The 'shadow car' could also act as a radio relay, as the car radio set should be pushing out much more power.

Returning to your Vehicle

- Handover the eyeball to a mobile operator who is covering the target car as soon as possible. The foot men will want to get back to their vehicles.

- Turn your covert radio off (it will interfere with your car set)

- Take a look around you, think third party

- Lock your doors

- Tell the team that you are 'complete' (back in the car)

Note Taking

During a foot surveillance it is difficult to make written notes of the target's movements, locations and contacts. Therefore it may be wise for one member of the team to carry a dictaphone on which to record events, but ensure that the recorder is reliable and that the batteries work. Alternatively, one of the mobile units could keep a written log by listening in to the radio commentary as they proceed.

Chapter Seven
Mobile Surveillance

Mobile surveillance is probably one of the most difficult types of surveillance to carry out, as there are so many factors that are against you whilst following a mobile target. The target has to be followed without detection and without you losing contact with him. At the same time you have to keep a log of events and actions, communicate with the other members of the surveillance team, navigate, photograph and consider the targets future intentions.

A mobile surveillance should not be a 'mad car chase', driving at excessive speed, screeching brakes and handbrake turns, but is done in a calm, relaxed, professional manner and most importantly, being in control.

The Surveillance Team

We refer to a mobile surveillance being carried out by a team rather than an individual. Carrying out a surveillance on your own is asking for trouble as the risk of compromise is very high from the outset and loss of contact in traffic is inevitable.

An operator on his own will soon be spotted and would therefore jeopardise any further surveillance, he may also lose the target at the first road junction he approaches. The success of a surveillance is dependant on how many operators are used, a combination of cars and motorbikes provide an effective surveillance team. However, I have worked in a team of six operators and a loss has still occurred.

It is appreciated that in the commercial sector, clients are very cost conscious and that a surveillance can be expensive to carry out. If you have to supply a potential client with an estimate of charges it is essential that you inform them of the importance of using a **minimum** of two investigators to carry out a mobile surveillance, which will reflect in the costs.

The Team

Prior planning would decide on the size of the team. Factors to consider are:

> • Is surveillance the answer? Can you achieve your aims by any other means?

> • Costings per surveillance operator

> • The targets awareness level

> • Area that the target is likely to be in, for instance, town centres, rural or motorway and the likely areas he may visit, you may need a motorbike or foot men

> • Whether a static OP is required to act as 'trigger'

> • Is a footman required to double up with a mobile operator?

A well trained and exercised surveillance team will enable a mobile surveillance to be carried out with the minimum of effort. Members can act on their own initiative without having to be instructed by the team leader, especially when the target comes to a halt and the team splits to surround him or 'boxes him in'.

Whenever possible make use of a static operator in a van or an OP to give you the 'trigger'. The most likely time to lose a target is within minutes of his departure, especially if his departure time is unpredictable and he knows his own area well. Surveillance is normally considered easy or difficult from the way that it is triggered.

Type of Vehicles

Ideally, all of the team's vehicles should be different in all respects, it would be a waste of time having two red Ford Escorts on the same task! Ideally the colour of the car should be a dark shade, obviously a bright orange car will soon stand out. A black car may give a sinister appearance; a white vehicle seen in the rear view mirror may resemble a Police car and make the target look at you more than once.

An ordinary production line saloon car with a reasonable sized engine should be used. We are not embarking on a mad car chase but if you become detached from the team, you need some power under the bonnet for you to overtake other motorists, especially large slow moving vehicles and so a 1.8 or 2 litre engine should suffice. Colour and appearance should be neutral and as nondescript or as commonplace as possible.

A vehicle will be seen but should not be noticed, so do not try to alter its appearance with extra lamps or mirrors (exterior or interior), as they will only make it distinctive. Likewise; scratches, dents, damage and malfunctioning lights will also help to identify and make the vehicle more noticeable. Ensure that all the wheel trims are present and are of the same style.

It is not recommended to use vehicles with personalised registration plates, or those that will easily be remembered such as having the letters ROD, BAT or SPY.

Weekly Maintenance

A white car can be mistaken for a Police car

Obviously, your vehicle has to be road worthy at all times and you should make a habit of checking your car on a regular basis; points to look out for are remembered by the pneumonic POWER;

P   Petrol. Ensure that you fill up with fuel every morning of surveillance and have a spare can in the boot.

O   Oil. Check the oil level at regular intervals.

W   Water. The coolant water needs to be topped up to prevent overheating and the screen washer needs to be kept full, especially in the winter months.

E   Electric's. Ensure that the lights work correctly, especially if driving at night. The target may notice if you have a light out and you also run the risk of being stopped by the police if you have a tail light out.

R   Rubber. Ensure that your tyres have enough tread and the air pressure is correct, especially if you are driving at speed. Do not forget to check your spare tyre as this is often overlooked.

Think also about the cleanliness of your car, inside and out. The interior should be kept clean and tidy but not too immaculate, you do not want the car to look sterile but at least lived in and used. If it is too untidy, and I have seen many cars full of old newspapers, magazines and a week's worth of fast food wrappings, it will attract attention to someone who is aware. If I were searching for a surveillance operator's car, this would be the one that I would look out for and take notice of. Any items of importance should also be kept out of view such as maps, brief sheets and radio parts.

The cleanliness of the exterior should also be considered. If you were working in an area that is more '*up-market*' then you would not want to be driving around in a vehicle covered in dirt and grime as you may look suspicious and be reported. On the other side of the coin, if you were operating in a more rough area driving about in a shiny-waxed vehicle, you will also stick out and thus be noticed.

Safety Equipment

In addition to your car bag containing your radio, maps and cameras, there are certain items that you may want to keep in your vehicle for safety's sake.

• Day Glow Jacket.

By wearing this you can sit and wait for hours in some places without being bothered. If you are not using it, then get it out of the way as it will show out.

• Torch

This is obviously useful at night and a large heavy torch such as a 'Maglite' may come in handy for your own protection.

• Windscreen Wash

A bottle of screen wash and rag should be handy in order to keep the inside and outsides of the windows clean. Dirt and dead flies will play havoc with your camera if you are using auto focus modes.

• De-Icer Spray

Not only does it clear your windows quickly in cold weather, but as a last resort it could be used for self protection as the aerosols have quite a powerful spray and will keep an attacker at bay from a distance.

• **First Aid Kit.**

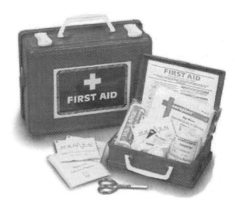

• **Roadside Assistance**

This is probably the most effective insurance policy that I have ever taken out. Of the times that I have broken down, three out of five happened when I was on my way to somewhere important or I was in a remote area. Unless you are a good mechanic and for the sake of a small cost, membership of one of these organisations is a must.

Personal Safety

Lock Your Doors

This is totally a personal preference but it is advised that you lock your car doors whenever you are inside, especially in built-up areas. In the past I have seen suspicious third parties actually go up to a car, open the door and confront the driver and it was quite frightening for them. There are some 'hard' people about especially in some rough estates who would not think twice about having a go at you. After all you are in their area, you may be interrupting their activities and they do not want you there, whoever you are.

Even worse, is having the actual target approach you and pull open your car door, you can consider yourself well and truly compromised if this happens. Do not forget to lock the rear doors as well; it can be even more embarrassing if the target gets into the back seat!

If you are concerned that if you lock your doors and end up in an accident and you can't get out, then don't worry. If you have had an accident to the extent that your car is likely to be damaged, a bit more damage by having the window popped open may not make much difference to the insurance companies costs. If the accident is so bad, the emergency services will just cut the roof off anyway.

The police actually advise to lock your doors if you are in a built-up area, if travelling on a motorway, then have the buttons up. If you are in an accident and have central locking, the damage caused by the impact may cause a delay in getting you out. However, if the damage is that bad, they will still cut your roof off.

Mobile Communications

Many operators and agencies adopt their own style of radio call-signs and codes and so there are no hard and fast rules regarding this. Use whatever system you are used to or happy with.

In simple terms, each vehicle could be termed; Car 1, Car 2 and Car 3. If you are using a hand held radio (or a fist mic) try to keep the radio set below the level of the dashboard and not bring it up to your mouth, if your target is checking his mirrors he will see you. In a similar vein, do not make the habit of bobbing your head down whenever you speak on the radio, this too looks peculiar, and may be noticed.

When you are static, ensure that your radio equipment is out of view and that radio transmissions cannot be heard by third parties through open windows.

The Crew

Generally, you may find yourself on your own but a vehicle crew can consist of a number of operators. Remember that even two operators in a vehicle (two up) can arouse suspicions, especially when waiting for a 'trigger'.

Four men in a vehicle can look 'hostile' so be aware of how you look to third parties. It is recommend that one operator per vehicle is used at most times, unless an extra operator is required to deploy on foot at short notice.

If two persons are used (as is often the case in the Police and other Enforcement Agencies), decide on the tasks of driver and footman/radio operator. Their appearance should fit with the vehicle and area of operations. The second operator during the mobile phase could sit in the rear seat behind the driver in order to remain out of view and giving the appearance of being 'one up'. If necessary, he can switch to the other side temporarily to show the vehicle 'two up'. In addition the second operator sat in the rear can easily take covert photographs or video when necessary. Should you have two operators in the same vehicle, consider them being different sexes, which appears more natural to an onlooker.

Enforcement Agencies will often use two operators in order to share responsibilities, so that one person concentrates on the driving whilst the other operates the radio and provides the commentary. This has its 'pros and cons' and may arouse suspicion from some 'aware' targets.

If you have to sit in your car for a period, (even if it's a short halt whilst following) try and move over to the passenger seat. If the target (or anyone else) sees you sat there, they would naturally presume that you are waiting for your driver to return without arousing too much suspicion.

Do not wear brightly coloured clothing or have anything notice-able on the dashboard that draws the attention. A change of jacket or the wearing of a hat for a short period is advisable, but do not wear sunglasses unless every-one else on the road is also doing so. Do not fall into this false sense of security by hiding behind a pair of *Ray Bans* sunglasses, for example.

The Mobile Surveillance

Considering the three phases of our surveillance operation, (Pick Up, Follow and Housing) we will now discuss the tactics used in a mobile surveillance.

Plotting Up and 'Boxing' the Target

On arrival in the area of where a surveillance is to commence, you will probably meet up with the team at a pre-determined rendezvous (RV). The team members would now carry out a recce of the general area to familiarise themselves with the layout of the estate and escape routes. You need to carry out a recce of the target's address by carrying out a drive past and also a walk past.

If you have a sketch map drawn at the initial recce, use it in order to identify where the target address is before you actually get to it. The last thing you want to do is drive down the target street, crawling at 5mph whilst trying to identify the target property, as you will be noticed. If you consult your sketch plan, you can see which side of the road the target is on, how far down it is and therefore identify it from a safe distance before you get on top of it.

On a drive past you need to be looking out for particular circumstances:

> • Any sign of life or activity such as: lights on, windows open, curtains open, or milk on the doorstep

> • Any vehicles, their details, how they are parked and which way they intend to go

• Any trigger positions where you can plot up or put the van in, as described earlier

• Check and double check that the address you have identified is the correct one

• Consider dropping off a foot person in order to take a closer look and obtain more detail

The Trigger

Once you have the trigger in position, it is his job to maintain the eyeball on the property and report any events to the remainder of the team. Nothing may happen for a number of hours and so the task requires much concentration. If nothing happens, then report to the team, 'No Change, No Change' often. This not only informs that team that you are still in control but also keeps them up to date and doubles up as a radio check.

If there is a problem with communications such as being out of range, it is the mobile units that have to move to a better position, as the trigger person cannot move.

The mobile units have to 'plot up' in a position that is safe, where they will not arouse any suspicion from third parties. These units do not have to see the target address but have to get off the plot completely and be in a position to take up the follow when the target moves.

The Plot Up

In the diagram, the trigger is located out of the '10 - 2' and also positioned behind the target, as you do not want the target to drive towards you and pass you (you will loose a life). You will note that there are only two exits out of the estate and these have to be 'covered' by the mobile units. By this we do not mean that Car 2 and Car 3 actually sit on the junction.

It may not be physically possible (double yellow lines, busy traffic for example) or practical. What it does mean, is that the mobile units can park anywhere they like (so as long as it is safe and away from the plot) as long as they can get to their respective 'pick-up' points in time, on a standby.

• **Car 1** has the trigger. He has to be close enough to be able to identify the target but far enough away not to be noticed. Remember, if you can see the target, he can see you.

• **Car 2's** responsibility is to 'cover' the north exit and is parked up in the supermarket car park. This is a safe area where he can wait all day without being noticed or bothered. Caution has to be maintained in the event he gets blocked in by shoppers and so he has to keep an eye on the traffic flow. On a standby, Car 2 can pull forward and get a view of the north exit and so call the target's direction of travel.

• **Car 3** is covering the south exit from a lay-by. Again, on a standby, he can move forward and give a direction of travel if the target takes the southerly exit.

Choke Points (Secondary Stakeout)

Sometimes it is not possible to trigger the target when he initially goes mobile from an address. Therefore he may have to be picked up somewhere along a route that he is known to take regularly, especially if the target's address is in a cul de sac. This 'choke point' may have to be identified by examining a map or by driving around the area.

The Pick - Up Phase

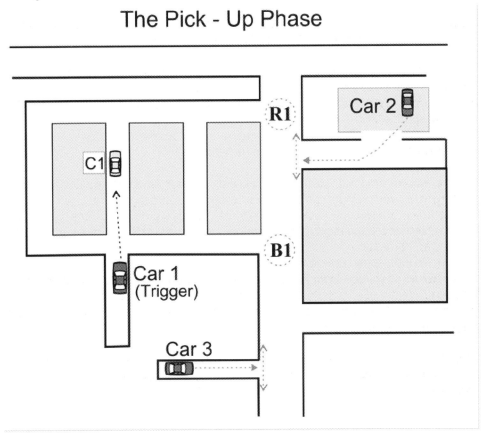

When picking up a target in this instance, the cars must be distributed along the route in such positions that the crews can see the target as it passes, but they are not themselves noticeable to the target.

As soon as possible after the pick-up, a team member should attempt to identify that the driver (or passenger) is the actual target to be followed. You could consider having an operator drive towards the target in order to have a 'head on' to identify him as he may be checking his mirrors, or wait for the target to turn right in order to get a look at him from the side.

Action on a 'STANDBY STANDBY!'

As soon as the target appears out in the open or there is signs of movement, the trigger person should call, 'Standby, Standby' and commence a running commentary on the targets activities and movements. This 'standby' is a wake up call to put the rest of the team on alert.

As soon as the trigger gives a 'standby', the mobile units should carry out the following:

> • Instantly acknowledge with your call sign (in alpha numerical order). When the team moves, no one should be left behind

> • Turn your engine on

> • Listen very carefully to the 'triggers' radio commentary, he will be giving descriptions, vehicle details and directions

> • Move from your 'plot up' (or Lie Up) position and draw near to the spot where you intend to pick up, or intercept the target

> • Be prepared to pick up the target and take the first follow or act as back-up

> • Do not come up on the radio to ask 'what's happening?' If there is a period of silence from the trigger, he may be filming or taking photographs

If a standby is a false alarm, the trigger should call '**CANCEL STANDBY**', to which the team acknowledges and return to their 'lie up' positions (LUP's).

Triggering from your Mirrors

Quite often you will be in a position where you are observing the target through you rear view mirrors. When he goes mobile, you may have to call a direction of travel such as Left or Right. Be careful not to get Left and Right mixed up as it is very easy to do so when looking in mirrors. Rehearse and think to yourself, what am I going to say on a standby. 'If he comes towards me he has gone Left Left and if he turns away from me he has gone Right Right'. It pays to mentally rehearse to yourself and to get it right first time.

Trigger Person Do Not Move!

Remember that surveillance is all about team work, when the target moves off inform the team of the direction, if he goes out of your view let them know that you are 'unsighted', this is their cue to take the eyeball. If a team member hears the phrase, 'unsighted to me', he will realise that the target is out of view or someone's control and therefore the eyeball is 'up for grabs'. Whoever sees the target first can take over the commentary.

Most compromises by inexperienced operators occur when the target initially moves off. The first thing the target does when pulling out, is to check his rear view mirror, especially if he is aware.

As Trigger, never move off until you are out of the target's mirrors

Referring back to the diagram, if the target moves towards the north exit to the estate, it would be **Car 2's** responsibility to pick him up and call a direction on the main road. If he goes left towards the mini roundabout, **Car 2** can call this and **Car 3** can come round and take the first follow. If the target takes a right on the main road, **Car 2** can call it on the radio and so **Car 3** can stay where he is until the target passes and then takes up the follow. This is operating as a team should do, passing the target from one person to another. Up to this stage, no one has actually 'followed' the target but surveillance has been 'imposed'. At your briefing, it would have been decided whether the trigger vehicle

(especially if it is a van) is to stay where it is, or whether it joins in the follow.

Quite often, we will leave the van where it is until the target has cleared the area (in the event the target returns). It is useful to bring the van with the team as it can take part in the follow (with caution) and it can also be used to re-trigger the target when he has been 'housed'.

Team Positions, The Surveillance Convoy

Once on the move, the lead vehicle or 'eyeball' should be in control of the surveillance and at that moment in time is in charge of the radio net. He should now be giving a running commentary to the remainder of the team, to which no one should interrupt.

As lead vehicle, always drive 'normally' and be confident. Obviously you do not want to be right behind the target when there is no need to, but common sense prevails and this is dictated by the terrain and area. In built-up areas you need to be close as possible, whereas in rural areas you need to be further apart. As a general rule, always attempt to use at least one vehicle for cover (unless it is a learner!).

If approaching an obstacle such as traffic lights, a junction or a roundabout, you may need to be as close as possible to avoid being held back. On approaching an obstacle 'never crawl up' behind the target, if you do this you will soon be spotted or have the targets suspicions aroused. Remember, you are a public road user going about your normal daily routine and therefore you have to act normally.

If your team members have not acknowledged that they are with the convoy, carry out a radio check to ensure that the team is with you. Hopefully you should get the response, **'Kilo's backing, Romeo's tail end'**, depending on what call sign system you are using. Some Enforcement Agencies used a system called a 'Convoy Check' that can be useful when operating in large teams. During a 'convoy check' each car in turn comes up on the radio with their call-sign followed by their position in the convoy. For example, **'Car 2's back up, Car 4's third in line, Car 1's tail end charlie'**.

This method of mobile surveillance (when we are in convoy) is considered as 'reactive' as the team is reacting to the target's movements and is a common type of surveillance. At a further advanced level, especially when the team know the ground very well and their driving skills are good, they can carry out 'active' surveillance. Mobile surveillance carried out this way can be conducted by the operators running on parallel roads and heading off the target at intersections and roundabouts. Obviously there still needs to be an eyeball, either behind with cover or from the air.

Keep Your Distance

Very often you will come to a halt whilst waiting in a queue of traffic, you may be directly behind the target or have a vehicle for cover. Either way, do not get too close to the car in front for safety reasons. If you are too close, you will not have enough manoeuvring room to be able to pull out in an emergency. As a general rule, make sure that you can at least see the tyres of the car in front or at least a piece of the road surface.

If you are driving in rural areas, try not to be constantly in the mirrors of the target if you have no vehicles for cover. Use the road, hills and bends in order to catch glimpses of the target as he encounters them thus 'clipping' the sight of his rear bumper. For the remainder of the team, do not be too evenly spaced apart as this could look unnatural and make the convoy appear to be in formation.

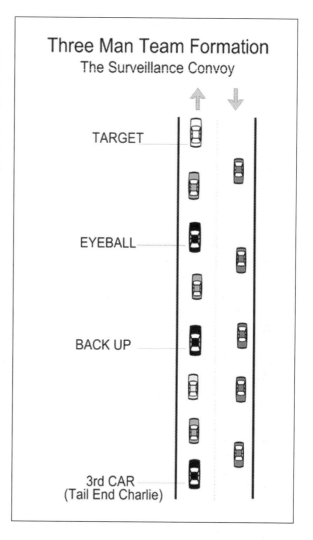

Three Man Team Formation
The Surveillance Convoy

TARGET

EYEBALL

BACK UP

3rd CAR
(Tail End Charlie)

Do Not Be Too Kind

If you are in a long queue of slow moving traffic, it helps if you have one vehicle for cover. If you do not, consider letting a car come in between you and the target from an adjoining side road. Only do this if it is to your advantage. If you do want a car to pull out, do not flash your headlights but give a discreet wave to let them out.

Be very careful if you do this, as the driver that you have just let in will now be in a good mood because they have just been let in. If they also decide to let someone else in further up the road, and then they let someone in, before you know it you are four or five cars behind the target, so be very careful if deciding to let someone in as cover.

Safety Gap

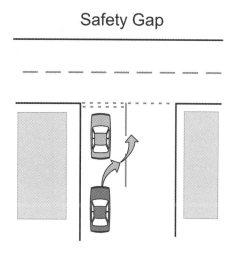

Leave a gap in order to pull out quickly

If you are in a long queue of traffic (waiting for lights or approaching a roundabout) and any of your team members are being held back, do not be afraid to call them forward on the radio when the traffic conditions are safe. Provide a gap and let them come in front of you. Obviously you do not want to carry out this procedure in the target's mirrors.

Mobile Commentary

Whilst carrying out a mobile surveillance, the commentary given by the lead car to the other members of the team should

be precise, straight to the point and given instantly. Whilst you as eyeball are in front, the remainder of the team may not be able to see the target and be some distance behind you. The commentary is for their benefit.

Certain phrases and descriptions are used to simplify messages and to assist the operators because they will not have any visual contact with the target. Although these phrases may appear obvious or unnecessary, they are to assist you and the team to prevent any confusion and subsequent loss of contact.

All messages are to be kept short and accurate. A message lasting half a minute could mean that the target has travelled half a mile in that time and changed direction, so do not waffle on and repeat yourself unnecessarily.

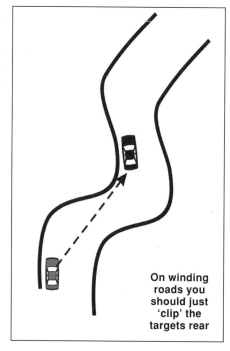

On winding roads you should just 'clip' the targets rear

You should keep the team up to date with an accurate running commentary giving details of the targets:

- Direction of travel

- Speed

- Intentions to turn (which are indicators used)

- Any deviations made

- Current position in relation to local landmarks (his position, not yours)

- Any unusual driving tactics.

- Loss of contact, temporary or otherwise

Direction of Travel

When giving the direction of travel use large visible local landmarks as an aid, as street names can lead to confusion if you are not familiar with the area and can be difficult to spot. The direction of travel may be given in the form of:

'That's following the signs marked A629 Halifax...'   or
'No deviation, windmill on the nearside...'   or
'Continuing straight'

Left and Right, Nearside and Offside

When giving any indication to the target's movements they should be repeated to make sure that everyone is in the know at once. This eliminates other team members using 'air' time by asking for repeated messages. For instance if the target turns Right, he's turned '**Right Right**'. If he stops he's come to a '**Stop Stop**'. We repeat the call two or three times in the event the operator is 'clipping' their calls and the call is possibly missed by the team.

The terms Left or Right should only be used when describing a change in direction and should not be used when pointing out a landmark. For example

'Target passing church on the Left'

is wrong but should in fact be said

'Target passing church on the Nearside'
(or Offside as applicable).

The reason for this difference is so that any team member who may be held back in traffic and may possibly be getting out of radio range, can still attempt to catch up with the surveillance by listening to the commentary (which is the whole idea). Should the radio message be 'broken' and all that is heard are the words '**Church./ /.Left**', he would presume the target has turned Left at the church. Whereas if he only heard the words '**Church.//.Nearside**' he would decide to continue straight with no deviation knowing that a landmark (the church) had been indicated on the nearside.

Should the target use his indicators at any time, inform the team of his intentions, for instance, 'Target's held at a 'T' junction with a nearside indicator'. This enables other operatives to prepare for the turn by getting into the correct lane or taking other action.

If you are behind the target vehicle who is at a junction or crossroads and indicating to turn, do not indicate the same yourself. Should the target decide to drive straight across at the last second, you will be committed to making that turn (because you indicated), which you will have to take, in the event the target is observing you and carrying out anti-surveillance.

When a change of direction is made, make a reference to where the turn occurred, as you would not want the team taking the wrong turning. Use features or road signs so that you may hear the commentary:

> **'That's gone Left Left at the Post Office'**

> or

> **'That's gone Left Left into Cumberland Close'**

Reference Points

As the target vehicle passes identifiable landmarks (reference points) the Eyeball should pass this on to the remainder of the team. For example '**passing church on the nearside**'.

These reference points should be large and prominent so that as the operators can easily see them from a distance and be able to establish how far the target is ahead of them. This way, they can decide whether to close up or hang back as necessary. Do not use moveable objects as reference points such as '**passing Telecom van on Nearside**' as it will have probably moved by the time the last man gets to it. Features such as phone boxes, advertising boards, buildings, shops and churches are ideal.

Be careful of using street names as reference points (unless you are familiar with the area) such as, 'passing Station Road on the nearside'. If you are back-up, the last thing that you want to do is have to slow down to find and locate the small street sign in order to read it, so use large prominent features.

Advance Warnings of Obstacles

Should there be some form of obstacle or hazard to your front such as a set of traffic lights or a roundabout, inform the other team members, such as 'approaching a roundabout / crossroads / set of lights'. This will allow the team to close up, as there is a possibility that a loss could occur here.

Also warn of obstructions such as roadworks, tractors, learners, cyclists and pedestrians that may be a danger to the team. If there is a speed camera or a Police car travelling towards the team, then let them know as you would not want them to risk a speeding ticket or be overtaking at speed with a Police car coming towards them.

Traffic Lights

On approach to traffic lights pass all relevant information back to the team regarding their state. The other members may be required to accelerate to catch up so as not be held by the lights. Let the team know the sequence of the lights as they change, and the target's position in the queue of traffic. 'Tail End Charlie' should inform you of his position and when he is through the junction.

Speed and Lanes

Relay the speed of the target frequently, but more especially when the speed changes. We tend to 'bracket' the speed such as, '**three zero to three five**' (30-35mph). Inform the team in which lane he is travelling (such as motorway or dual carriageway) or on approach to a junction or roundabout with more than one lane. On a road with multiple lanes such as a motorway, we could nominate the three lanes; the nearside, the centre and the offside but this can get confusing when there are four or more lanes. For this reason we tend to number the lanes from the nearside lane

so that if the target is in the centre lane of a three lane carriageway he would be in lane '2 of 3'.

Roundabout Procedure

When the target approaches a roundabout, the team must be given plenty of warning in order for them to close up, especially if the roundabout is busy. The position of the target must be given as he approaches the roundabout, when he is on it, when he passes exits and most importantly, when he exits off the roundabout.

In a similar fashion mentioned earlier, when referring to using the terms Nearside as opposed to Left Left, we adopt similar procedure to identify which exit the target has taken off a roundabout. This procedure avoids confusion especially if a team member is having difficulty receiving the radio commentary.

If we suggest that the target vehicle is onto a roundabout and he takes the third exit (Right) the mobile commentary would be as follows:

> **'That's up to the roundabout'**
> **'That's at the roundabout and held, wait'**
> **'That's onto the roundabout'**
> **'Not One, Not One',** as he passes the first exit
> **'Not Two, Not Two',** as he passes the second exit
> **'Taken Third, Third on the A629 towards Leeds',** as he takes the third exit

Roundabout Procedure

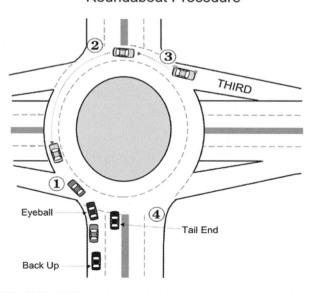

You will notice the change of phrase between using the terms One, Two or Three and First, Second, Third. Each exit is numbered in a sequence of One, Two, Three as the target passes it, but if he takes a particular exit the phrase changes to First, Second, Third and so on.

This system was devised in the event of poor communications. If a team member was having difficulty receiving the commentary but heard '**Second, Second**', he would automatically know that the target has taken the Second exit whereas if he heard '**Two, Two**' he would know that the target had passed option two and was continuing round. In order to add credibility to your commentary, it may be worth adding that extra bit of information such as the road name or direction, so we may hear:

> **'Not One, not One,'**
> **'It's the Second, the Second, A610 towards Nottingham'**

If there is a 'No Entry' from the roundabout (traffic can join but not leave) then this is not counted as it is not an option that the target can take.

Handovers

Every now and again you will need to change lead vehicles (the Eyeball) in order to prevent being noticed. These changes (or Handovers) should be carried out at natural places such as roundabouts and road junctions. Avoid pulling into the side of the road (to let your back up come through) unless you are out of sight of the target, such as behind a row of parked cars. Never rejoin the carriageway whilst still in the target's mirrors, he may notice you, wait until he is out of view before you pull out.

As back up, (who should be behind the eyeball with one or two vehicles in between), you should be ready to take over as eyeball at short notice in the event that the target suddenly turns or stops (an unplanned handover). Your concentration must be on the target's actions and the eyeball's commentary and therefore you have to think ahead at all times.

As eyeball, you should decide when to hand over and this should be carried out frequently, depending on a number of factors. Essentially we would carry out a handover at the following times:

> • When you have had the eyeball for a while and there is risk of compromise if you stay with it any longer, especially if you have been directly behind the target with no cover.

• Whenever there are two or three changes in direction. As eyeball, you do not want to take the target around one corner, then another and then another, you will alert the target. If he is carrying out some type of anti-surveillance, you will only confirm that you are following him, so hand over after changes in direction.

• When the target stops (at the side of the road for example). It may look a bit obvious for the eyeball to stop directly behind him. So in order to act naturally, the eyeball should overshoot and hand over the eyeball to the back up. If the vehicle moves off again, you then have a different car taking the eyeball and triggering it away.

• On entering a car park. If a target is suspicious, he may pull into a car park to see if you follow him in. Therefore we normally hand over as the target enters.

• When you are compromised. If this situation occurs, you will have to clear the area and so your back up may keep an eye on the target, it may be a case that the whole team disperses.

Where to Hand Over

There are certain places where a handover can be carried out without being obvious to the target. What we would not expect to happen, is for you to ask for a hand over, move over to the nearside and let your back up come screaming through by overtaking you. If this were to happen and the target were to see it in his rear view mirror, he would probably expect the 'boy racer' to overtake him also, but when he doesn't but hangs onto his bumper, he soon becomes suspicious.

For this reason we need to hand over at 'natural' points where the eyeball can naturally peel off the road. In order to instigate a handover, the Eyeball should come up on air and ask, '**Back up are you in a position?** (to take the eyeball)'. If they are, you should hear the

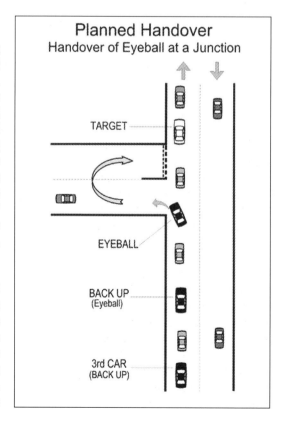

Planned Handover
Handover of Eyeball at a Junction

TARGET

EYEBALL

BACK UP
(Eyeball)

3rd CAR
(BACK UP)

response, '**Yes Yes**'. Locations for handovers can be:

• Nearside Junctions

As the eyeball, all you have to do is turn left off the road and let the back up vehicle take over the eyeball, tail end Charlie then becomes back up. The new eyeball should keep his distance from the target and try not to close up on him unnecessarily.

Ideally the previous eyeball should now become tail end Charlie but do not rejoin the carriageway until you are out of the target's mirrors.

We try not to handover using an offside junction for a number of reasons. Firstly, the Eyeball has to cross over traffic in order to turn off. In doing so he may encounter oncoming traffic and subsequently hold up the team. If he manages to cross the road, he may encounter getting back again difficult as he has to cross the traffic.

• Petrol Stations

In a manner similar to the above, all the Eyeball has to do is pull into a petrol station and let the back up come through. Again, do not pull out onto the main road until you are out of the target's mirror.

Protocol dictates that you should now become tail end Charlie. However, if the back up car has been detached and is not in a position to actually 'back' the eyeball, then you must get out and act as back up straight away. You can always change over positions at a later time.

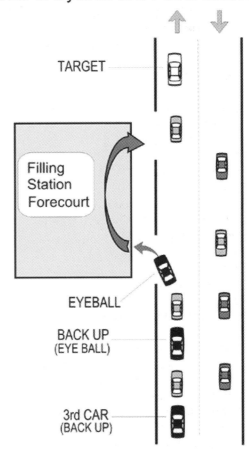

The Planned Handover
Handover of Eyeball at a Petrol Station

TARGET

Filling Station Forecourt

EYEBALL

BACK UP
(EYE BALL)

3rd CAR
(BACK UP)

• Roundabouts

Roundabouts can also be a natural place to handover. As soon as you see the sign prior to the roundabout, you should offer up the handover and check that your back up is in a position to take over.

There are essentially two ways of handing over at a roundabout. Firstly, the eyeball can take the target onto the roundabout, call the exit and then continue going around the roundabout letting the back up take over. Secondly, the eyeball can peel off at the first exit (if the target hasn't taken this one) and hand over this way. If you do this, ensure that you can turn around and get back in the convoy quickly. You do not want to find yourself joining a dual carriageway and not being able to turn around for miles on end.

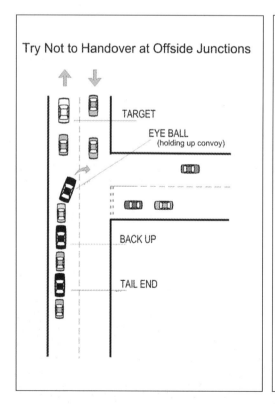

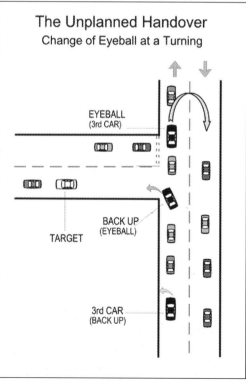

• Laybys

Caution should be used if handing over at a layby, if there are cars already parked there, they will afford you some cover but empty ones may not. As eyeball you can pull into a layby and let your team come through, whatever you do, do not pull out again if you are still in the target's mirrors.

Where and When Not to Hand Over

• Turning into offside junctions. You may hold the team up as you will have to cross oncoming traffic

• Do not bring teams through. The backing car should not overtake you and then slow down behind the target

• Do not hand over at traffic lights. As you turn off and handover, you may get held by the same lights and so become detached

• Hazards. Anywhere where traffic is heavy and prevents you from rejoining the team

• When there is heavy traffic behind you, check your mirror before a handover. If there is heavy traffic behind you, you may not be able to rejoin the convoy for a short while

What Happens When The Target Stops

Whenever the target vehicle stops, the eyeball must immediately transmit the message '**STOP, STOP on the Nearside** (Or applicable)'. Although the eyeball vehicle may have to keep moving and pass the target, it is important that the other vehicles stop quickly or take appropriate action. If the eyeball has had to overtake the target, the back up vehicle naturally then becomes 'eyeball' and the third man as back up.

PETE'S TIP: Remember that when a driver is driving fast, he is more likely to be looking ahead of him rather than in his mirrors.

This should be practised and carried out as a drill whenever there is a stop. In addition to stating that there has been a stop, also indicate whereabouts in more detail in order to put the team onto the target, **'It's a STOP STOP on the nearside at a newsagents'**.

We are now into the 'Housing' phase of our surveillance and so we now have to re-plot for the 'Pick-up' phase.

The eyeball can give a commentary on the target's actions if he gets out of his vehicle and the team leader can decide on what course of action to take, such as put footmen out. Whilst the commentary is being given, the previous lead car should take a position ahead of the target and tail end Charlie hold back and take up a position behind him.

When the target goes mobile again on the original direction, (remembering that the trigger never moves) it should be Tail End Charlie that comes round and takes the first follow. Remember that it was the previous eyeball that had to overshoot when he stopped and so does not want to take the follow again.

Every situation is different but the main aim is for an operator to re-trigger the surveillance and the other team members to cover the possible routes the target may take. On a standby or when the target moves off, ideally it should be a fresh vehicle that takes the first follow rather than the one that had the previous eyeball when the target stopped.

Stopping in a Car Park

We normally carry out a hand over when the target enters a car park, this effectively is a stop and so the eyeball should not follow him in but hand over to the back up. An aware target may be checking to see who follows him in.

- The eyeball should overshoot and find a plot up location

- The back up takes the eyeball and controls the target in the car park. If the target enters a car park, it is fairly likely that he will get out on foot. When the target comes to a halt, inform the team of his whereabouts in the car park using the 'clock ray' method as shown in the diagram. If footmen have been deployed, they do not want to be running about the car park attempting to locate the target. If they can enter the car park knowing that the target is at 2 o'clock, it saves time and effort.

- The eyeball (trigger) vehicle should now position himself so that he can clearly see the target and also the exit to the car park. This way, not only can he give a standby but can also give a direction of travel on as he exits the car park

If the car park has multiple exits, these should be identified as soon as possible and relayed to the team who must then get in a position to cover them. In large car parks, it may be necessary to have more than one car in there.

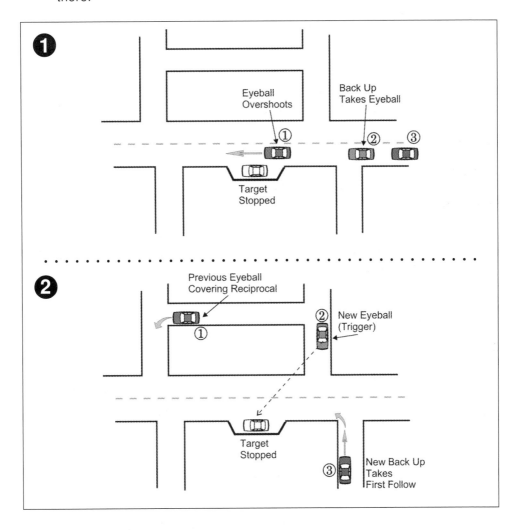

The Cul-De-Sac and Dead End Streets

The target may drive into a cul-de-sac to either visit an address or to carry out a counter surveillance manoeuvre. Two scenarios can be envisaged:

when you know that the road is a dead end, or you have been caught unaware and do not realise that it is a dead end until you are into it and it is too late.

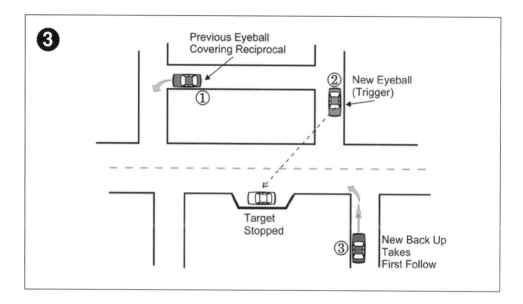

The following actions can be taken when the target turns into a cul-de-sac:

• If the he cul-de-sac is recognised as being so

• The eyeball is to continue straight, driving past the turning and check if there are any routes out at the rear by car or on foot

• Back up to carry out a drive past of the turning to identify where the target has stopped and get a trigger on the entrance/exit

• Tail end Charlie to enter the cul de sac to positively identify where the target has stopped. This can be done either by driving in or by going in on foot. This is not always possible, especially if the cul-de-sac is only a short one

• The team should reorganise to pick up the target when he goes mobile again

• If the house or premises is unidentified, an operator may have to check it after the target has gone mobile or return to it at a later time

• The cul-de-sac is not recognised until you have turned into it

• Don't panic and act naturally

• Consider if doing a three point turn and driving out will arouse suspicion. If possible do this out of sight of the target

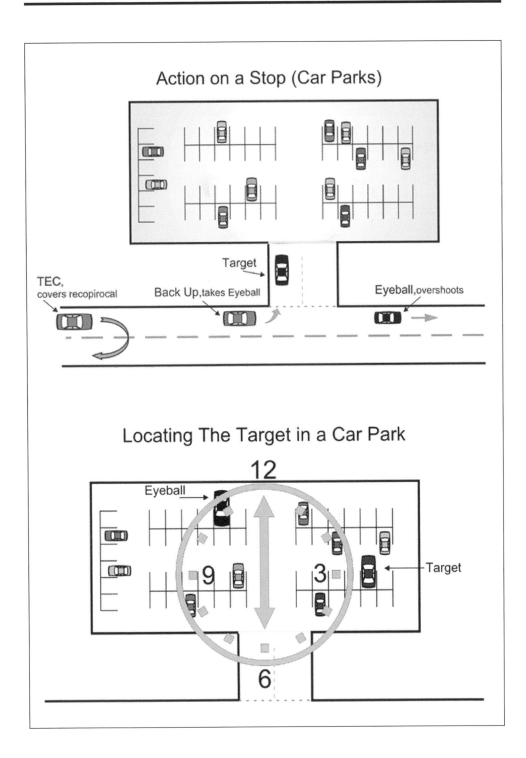

Action on a Stop (Car Parks)

Target

TEC,
covers recopirocal

Back Up,takes Eyeball

Eyeball,overshoots

Locating The Target in a Car Park

12

Eyeball

9

3

Target

6

• Park naturally on the roadside and walk away from your vehicle out of sight, possibly through a foot path if there is one

• Drive onto a resident's driveway and make a pretext call at the front door. You can then depart, driving out of the cul-de-sac

• Act naturally, do not look or pay any attention to the target and avoid eye contact

The Fast Driver

Some targets will drive like maniacs, not just because they suspect that they will be followed, but because they do this as their normal pattern of behaviour. So it may be worth inquiring at your briefing stage on how your target is likely to drive.

Fast speeds on the road can be the cause of fatal accidents and so I would be inclined to think to myself 'Is the job really worth it, do we really have to push ourselves at the risk of an accident?'

These drivers can be difficult to put under observation and so a pattern of movement may have to be established so the surveillance can be carried out in stages.

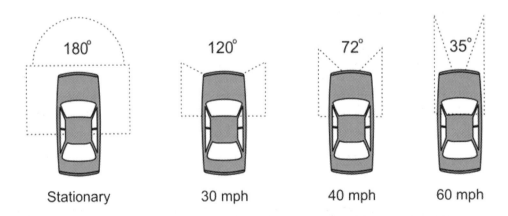

Your field of vision narrows the faster you travel

Loss of Contact

Action on a Loss at a Crossroads

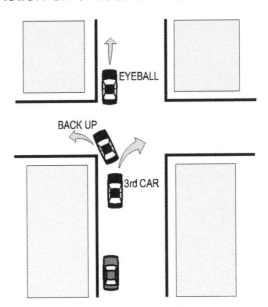

Losing contact with the target is inevitable from time to time and happens often, it is an occupational hazard in surveillance. You can have a team of six cars and two motorbikes, this will greatly minimise your chances of losing the target, but it can still happen. I know of a surveillance team on the security circuit that claims to never have had a loss..., in this industry there are only two types of surveillance operators, those that have losses and those that tell lies.

A loss will occur for many reasons, such as traffic congestion, busy roundabouts, traffic lights and more importantly, lack of concentration. If you hear the call, 'Temporary Unsighted' you would normally expect to hear, 'Eyeball Regained', shortly afterwards. If the 'unsighted' calls come one after another, expect to hear a 'Total Loss, Total Loss' shortly afterwards.

The longer the target has been 'unsighted', the further he may be getting away from you and therefore, the more difficult your task becomes in picking him up.

When a '**total loss**' is given by the eyeball, the following procedure should then be put into action: The eyeball will state where the total loss occurred then a search pattern should be adopted as follows:

- Eyeball call the 'total loss' and to continue in the original direction or the most logical and fastest escape route

- Back up vehicle to take first nearside turning after point of loss or the second most logical escape route

PETE'S TIP: *It is worth remembering that whilst travelling at 60mph in a vehicle, you will travel one mile in one minute.*

• Third vehicle to take first offside turning after point of loss or the most logical escape route

• Fourth vehicle to remain at point of loss and check immediate area

Common sense should prevail as to the time and distance travelled along these routes relative to the speed of the target. If you feel happy that the target has definitely not taken your route, you should inform the team leader, and cover the direction upon which you have been checking or continue searching in another, that has not yet been checked.

The operator who is covering the point of loss remains there for a number of reasons:

• The target may travel back though the same location or may have stopped in the vicinity

• From this position you are able to relay radio messages as the team may now be getting further and further apart

• You will be in the best position to 'back' the eyeball when contact is regained

If the target is located, the eyeball should immediately call '**CONTACT, CONTACT**' followed by the target's location and his direction of travel.

Keep it in mind that some of the team members, during their search may now be out of radio range and so the location and direction of the target should be repeated over the air. If necessary you may have to use your mobile phone.

If the loss occurs at a roundabout, you should treat this in the same way as you would at a crossroads or junction with multiple exits, each one should be checked.

Never let over enthusiasm of not wanting to lose the target by being too close, result in 'showing out' and compromising the surveillance.

Multi-Storey Car Parks

Multi-storey car parks can be tricky to cover, especially when there are multiple exits. When the target drives into multi-storey car park, expect him to find the first available spot and park in it. If you can obtain a spot close by, all well and good, but quite often you may have to rise one or two floors to obtain a space.

Every situation is different but the following is a suggested procedure:

• Upon the target entering, the Eyeball vehicle hands over to the Back up then remains on the outside of the car park, checks and covers the exits

• New Eyeball takes the target into car park, reporting where it stops

• Footmen are deployed to take the eyeball as the target goes on foot

• Tail End Charlie, remains on the outside of the car park. If necessary, he can take up a position on the top floor where he can relay radio messages

• The footman having made contact with the target in the multi-storey will remain with him and follow him into street

• Be aware of the target returning to his vehicle after collecting a parking ticket

• Remember to examine the target vehicle for the amount of time parked and note anything of interest that is possibly left on view inside. You may also want to make a note of the mileage but do this only if it is safe to do so.

Indoor Shopping Centres and Airport Car Parks

Be aware of the car parks where you obtain a ticket from a barrier upon entering. Usually you have to keep your parking ticket with you and pay at a machine located in a nearby building or at the stairwell to the car park just prior to departure. This means that you have to pay on returning to your vehicle, which may cause difficulties in keeping control of the target.

After paying, you normally have a 15 minute period to actually leave the car park before the barrier refuses to let you through the exit. **Remember where you have parked your car!**

Showing an Empty Car

At times you may have to let the target pass you whilst you are stationary, you may be giving the trigger from within a long cul-de-sac for example. If so, you may want to show an empty car to make it look unoccupied by 'ducking down' before the target passes you.

If you do this make sure:

- That no one sees you, have a quick look around you, think third party [1]

- Turn your engine off and your wipers off

- Switch off your lights

- Make sure that your foot is off the brake pedal or the rear lights will flash bright

- Do not have your windows wound right down, except for a small gap, you may want to hear when the target car has passed you. You do not want to miss it

Revision So Far

- On the trigger giving a 'STANDBY', all call-signs should acknowledge. No one should be left behind!

- The vehicle nearest the target is the 'eyeball' or the vehicle that 'HAS'

- During the follow, the second (back up) and third cars will be at the rear, often out of sight

- The operator in the eyeball vehicle will give radio commentary on speed and direction of the target and of any road hazards

- Cars will change positions as dictated by the eyeball

- In rural areas and motorways a greater distance can be allowed between target and eyeball. Bends in the road, hedges and other vehicles can be used as cover

- In built-up areas and especially busy towns, surveillance vehicles must close up and the eyeball should be very close, at times being directly behind the target

- Cars should keep to the nearside of target's rear when in close proximity to lessen chance of attracting attention. People tend not to use their nearside mirrors as much

• If one has to stop immediately behind the target, drive and act naturally. The driver should 'minimise' on the radio and back up vehicle should take over the commentary for the time being

• At night time, it is more difficult to tail in country areas without showing out

• Drive with normal lights, ensure that they all work properly

Motorway Driving

Surveillance on a motorway can be easier or more difficult, depending on your outlook. Although vehicles can travel at much greater speeds, they can only go in one direction and only leave the highway at certain points, and so they are 'contained' to a certain degree. With this in mind, we have to realise and appreciate the problems that motorways and motorway service areas can present.

If your target's base is close to a motorway, be prepared for him using it and ensure that you have a full tank of fuel. Remember, if you have to peel off from a motorway to obtain fuel, your target and the team can be miles away by the time you rejoin the carriageway, and you will have to drive at breakneck speed in order to close up.

Speed

The change from rural and urban driving to motorway driving is obvious and it must be appreciated that we can travel a long distance during a matter of minutes at high speeds. Therefore it is important to be able to correctly assess and judge the speed of the target vehicle, so that the convoy does not become too 'strung out'.

Because motorways stretch for many miles, the eyeball can be retained for longer periods by the same vehicle but only when there is plenty of cover from other vehicles. Each vehicle in the convoy can allow a greater distance between one another and from eyeball to tail end Charlie, the distance can be as much as a mile or more. So long as radio reception is still good, there are no road hazards imminent and all the vehicles have the power to close up when required, you can keep well spaced.

Speed indication should be given often on the motorway. Should the target increase his speed from 70mph to 90mph, you may find that tail end Charlie is having to do 100mph in order to close up. This is given as an example only and not intended to entice anyone to speed.

Mirroring

As with urban driving, it is important for the eyeball on a motorway surveillance to make sure he does not copy or 'mirror' the actions of the target vehicle. Should the target pull out and enter another lane, the eyeball should maintain the same speed but remain where he is until such times as it appears safe to move out into the same lane as that of the target. If you think ahead and anticipate that the target is just overtaking another vehicle (such as a slow moving truck) you should stay where you are until the target has pulled back into the nearside lane. An inexperienced surveillance operator will often inadvertently mirror the target's movements.

Motorway Signs and Marker Boards

Describing terrain and 'reference points' when travelling on a motorway can sometimes be rather sparse. Bridges and National Grid pylons can be used as reference points as they are high up and can be seen from quite a distance.

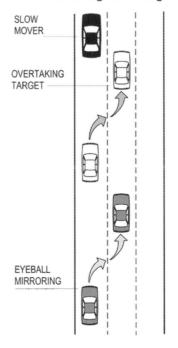

Mirroring The Target

SLOW MOVER

OVERTAKING TARGET

EYEBALL MIRRORING

As we approach the exits from a motorway, we are given warning by directional signs which are placed at one mile and half mile intervals (in some cases 2/3 and 1/3 mile) prior to the exits. Each of the exit warning signs details the distance, junction number and road classification number coming up.

You must remember that vehicles on motorways can only go one way until such times as they get to exits. If following slow moving targets, much discipline is required in order to prevent 'closing up' on the target and being forced to overtake. If the eyeball on the motorway does become too close, they should not hang on to its bumper but they should overtake the target and position themselves at the next exit in order to get behind him as he passes. At this junction the operator must also prepare for the target leaving the motorway here as well.

Never simulate a breakdown on the hard shoulder in order for the target to overtake you (for you to get back behind him), you will be noticed.

Approaching Junctions

On approach to a junction the Eyeball should always give prior warning and the team should close up. On passing the countdown markers the Eyeball should be giving a fast commentary as he approaches each, stating the lane that the target is in and his speed. For example:

> '1 mile marker board, junction 6, speed seven zero (70)'

> '1/2 mile marker board, junction 6, nearside lane, speed seven zero (70)'

PETE'S TIP: A GPS receiver is very useful for marking 'waypoints' when surveillance is on the move. You can quickly 'mark' points of interest and view your route or download it onto a laptop with mapping software.

'Countdown markers, three hundred nearside lane, two hundred, nearside indicator, one hundred, gone left, left, at Junction 6'

OR

'Countdown markers, three hundred, two hundred, one hundred Committed, Committed, continuing straight'. If the target does not deviate and continues on the motorway.

Handovers

When following along motorways let the handover occur by the Eyeball vehicle leaving at a junction and then rejoining the carriageway whilst the back up takes over as eyeball. Ensure that you have read your map and established that you can rejoin at the junction.

When the target leaves at a junction, it is likely that he will encounter a roundabout or a junction at the top of the slip road. This would be a good time to carry out a planned handover so you are not seen to take the target off the motorway and then follow him as he changes direction.

Motorway Service Areas

These areas usually have a large cafeteria or service areas and give access for members of the public to park their cars and seek refreshment before continuing their journey.

Because of the proximity of the parking areas to the motorway and the possibility that a target can change the direction he is travelling by using the service roads. We have to cover the options which are open to him by deploying the various operators in the following positions.

• **Upon entering a motorway service area, a three car team should:**

    • Eyeball should carry out a handover and take up a position in the area of the filling station or exit to the motorway

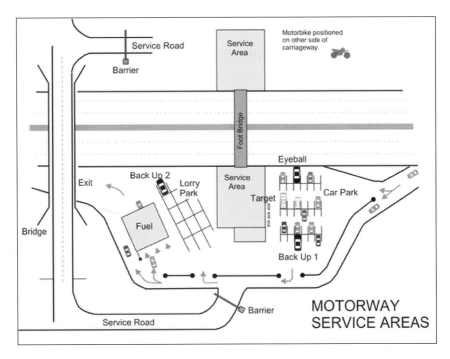

• The new Eyeball takes the target onto the service area and keeps him under control

• Back up vehicle should deploy a footman and cover any other exits away from the service area such as service roads to hotels and so on

• Consider sending a motorcyclist or any other vehicle to take up position on the other side of the carriageway, in the event the target takes a footbridge across and meets with an associate on the other side

What if the Target Stops on a Motorway

If the target pulls over into the hard shoulder, it could be for a number of reasons, he could have broken down or he could be carrying out some form of anti-surveillance. If this happens, act naturally and continue past. Whatever you do, **DO NOT**, simulate a break down and pull up on the hard shoulder some distance behind, you will be noticed. If the target has genuinely broken down, he may walk towards you for assistance. If he is carrying out anti-surveillance, you have now compromised yourself!

The team should continue past and deploy to cover the next junction (the target can only go one way). The team should position themselves in order to see when the target approaches the junction, possibly by a foot person being dropped off. The cars should then position themselves in the best possible place in the event

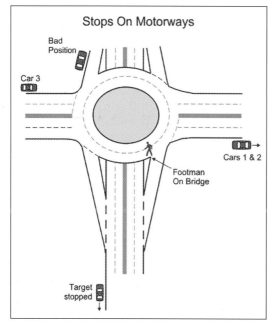

Stops On Motorways
Bad Position
Car 3
Cars 1 & 2
Footman On Bridge
Target stopped

that the target continues on the motorway. They should also be in a position to cover the eventuality that the target leaves the motorway at the same junction that is being covered.

Do not just expect the target to drive past after a short period. If he has genuinely broken down, you could be in for a long wait. If you are the one observing the motorway, do not forget to check any breakdown recovery vehicles that pass you, as your target may be on the back of it.

If junctions are not too far apart or you have a motorcyclist, it may be worth sending an operator to do a drive past going the opposite way, in order to establish what the target is doing.

Driving At Night

When driving at night, it is very difficult for the target to identify the vehicle or occupants in the car behind, especially when you are close. As the following cars headlamps are so bright, we tend to be blinded to anything but the lights themselves and so in busy times such as 'rush hour' we can afford to get closer to the target's vehicle.

and it may not be practical to 'hang back' too much. Ensure that any handovers are carried out frequently and always in the mirror of the target. This should satisfy the target's curiosity if he suspects that he is being followed.

Ensure that all your sidelights and head-lights are all working properly as a faulty light will soon be noticed. If you have to navigate by reading a map, try to refrain from using the 'courtesy' light as this will light you up like a beacon and ruin your night vision, use a small pocket torch if possible.

Quite often, the back up or tail end Charlie will have difficulty seeing where the other team members are in the convoy ahead of them. The call '**Touch Red**' on the radio is often used requesting that the eyeball (or person in front) tap their break pedals in order for those behind to see the brighter glow of the brake lights and thus indicating where they are.

In the past I have seen operators from particular agencies attach a small strip of reflective tape to the underside of the rear bumper. At night this can be seen from a distance and be a good indicator to the target's location. However, you would be risking compromise when attaching it and also if it is found by the target.

Lights Away!

Let's say that the target has entered a pub car park at night and you can only trigger the entrance from a distance away or from a standing O.P. It would be difficult to identify the target as other vehicles may also leave the car park. Due to this, if a vehicle leaves we call '**Standby Standby, Lights Away**'. This means to the team that a vehicle has left but cannot be identified, therefore a team member has to check it and confirm.

If you are also carrying out footwork at night, you may consider removing the courtesy light bulb altogether, so it does not to light up the car when you get in and out. Do not slam your car doors shut but gently push them to and then 'click' the door shut by pushing it in with two hands or your backside.

Motorbikes

The use of motorbikes provides an essential aid when carrying out mobile surveillance in heavy traffic in busy towns and cities, but they can have their limitations. In their favour they are harder to notice, they are fast with good acceleration and they can access where cars cannot. Using a motorbike greatly minimises the risk of a loss.

A surveillance rider's task is fairly specialised and requires much training and experience. The rider has to be very proficient in bike handling as his task is

probably one of the most dangerous on the team. A good rider will be able to act on his own initiative without having to be tasked by the team leader, he will know when to hang back or come through and take the eyeball.

Not only can he take part in the surveillance but he can also provide support to the team. For example, if you are tail end Charlie and held back in heavy traffic but need to close up but cannot get around it, the motorcyclist can help. If he cuts through the queue of traffic, pulls in front of someone and applies his brakes he can hold back the traffic and prevent them from moving forwards. As a gap appears, the biker calls forward the team member who then overtakes the held traffic and jumps into the gap created by the biker. In a similar manner, if the convoy are struggling to get out at a road junction, the biker could position himself in the middle of the adjoining road, hold any oncoming traffic back and let the team come through. As I mentioned, a bikers task can be a dangerous one!

The biker should be used:

• In heavy traffic such as busy towns and city centres, especially when there is a chance of the Eyeball losing control

• At major roundabouts and junctions controlled by traffic lights

• To provide suitable support to the mobile team

• To take the most direct and logical route when a loss occurs

• When following very fast or very slow targets

• To back up a footman who may be on a bus or train. It may be that your biker has to travel to the target's destination and arrive before him

• To pick up a foot person and re-deploy him

• To provide a trigger when the other vehicles are 'warm' or cannot obtain a good trigger position

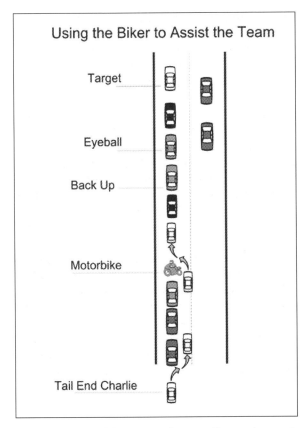

Using the Biker to Assist the Team

Target

Eyeball

Back Up

Motorbike

Tail End Charlie

• To cover the opposite side of a motorway service station

During the 'pick-up' phase or 'stakeout', the biker has to find an ideal place to lie up in whilst waiting for the standby. Sometimes this can be difficult but he can afford to be further away from the target than anyone else, as he has the power to accelerate and get to where he is meant to be quite quickly.

Some bikers will co-locate with one of the mobile units (in the back of their car). The biker can then relax as he does not have to be 'attached' to his bike in order to receive comms. You will find a biker doing this quite often when the weather is bad.

The professional surveillance rider will have his bike and helmet fitted with appropriate radio equipment. His radio will be worn about his person or he will have it fitted and powered from his bike, in some cases the biker will have one of each so that he can deploy on foot.

During the follow, the biker should pay attention to the commentary and should act on his own initiative. If the target gets held at a set of traffic lights, he should automatically close up in the event any of the team becomes held. If the lights change against the team, the biker can quickly clear the lights and take control. The rider will want to hand over back to the car team as soon as possible afterwards.

He can use other vehicles for cover but should also be courteous and safe. If the biker starts to annoy other motorists they will try to bump him off the road, flash their headlights at him or beep their horns, which will only attract attention.

Take care of your biker and he will take care of you

Standing Down The Surveillance

At the end of the surveillance, the team leader will order the team to 'Stand Down' and lift off from the surveillance. When doing so, a meeting point or RV should be nominated where all the team can meet up prior to debriefing and leaving the area. This RV should be an area which is safe and away from where the target or his associates are likely to visit or pass, so clear the area before de-briefing.

Log Writing

Obviously a record of events should be made during a mobile surveillance just as they would if you were on a 'static'. Use of a dictaphone is ideal as you can give a running commentary making a note of the times and events taking place whilst on the move. It may not be wise to write up your log sheet whilst in the middle of a surveillance at a temporary stop in the event that you may miss seeing something. Save the writing up of logs and reports once back at your base or as soon as practically possible. After the surveillance, it may be wise to plot the target's route on a map. This will reveal any patterns or unusual routes that they may have taken.

SINGLE HANDED MOBILE SURVEILLANCE

After my previous book 'Covert Surveillance' was published, I received criticism from some quarters who said that the book did not cater for carrying out a mobile surveillance single handed. A good point, but in my opinion, if you consider yourself to be a professional investigator, you would not be professional by carrying out a surveillance single handed, not intentionally anyway.

I often receive enquiries asking how much it would cost to carry out surveillance and always answer the same way. Stating that, 'You will need two or more surveillance operators in separate vehicles in order to minimise the risk of losing contact, and more importantly minimise the risk of having a compromise. Anyone stating that they can do it cheaper by only using one person does not know what they are doing and should be treated with extreme caution'.

When the client says, 'I can only afford one person', I turn the job down and recommend that they find someone else out of the telephone book, and wish them good luck.

That's my sales pitch, and over the years it has shown that the serious client understands what you are telling them and agrees to your suggestion. Therefore as a professional, it is up to you to educate and convince the client for the need of two or more operators to do the job properly. Although more expensive, it is cheaper in the long term and your evidence will be that much better especially if you are carrying out 'personal injury' type surveillance. You should certainly highlight the problems that will be encountered when operating on your own.

Even as a member of a surveillance team, at times you will find yourself having the 'eyeball' with no back up, as the remainder of the team is detached and so in effect you are carrying out a single handed surveillance. I, and many of my colleagues have had successes during single handed follows over long or tricky journeys, but not very many, often with the target being lost before being compromised, the better of two evils.

Failing to Plan is Planning to Fail

Prior to any surveillance, plan for it properly and get know the targets awareness level, has he been followed before, will he be checking in his mirrors, or will he be totally oblivious to a surveillance? Carry out a full recce of the target address or

the premises from where he is to be followed. Identify the vehicle or mode of transport likely to be used. If parked up, which way is it intending to travel, it may be better to 'pick up' the target at an obvious road junction he takes, rather than sit near the property.

Remember that we are talking about single handed surveillance, consider carrying out the surveillance in stages if at all possible, in order to minimise compromise. Let's say that we are trying to establish where a target is working. It may be possible that on one mornings surveillance we make it our objective to; identify the target, establish what vehicle he is using (or other mode of transport), the time that he leaves and the direction that he travels in. On the following day, we could make it our objective to plot up in the direction he intends to travel and then carefully follow him to his destination.

Plotting Up

Do not sit close to the target's address, the further away the better, remember if you can see him, he can see you. Be very third party aware and adopt an identity by giving yourself a reason for being there. Don't make it obvious that you are watching a particular address and use hedges and walls to provide you with some cover to avoid prying eyes. Consider sitting in the passenger seat to give the impression that you are waiting for someone. At night, avoid parking under street lamps and if you have the equipment, consider using a 'technical triggering device' to give you warning that the target vehicle is about to move.

When the target goes 'mobile', do not pull out directly behind him as you will be spotted, especially by an aware target. We only get one chance, so if at all possible, wait until the target is out of view before pulling out. Use another road user as cover or alternately, cover the first or second junction on his intended route.

During the Follow

If you are behind the target and have no vehicles providing cover, peel off at regular intervals and put another road user in between you. Whatever you do, do not rejoin the road if you are still in the target's mirror, if he is aware, he will be checking to see if you pull out. Try not to peel off if there is a string of traffic behind you, you may not be able rejoin the carriageway very easily.

Depending on the amount of traffic, you may afford to have two or three cars providing cover, but remember that if you hit a roundabout or a junction you need to keep control of the target as these are high risk areas where a loss is possible. If you lose contact, it may be difficult to locate him when you are on your own. Logically you should search along the most likely route travelled on, or make your way to any known possible locations that the target is known to visit.

Always act naturally, if the target is held in traffic, avoid 'creeping up' behind him in the hope that you will not be noticed, you will be. If the target is held at a junction and indicating to turn, do not indicate yourself as previously mentioned, and try to avoid 'mirroring' the target's movements.

At night time, you can afford to get close to the target in busy traffic, as the target will only see a pair of headlights and not the colour/type of vehicle you are using. Ensure that all your lights work correctly. If the roads are sparse with traffic, you will have to 'hang back' and turn off frequently.

Action on a Stop

When he comes to a stop, don't pull in directly behind him. Use cover to park behind or peel off to one side, if you are too close, act naturally and drive past before stopping and avoid eye contact.

When the target stops, you have to consider will he get out on foot or will he drive off again. Keep your eyes on the target and try to anticipate by reading his body language, actions and intentions such as removing a seat belt, turning the engine off or retrieving items from the passenger side.

Always have your 'working tools' close to hand so that they can be used at short notice. Your camera, binoculars, dictaphone, notebook and pen should always be within easy reach but remember not to have them in view so that passing third parties can see them.

The target may enter a car park (multi-storey or open) and it is important that you keep him under tight control. If he is entering a car park you can expect him to get out on foot and so be prepared and adopt a sense of urgency and park up quickly before the target disappears. Decide whether to obtain a ticket from the machine. Whilst you are looking for change and putting a ticket on your windscreen, the target could be away and gone forever. If you get a parking fine, add it to your invoice!

Do not take unnecessary risks and do not over expose yourself. Remember the aims and objectives of the surveillance and stick to them. If the brief is to establish what software the target buys at the computer shop, we don't need to follow him into the newsagents, the chemists and the bookmakers, so let's stay outside and get in close only when it is necessary.

The FBI's floating box method which requires many vehicles and practice.

FBI Floating Box

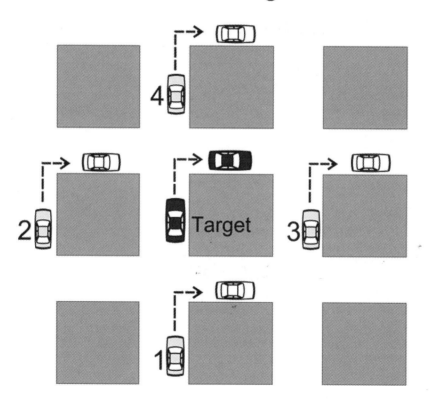

Acting as a team, surveillance is 'imposed' on a target, when on your own a target is 'followed', tactically this is a vast difference, fraught with danger and goes totally against the grain. Mobile surveillance is not easy, it requires the right training,communication and much practice.

Chapter Eight
Static Surveillance

Much surveillance work involves a static observation in order to carry out a continuous watch on an individual, a premises or objects. The static Observation Post (OP) is where we are in a fixed position with no requirement to follow the target. We could be tasked to observe a warehouse to note all deliveries made, or to watch a private house to photograph the occupants when they leave. The reasons for carrying out a static surveillance are many and the methods used to carry out such a surveillance are described in this chapter.

In addition, use of the static OP may purely be used to provide a trigger as previously discussed. The surveillance van (if used as an OP) can follow on behind a mobile surveillance (or even take part in it if used carefully) and move into a new static position when the target arrives at his destination.

What is an OP?

> • A static position from where you can observe, report and photograph activity
>
> • It can be Covert or Overt
>
> • Long or Short Term
>
> • Urban or Rural
>
> • Located in Buildings, Vehicles or Rural 'Hides'
>
> • Located on foot for short term measures

Vehicle OPs

As described in Chapter Five on Surveillance Equipment, a fully equipped surveillance van is worth its weight in gold to the surveillance team. Having the ability to move your O.P. into a position, observe and photograph the targets and then depart without arousing any suspicion from the target or locals, is paramount to a covert investigation.

It can be difficult to sit in the front of your car on a housing or industrial estate and carry out observations. It is extremely difficult to last for any length of time before you are reported to the Police or arouse third party suspicions. With an increase in crime rates, the general public are normally on their guard to anything suspicious.

Occasions do arise when it is necessary to observe for long periods from a car and the operator can feel exposed and uncomfortable when doing so. If you have to, try and sit as far from the target as possible, preferably having to look obliquely at the target rather than straight at it. Use any cover that may shield part of the car such as other vehicles, walls, hedgerows and trees. If you are sat in the passenger seat this will give the appearance that you are waiting for the driver to return. If sat in the rear, use a jacket on a hanger to provide you with some cover. Many motor accessory shops sell small roller blinds that attach to car windows to act as sunshields. These are effective for providing temporary cover, especially when attached to the rear windows of the car.

What if I am challenged?

If you are challenged by a member of the public, have a good cover story ready and make it sound realistic and convincing. On occasions, it may be worth telling the curious person that you are waiting to 'serve' Divorce Papers on a person and you are waiting for them to return home as they are being evasive. Use your imagination but do not let it run away with you.

Surveillance Vans

During your pre-surveillance, you decide that the only way to observe the target premises is by use of a surveillance van. The vans position is important and you must decide whether to observe though the rear window or through the front or sides.

When positioning the van, consider:

- What is your reason for being there?

- Your OP position in relation to the target, can you see the target clearly, are there likely to be any obstructions. Can you identify who leaves the property and in which vehicle

- Is your position obvious? If there are no other vehicles on the street, you may show out

- If the target goes 'mobile' are you able to give direction of travel to the remainder of the team?

- Does the target have to pass you on his way out?

- Does the van intend to join the team and follow the target when he leaves? If so, does the van need to be facing in the intended direction

- Are you in a cul-de-sac with only one escape route? If so, park facing outward in the event you have to extract quickly

- Is it feasible to 'self extract' or is it too risky?

The Insertion

If possible park the vehicle where there is some cover from the view of others, especially in residential areas. If you have to park outside a house such as a semi-detached or terraced, then park between the two properties. One neighbour may think that the van is connected with next door or vice-versa and so possibly limit suspicion about the van.

If it is difficult obtaining a parking position, it may be necessary to park the van or another vehicle the day before the surveillance in order to 'reserve' a space. If a car is used, it can be driven away to make a space for the van the following morning. If it is not possible, you may have to wait for residents to depart for work and then jump into their space.

Before moving into position carry out a recce by driving past in another operators car rather than using the van. Carry out a foot recce if required, find the most suitable spot to position the van so that you get the best possible view. Note anything about the target premises; are they occupied, what vehicles may be parked out of view, is there milk on the doorstep, are any windows or curtains open.

Moving into position can be done in one of two ways. You can either have a partner drive you into position and then lock the door and walk away from the vehicle, or you can drive yourself in and then hop into the rear of the van. Obviously the first choice is recommended and much safer.

If possible, blend in with other vehicles

Should you be seen to crawl into the rear of the van, the surveillance would be compromised before it has even begun.

Always leave the ignition key at a place under the dashboard or in the glove compartment where you can easily reach it if you have to depart from an area quickly. A team member should also carry a spare set that he uses during the insertion and extraction.

The Van Observation Platform (OP)

When the surveillance is being carried out in what would be termed as a 'risky or hard' area, back up and radio contact between operators is essential. At any sign of compromise or trouble then it would be wise to terminate the surveillance and leave the area.

In the past, the following encounters and problems have occurred when using surveillance vans:

- Neighbours stood beside the vehicle discussing its presence

- Arrival of Police after being called by suspicious neighbours

- Curious people attempting to look into the one-way glass

- Children playing and shaking the vehicle in an attempt to set off the car alarm

- Tyres being deflated by playing children

- The vehicle being accidentally blocked in

- Attempted break-in of the van

- Parking tickets issued whilst an operator is in the back

- A ladder on the roof rack (placed as part of cover) being stolen

You may be working on an investigation where you will only get one chance to watch for the information that you need, and so remaining in position all day is vital. However, the safety of the operator should be considered and the surveillance terminated should any problems occur.

Once in position you can set up your OP for your requirements. Start the surveillance log detailing as much information about the target area as possible. Set up the video camera on its tripod, set camera for correct exposure and focus, adjust any other special equipment that you may need and have it organised so that you know where it is when you need it. Also inform the team leader when you are established and report anything of interest. Ensure your radio  volume is turned down and your phone ringer switched off.

If there is no activity, report a '**No Change**' to the team leader at regular intervals.

Amount of Time Spent in the Van

Once set up in your observation van you can be totally self contained and remain there for as long as you wish. It is not uncommon to find observations being carried out for periods of twelve hours or more and it takes a committed operator who can cope with the demands of the task, whilst being in a confined space with long periods of boredom.

Should the OP be in for long periods, you can either change the operator and his vehicle or just change the operator and use the same vehicle. When a change of operator is made it is better done by driving out of the position, making the change and then returning. Whilst the change is being made, another operator should move into the same spot to take a temporary trigger and to reserve the parking space if need be.

Should there be some local information to pass onto the 'fresh' operator, you can brief him during the time away from the target area.

This American designed surveillance van could be slightly obvious in some areas

On one surveillance task in the past, a van was used for a period of three weeks to observe the comings and goings from a house in Lancashire. The residents of the street appeared to not notice the van but the target gave it more than the occasional glance a few times. One morning when it was known that one of the targets would leave the house, the rear doors of the van were left open with a number of cardboard boxes in the back for him to see.

The target had seen us moving the boxes about and this hopefully satisfied his curiosity. After he had departed the cardboard boxes were flattened and the observations of the house continued from the rear of the van.

Vehicle Disguises

For most purposes a plain unmarked van is sufficient to carry out observations from. Should you feel the need, then it could be disguised in a manner of ways:

Magnetic signs advertising a fictitious company *(Mark Birds Plumbers)* are useful and can be attached and removed within seconds. It would not be wise to have a fictitious address on the sign in the event a suspicious person decides to check it. A mobile telephone number would not seem out of place and could be included on the sign. Should anyone be suspicious of the vans presence, they may telephone the number written on it. If they do, an excuse can be given as to why it is in the area and you will also know that certain residents are suspicious and aware of it being there.

Fitting the van with a roof rack holding a ladder or copper pipes, gives the van an appearance of having a purpose and so people would not think twice about its presence. If you do this, make sure they are secure and are not prone to being stolen!

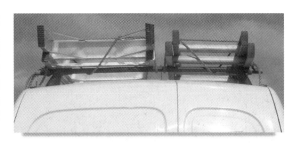

Use of Van in Mobile Surveillance

Should the van be used as a static OP or trigger, and thereafter be used as a mobile unit, caution should be taken so not to 'show out' and the vehicle should be used as little as possible.

Should the van be required later to act as a trigger or move into a position to obtain evidence later on in the surveillance, it should remain at the rear of the 'convoy' until required. We try to have a van on every surveillance team for this purpose.

On an investigation involving personal injury fraud, we had to establish that the target was physically able to drive a car. (She had suffered a broken wrist and had a neck injury due to a road traffic accident).

Using the surveillance van with an operator in the back, the van was driven in front of the target and she was 'followed' from the front. Video film was obtained of her being able to drive competently. She was shown to be able to steer, change gear and indicate during busy town centre traffic thus disproving her claim of a neck and wrist injury and being unable to drive.

In another instance, we drove right into a factory through the roller shutter doors in order to obtain photographs of machinery within. The driver left the van (with an operator in the back) who went and 'blagged' a member of staff. Whilst doing so, video film was obtained from the back of the van.

Why Do Van OPs Become Compromised?

At times the surveillance van will become compromised for a number of reasons, and more often than not by third parties rather than the target. If a compromise occurs, the vehicle should be extracted as soon as possible to prevent any risk to the operator inside.

The van OP may be providing the trigger to the surveillance and so this is the most important asset to the team. Therefore care should be taken in its placement, the way the operator inside acts and they way that it is extracted.

The reasons for compromise are many but we can minimise the risk of compromise if we look at the reasons why the Van OP is brought to another person's attention.

Operators Own Fault

• Position

Ensure that the van is parked 'naturally' and has a reason for being there. A van that sticks out like a sore thumb will soon attract unwanted attention. If you feel that the van will stick out then do not use it, attempt to get 'eyes on' by a different method or from a different location. Be aware of 'stealing' someone's parking slot, some people are very possessive of a gap in the roadside and will not like someone else parking in 'their' space, even if it is public right of way and access.

• Insertion

Try not to 'self insert' the van and then climb over into the back unless you are absolutely sure that you are safe to do so. If it is early morning, remember to switch off your sidelights. If being driven into position, the operator driving you in should not be seen to sit in the front and talk to the operator in the rear, if the driver has to talk, have a reason to do so, for example, pretend to be on your mobile phone.

When the driver gets out, think 'third party' and do not appear to rush away from the van. Have a reason for being there and choose a route to walk away so that it looks natural.

• Movement

When in the back, keep still! There should be no reason for any sudden or violent movement as any rocking of the van will be noticed by an observer. It has been known for some vans to be fitted with damped shock absorbers to prevent rocking but personal discipline is most important not to move about.

• Noise

Noise can be a contributing factor to compromise if you are on the radio or a mobile phone. Remember that there is only a thin piece of tin (unless insulated) between you and anyone stood nearby and your voice will carry, so be careful.

• Sightings

Make sure the observer or the target themselves do not see a camera lens poking through. If you have to shoot through the front try and be a few inches away from the viewing aperture. Do not lean into the front if you have forgotten you mobile phone or map as you will be seen.

• Smoke and Smells

Only personal discipline will stop a hardened smoker from lighting up in the back of a van. As a non-smoker, I can smell a cigarette from quite a distance. The sight of cigarette smoke or the smell of it wafting from the van can almost certainly give you away.

• Silhouette

Be careful, as in some light conditions an observer can see in through reflective mirror tinted windows, especially in low light. In addition, if you are shooting through the front, have the rear windows shielded by a curtain as the shape of your body will be silhouetted.

An OP was put under these road markers in order to observe a nearby farm entrance

• Re-supply

When the van is inserted, it is up to the 'van man' to be totally self sufficient whilst carrying out his job. He should be inserted into position with enough to eat, drink and have facilities for going to the toilet and have a supply of films, video tapes and batteries.

In the past, I have seen so called 'professionals' have plated meals from a nearby supermarket delivered to the van so that the 'van man' can have his breakfast! Not only does this attract attention by the comings and goings from the van but also whilst the van man is tucking in and pouring on the ketchup it detracts from what he is supposed to be doing.

Other Peoples Fault

• Children

Children can often be inquisitive of the reflective window and attempt to see through it out of curiosity. Therefore have a curtain or other method to prevent anyone from looking through the glass.

• Dogs

In the past we have had an operator quite happily in the back of a van when all of a sudden a passing dog would go wild and start barking at the van. This does not do anything for the van man's confidence and could arouse the owners suspicion. There are various reasons why a dog should react, your smell, noise, even the inaudible sounds from your video camera and there is very little you can do to counter it.

What to do in the event of a compromise

At the first indication of a compromise, inform the team so that they can close in to your location and prepare to extract you. You may have to resort to 'clicks' so that you do not have to speak.

The man in the van should not need a re-supply!

If you can, inform the team of what the problem is so that they can be prepared for it and take appropriate action. In the past we have had an attempted break in of the van and managed to prevent this purely by one of the operators driving up behind it and sitting in his car and thus deterring the would-be thieves.

The van should be extracted and driven to a safe area where the operator can extract. During this phase, ensure that you are backed by one of the team in the event that you are followed. If you are the person who has to extract the van, be prepared for confrontation with a resident and have a realistic cover story at the ready.

URBAN OBSERVATION POSTS

When we speak of urban surveillance, we mean any situation where a surveillance has to be carried out that does not involve the techniques described below in the section on Rural Surveillance.

An urban surveillance can take place in a village, town, city, industrial estate or housing estate, in fact anywhere which is built up. Obviously rural techniques can be deployed in an urban situation but the type of OPs used in an urban situation is different.

The urban static OP can take the form of many guises, the main two being the surveillance van and the room OP Other types of OP can also be used and are discussed later in the chapter.

Indoor Static OPs

The indoor or 'room' OP can be any form of building or structure from where you can carry out your observations such as:

- Hotel room
- Disused or used office
- Portacabin
- House
- Factory/mill/warehouse
- Shop
- Caravan
- Flat or apartment
- Boat
- Garden shed
- Loft space

In fact anywhere where you are not in a vehicle or hedgerow/undergrowth.

In the past we had to establish an O.P. to observe an inshore oil tanker which would moor up along a river quayside. There was nowhere to carry out observations from apart from an old school house (used for storage) located on a neighbouring company's premises.

Our client was granted permission for us to use the old school house. Once inside it was found that there was no upper flooring in the building and so we hired a scaffolding tower from a builders merchants in order to provide us with a viewing platform. The tower was approximately 40 feet high and we were able to view out of a 'crucifix' window and through holes made by removing roof tiles.

From the top of the platform we were able to covertly observe, photograph and video record the events that took place below us.

Hotel Rooms

We have put a few OPs in hotel rooms. This can be very useful so long as you obtain a room that overlooks the target area. Only a suitable pretext will get you the room that you want.

On one occasion, we required a specific room on one particular side of an hotel. One of the team members went to book the room and used the pretext that he was an ambulance driver away for a few days break but still on call. He stated that he had a poor reception on his mobile phone and asked if he could have a room as high up as possible. He was being shown the hotel rooms for suitability

This disused chapel was used as an OP site

Operators were able to observe from the crucifix window down onto the target premises

Inside the OP

The interior brickwork had to be chiselled away to provide a wider viewing area, without altering the exterior appearance of the crucifix

A scaffolding tower was hired and erected inside the chapel to provide a solid viewing platform

Observation were maintained by two operators in total darkness

and the first one shown was on the wrong side of the building. He told the receptionist that he could not get a phone signal in that room and so was shown another. He eventually got a 'good signal' on the correct side of the building and the hotel room was booked!

As with everything we do in surveillance, we have to have a reason for being there and this is equally important in hotels as the owners are often interested in people and what they do.

If you have to use an hotel for an OP you have to have a reason for staying in your room for long periods of time. Taking a laptop computer on the pretence that you are 'getting away' for a few days to get on with some work is realistic enough. If out of the room, be aware of inquisitive cleaners and staff, so ensure all your equipment and paperwork is out of sight.

Individual OP Tasks

The principal tasks of an operator in an OP are to:
  • **Trigger**, to give warning of movement (the Standby)

  • **Observe**, to observe and watch events

  • **Record and Photograph**, to compile logs and photograph/video activity

  • **Operate Radio**, to relay incidents to the mobile teams or team leader

  • **Sentry**, to warn of unwanted visitors to the OP

An experienced and well trained operator will be able to do all of these tasks to enable a minimum of two men to run the OP.

Manning Levels

Manning levels should depend on various factors listed below, but an observation lasting over a day should ideally be manned by a minimum of two operators. You should consider:

• Time spent in the OP (hours or days)

• The aim of the OP Is it a short term trigger or long term intelligence gathering?

• The size of the area to be kept under observation and the amount of activity to be recorded. One person may watch and photograph whilst the other records information and reports by radio

• The size of the OP site. Is there enough room for a team?

Re-Supply

On most occasions you should go into the OP totally self sufficient taking in with you enough food, water, films and batteries for the duration as any comings and goings may get you noticed. This is not always possible and so a re-supply may be necessary to bring items to you, or you may want to pass out surveillance logs or video/photographic films.

There are essentially two ways of taking things in and out of your OP by:

• **Live Letter Box (LLB)**

• **Dead Letter Box (DLB)**

The Live Letter Box is where a person would come to the OP or brush past, and in doing so, pass or collect items to/from the OP team. With the Dead Letter Box, an operator may have to leave the OP at night and then leave/collect the items in a secure pre-designated place. Another team member can then collect them at a separate time after the drop.

PLANNING THE OBSERVATION POST

Pre-Surveillance Report

As discussed in Chapter Two on planning, a thorough recce should be carried out of the area you will be operating in. The format below is a basic pre-surveillance report for siting an observation post.

PRE-SURVEILLANCE CHECK LIST

Address_____

Approach & Route_____

Recce 360 degrees from Subject premises considering:-

Primary and Secondary O.P. positions

Factors to be considered:-

    Routes in/out to O.P and drop off points

    Can you see the subject clearly

    Can you observe the approaches

    Are you overlooked

    Can the Subject see you - is it obvious

    Positions for support and back up

    Radio check and mobile phone signal

    Emergency R.V. Position

    How long to establish O.P.

    Note any hazards

    Rest areas, meals & toilet facilities

    Special equipment & aids

    Team base accommodation

    Any additiional information

Target Address/Location

Ensure that the address is correct and provide a description of it, especially if it is difficult to locate. If there is no number on the front door or gate, double check. Draw a sketch plan of the immediate area indicating all routes in and out by vehicle or on foot. Identify possible OP locations to trigger the surveillance and suggested 'lie up' positions for the back up units.

Approach and Route

Operators may have to make their own way to the target's location rather than be led there by the team leader. Directions should be taken from a main local landmark to the premises or to a central RV point. Obtain local street and Ordnance Survey maps and consider the use of aerial photographs if possible. Some aerial photographs can be obtained from the website ***www.multimap.com***.

Recce 360 Degrees

Carry out a recce 360 degrees surrounding the target premises (do not just consider the front of the premises, there may be hidden access to the rear) consider how many observation positions are available and their locations. Remember, the OP position could be in a van, car, hedgerow or building.

The following factors should be considered when choosing your OP location:

• Route In and Out

The route in and out of the OP should provide you with easy access and be covered from view of the target if possible. The route in does not always have to be the same route out and consider third parties. Identify areas where the OP team may have to be dropped off and picked up by vehicle.

• Can You See the Target?

Once in the OP you should be able to see the target clearly. If the target premises cover a large area, you should have a good field of view or even consider using two or more OPs to observe it. Consider whether your field of view will become obstructed by passing or parked vehicles, or any other obstructions.

• Can You Observe the Approaches?

The approaches to the target should also be able to be observed. This will assist when waiting for a target to arrive and give you that extra time you may need to have cameras up and running. On the targets departure you may need to inform the team of him leaving, giving his direction of travel. In addition you need to see the approaches to your OP in the event of a 'third party' approaching. All routes at the rear of the target premises should be assessed in the event the target departs from there.

• Are You Overlooked?

Should the OP be in a built-up area, be aware of anyone above you in buildings or offices. Likewise should you be in a rural situation be aware of anyone on high ground that may be able to look down onto your position.

• Can the Target See You?

Is your OP in an obvious position? You do not want the OP to be in a position that will attract and draw attention.

• Position for Back Up and Support

A suitable position should be found where your back up and mobile units can be located. The position should be

Be aware of overlooking CCTV cameras

close to the OP so the back up can assist you if compromised and can reach you quickly. The position has to be within radio range and should not attract attention from 'third parties'.

• Emergency Rendezvous

An emergency rendezvous (ERV) should be located and known by the surveillance team. In the event the OP is compromised or the surveillance team is split up, they can make their own way to the ERV to reorganise themselves and plan what action to take next.

• How Long to Establish

Estimate how long it will take to move into position and establish the OP to commence observations. This will effect your timings when planning the insertion. It could be a simple affair of driving a surveillance van into position or having to navigate across country, and then set up a rural hide.

• Likely Hazards

Note any particular hazards that may present themselves such as: parking problems, traffic conditions, security patrols, neighbourhood watch, wildlife and animals, floodlighting at night and CCTV cameras.

• Dead Letter Box Locations

If it is necessary to use a dead letter box a suitable location should be found.

• Rest Area, Meals, Toilet Facilities

Depending on how long your surveillance is going to be, you may require an area where you can rest, eat and go to the toilet within the confines of the OP In addition, the back up and mobile units will also require these facilities.

• Special Equipment and Aids

Decide what special equipment or aids you may need for the surveillance. Equipment such as tripods, powerful lenses, night vision scopes, electronic devices, screens or camouflage nets will need to be considered.

• Team Base Accommodation

An OP was put in the foliage on this modern industrial estate

Should the team be staying in the vicinity of the target area for a number of days then suitable hotel or accommodation should be found. When choosing a hotel consider the fact that you may be getting up fairly early in the mornings and that your comings and goings may appear suspicious to the staff. Motorway hotels and *Travel Lodge* type hotels are convenient and offer some privacy.

• Additional Information

Add any relevant information that you think is necessary such as any sightings of suspects, any vehicles noted at the time and whether a pretext visit was made.

On one occasion we carried out a recce for a task where the main gate and security lodge of a large company had to be kept under surveillance. This company was situated in a very large modern industrial estate where mounds of earth had been created to provide 'natural' divisions between the boundaries and were covered in bushes and small trees. It was our intention to put a rural OP in the foliage from where we could observe the main gate and security lodge.

Two of us went on the recce quite overtly, suitably attired as 'Highway Maintenance' workers, armed with petrol strimmers and the intention of clearing away over grown grass at the side of the road. Whilst one was able to get a close look at the target area and create a diversion with the strimmer, the other was able to identify an OP position and create a hide in the foliage. A string line was then laid to enable us to follow it in the dark which led us into the OP position.

Over the following three nights we were able to move into the position and carry out the surveillance without any difficulties.

Selection of an OP

The indoor room OP is used less often than the surveillance van as it is not always possible to obtain a good position from where the target can be observed. However, when carrying out your pre-surveillance, always consider the static OP.

> • Ensure that your routes in and out of the OP are protected from view. Insertion and extraction are the most vulnerable times when you are likely to be seen. Have your Back Up positioned nearby.

> • Make sure you can see the target and the targets approaches to the target area. Many room OPs are situated on upper floors and overlook the target area.

• Ensure that you will not be seen whilst observing. People in adjacent buildings, especially if they are higher up will overlook you. Site your observation position as far back from the window or viewing aperture as possible.

• Do not silhouette yourself by having a light background behind you or a bright window. If the room is darkened wear dark clothing, and make a dark background by hanging a length of dark material to screen behind you.

• If possible, fix net curtains over the windows, if not, a cloth screen hung between you and the window (a few feet back and not covering the window itself) will provide you with cover so that slits can be cut, through which to observe. House plants or ornaments on a window sill do not look out of place that will also provide you with 'natural' cover.

• Have an escape route planned in the event you need to leave the OP quickly.

• Check if there is a power supply to recharge batteries, what toilet facilities are available and if there is a water supply.

Eyes on Platform 2

A number of years ago we had to keep a business premises under surveillance for nine days. The particular targets (our clients former employees) were suspected of infringing our clients copyright by manufacturing the same products and attempting to sell them to our clients customers at cheaper prices.

We discovered that their business premises were located in an industrial unit adjacent to an unmanned railway station near Leeds. It comprised of a large yard area and a warehouse with large roller shutter doors which we needed to see into.

At first view it appeared to be very difficult to put under long term observation but an ideal OP position was found on the railway station platform in a disused toilet that had been boarded up except for a small square window. Inside it was dark, cold and smelly (it was February) and it was evident that a tramp had used it as a refuge at some time.

Over a nine day period, we would walk along the railway platform in our fluorescent jackets, enter the OP early morning, carry out our surveillance and extract after all the staff had gone home. The two of us would remain in there all day, totally self sufficient, as we could not leave as the small window faced on to the target.

An OP was sited in the white hut on the left looking into the roller-shutter doors of the industrial unit

A view of the white-painted disused toilet

Inside the OP

Views of the outside and interior of the target unit taken from the OP

Through two observation holes in the wooden walls, my partner Steve, would use the video camera whilst I took still photographs and made notes on dictaphone. We were approximately 70 metres from the warehouse and had a good view of the yard and inside the unit, at times the staff would be only 3 or 4 metres away.

From our cold OP we were able to identify what materials and machinery were being taken into the unit. As the targets new business started to unfold, we were also able to identify what products they were producing and where they were being despatched.

From the OP we had gathered a lot of information for our clients needs and over a period of months we would regularly go back to the OP to keep a check on activity. At one stage, a large white board appeared on the rear wall detailing the customer's orders that could be read with binoculars and photographed with a 600mm lens.

Our evidence was used in the High Court as it clearly showed that some of the machinery used had been built to order and infringed our clients copyright by design. The small building has since been demolished and replaced with a new one.

RURAL SURVEILLANCE

On occasions, a surveillance operation may be required in a rural setting such as having to watch a farm, or a premises located in the countryside. If the use of an observation vehicle is not practical, then the task still has to be continued. To establish a watch on the target it may be required for the operator to be totally camouflaged and concealed in his local surroundings for sometime to achieve his aim.

You do not necessarily have to be in the countryside to mount a rural OP The techniques and methods described below are equally utilised in cities or towns when the only position to carry out observations may be from a hedgerow, ditch, undergrowth or a small wood. Your OP may be required to solely provide a trigger for a mobile team.

In the recent past we have carried out many surveillance tasks which required to be completely camouflaged, three of which were in urban areas such as Salford,

Bradford and Chester. It may appear that it is verging on the extreme to be adopting these methods, but at the end of the day it is a means to an end. If you can achieve a result by photographing a target and the only way of doing so is by lying on your belly in a hedgerow then that is what has to be done.

Personal Qualities

For obvious reasons, this type of task is suited to someone with experience and more likely to be someone with a military background or who has had the relevant training. Some of the information in this chapter is taught to infantrymen during their basic military training and many of the techniques are also used by specialist troops, where it is essential that these methods are adopted to ensure their own survival. For the investigator (who is possibly less experienced) the techniques are essential to ensure being undetected.

Types of Rural Observation Post

As mentioned, the OP can be in a variety of places, a hedgerow on an industrial estate, a railway embankment, a ditch at the side of the road or in the edge of a wood. The best position to use will be determined by yourself and the circumstances.

The OP may be a short or long term position. In most instances it is possible to construct a simple OP using camouflage netting and then covering this with natural foliage. If you are in a hedgerow you will have to 'hollow' out a space using secateurs to form your hide and strengthen the foliage roof, to prevent it from collapsing.

There are various types of OP and their choice is normally dictated by the amount of cover available and probably more importantly, the amount of time that the OP is to be manned.

Types of OP

- Standing OP
- Surface OP
- Sub Surface Hide

• Standing OP

The standing OP would be a very short term measure rather than a full blown OP. It is more likely to be used to trigger a surveillance where an operator has minimum equipment such as a combat jacket, face veil and his radio. Imagine that you are on a mobile surveillance and the target drives from the main road into a premises located in a rural area. It may not be possible to trigger and observe from your car and so you will have to deploy on foot to get 'eyes on' from what we call a standing OP.

• Surface OP

As its name suggests, this OP is carried out by lying on the surface without having to dig down in order to create some cover. Ideally the position could be in thick undergrowth or in a dip providing you with cover. The use of natural cover (foliage) must be used together with camouflage nets to reduce the risk of compromise. The surface OP is used for short term measures or when the threat of compromise is considered to be minimal as you may be fairly exposed to a close observer.

A hide of this sort requires practice and experience to build and also to have confidence in your camouflage and concealment.

• Sub Surface Hide

Sub surface OPs require detailed planning and an experienced OP team in order to operate effectively. The team will have to take the necessary materials with them in order to construct the OP such as shovels, sand bags and camouflage netting. The OP may possibly be in a ditch and so suitable camouflage netting would be placed over the top followed by natural foliage.

If this is not possible, then a shallow 'scrape' may have to be dug out (during the dark hours) in order for you to remain concealed below the skyline. An area of turf is removed from the OP site, the ground is dug out to form a hollow and the soil removed from the area, a low roof is then built over the top. The turf and camouflage is replaced on top of the roof and a small entrance is made. The operators can then live in the 'hide' for a number of days without replenishment. Plenty of back-up in the surrounding area will be needed to protect the OP team during construction which is normally done at night.

This type of OP can be very hard work to set up and requires back up during construction, it is likely to be used for two or three days or even longer. In the commercial world, this type of OP is often used during long term surveillance of up to a week or more. It is more likely to be used by military close observation teams or Police CROP (Covert Rural Observation Post) teams.

Camouflage and Concealment

Camouflage and concealment is probably the most important factor in this type of covert role. You may be positioned within 10 metres or less of your target (or third party) and be required to maintain observations. Your target or any other third party should not have any indication to your presence, and this should be done by blending in with your surroundings. Camouflage and concealment is breaking up the appearance of people or objects to make them appear natural, and part of the terrain. It is an art which requires much practice and experience.

If we look at the reasons why we see things and what brings them to our attention, hopefully we will be able to counter them, and thus make ourselves become less visible. Things are seen because they are different than their natural surroundings. The main reasons things are seen are due to:

• **Shape** • **Shadow** • **Silhouette** • **Surface** • **Spacing** • **Sudden Movement**

A piece of netting over a lens helps reduce reflections

• Shape

Objects and people can be recognised instantly by their shape. Your body shape or outline is distinct and therefore has to be 'broken down' to look more like a 'blob' than that of human form. The head, neck and shoulders being the most important. This can be done using some form of camouflage netting attached to a camouflaged bush hat which hangs and drapes over the shoulders to break up the outline to which natural foliage can be added. Should you be using camouflage netting to make a hide, the outline should also be broken down with natural foliage. Especially attempt to break down any straight lines that occur.

• Surface

Many objects have a smooth surface but bushes, grass and rocks are irregular, therefore a camouflage jacket on its own may not be enough cover in order for you to blend in. By attaching irregular pieces of camouflage material to it, gives its surface an uneven texture. Local foliage attached to the person also assists in the breakdown of the surface and helps blend in with your surroundings.

Smooth surfaces are often reflective which means shine. Obviously anything that shines will be instantly seen. Shiny objects to be aware of are: camera lenses, binoculars, watches and jewellery. The forehead, face, hands and wrists also shine, so make use of camouflage cream/paint (camcream).

Camera lenses and optics should be fitted with lens hoods or attach a fine cloth mesh over the lens to reduce reflections.

These Arctic troops stand out due to their regular spacing and surface colour

An OP was once put in a graveyard at the end of this street

• Silhouette

When moving to and from the OP position and just as importantly, when in the position itself, attempt to keep below the horizon to avoid being silhouetted. Any object silhouetted against a contrasting background is clearly noticeable such as light coloured clothing in front of a dark background. When moving, make use of cover such as hedgerows and ditches, or crawl if necessary. When using cover to observe, attempt to look through the cover or around it rather than over the top.

• Shadow

In bright sunlight and moonlight nights, your body shape will give a shadow if you are walking or stood up which may betray you. Make use of shadow for cover whenever possible as it is difficult for an observer to see into shaded areas. Remember that when the sun moves so does shadow.

• Spacing

Natural objects are never regularly spaced on the ground, regular spacing means man made objects. If there are a number of you having to move across country, vary the distance between you so that the line appears irregular. Avoid any areas that provide isolated cover, a single bush in a field may seem an appropriate spot to observe from but it will stick out like a sore thumb becoming obvious, areas such as this are also more difficult to move in and out of to occupy.

• Sudden Movement

Humans are naturally predators and therefore the human eye is attracted to movement, especially if it is sudden. Movement is one of the most important give-aways to our presence. You may be totally camouflaged in your surroundings and made to be invisible, but a slight movement from the hand or turn of the head will catch someone's eye and you will be compromised. If you have to move, move slowly, deliberately, with stealth and the use of cover. Do not be afraid to crawl on your front or hands and knees and do not rush.

Concealment

Camouflage and concealment are two very important skills, which will enable you to see without being seen. Once camouflaged, you will need to conceal yourself by making the best use of cover without giving up a good field of view.

The following principles should be observed:

- Look round cover or through it, not over it
- Avoid skylines to avoid silhouetting yourself
- Make use of available shadow
- Choose clothing and equipment to match the background
- Avoid isolated cover such as lone bushes or trees
- Move carefully, especially when moving into or out of cover

Camouflage Paint and Face Creams

In order to camouflage the face and hands 'cam cream' will have to be applied. This cream is easily available from army surplus stores. Cover the whole face, forehead, neck, ears, hands and wrists with a thin base layer of brown cream so not to reveal any patches. Then sparingly apply more cream in dark patches at random to break up the shape of the face and possibly add a touch of dark green coloured paint.

Remember to do the 'V' of your neck and the back of your wrists, otherwise clothing will ride up and expose skin.

People with black or dark skin should also apply cam cream as the skin reflects light and becomes shiny, cam cream should be non-reflective.

Communications and Hand Signals

When working in an OP during daylight silence is essential and so communication may be achieved by using hand signals. When using radios, it is essential that you have comms with your back up. At times you will be lying very low on the ground or in ditches below ground level, therefore radio signals will be reduced. A 'mag mount' antenna attached to a hand set should be used to maximise comms and should be elevated if possible by putting it up a tree or attaching it to a fence post. The 'coat hanger' dipole mentioned earlier is ideal for this situation.

Why Are Rural OPs Sometimes Compromised?

As we have mentioned earlier, there are many reasons why OPs will become compromised by either the target or by third parties. The reasons for compromise are many but we can minimise the risk of compromise if we look at the reasons why the OP is brought to another person's attention.

Operators Own Fault

• Location

Sometimes it is very difficult not to put your OP in a position that is not obvious as the only cover available may be in the obvious place! Stay out of the '10 - 2' arc and avoid lone cover such as a clump of bushes in the centre of a field. Avoid being near routes that the public may take and ensure that you are not overlooked.

Troops have to be prepared for compromise at all times and be ready to move out quickly

• Insertion

Ensure that you are not seen entering or leaving the location. Use available cover, enter the OP at night or have a reason for being in the area before you slip into your OP. Be aware that on dewy mornings you may leave tracks to the OP site.

• Movement

As we discussed earlier, sudden movement is the biggest giveaway when trying to conceal yourself. You may have the best camouflage and be completely invisible but you will be noticed the second you move. Only personal discipline and training will help you to lie perfectly still for many hours.

• Noise

It is essential that you keep quiet in the OP. There should be no reason for idle conversation as whispers soon grow into loud dialogue. Be aware of your radio volume and your mobile phone should be in silent/vibrate mode. If using a radio or phone, keep watch of your voice level. Quite often you can start off a conversation in a low whisper but very soon you can find yourself shouting without realising it, the longer you are on the call.

• Smoke and Smells

Smoking is not advisable in an OP for obvious reasons, so if you are a heavy smoker, be prepared for a long wait. Not only will the smell give you away but at night, a cigarette tip will illuminate your face, especially when viewed through night vision optics.

• Silhouette

Your position should be so that you are looking through cover and not over the top of it or you will be 'skylined' by your silhouette. In addition, ensure that you blend in with your background and not be in contrast with it.

Remember to switch off
the recording lamp

• Re-supply

If you are in the OP for a long period, it may be necessary to be re-supplied with fresh batteries, films and food and for any waste to be taken away. This can be a high risk time and therefore do so with caution.

• Torch Light

Keep torchlight to an absolute bare minimum at night, you do not need a lighthouse beacon to read a phone number from a pad. Keep the torch lens as small as possible and get under cover when you have to use it.

Remember to turn off the red light at the front of your video camera and be careful that the light from the viewfinder does not illuminate your face.

• Lack of Camouflage

You will need sufficient camouflage on all sides and it has to be of the correct type. Camouflage nets covered in local foliage are very effective but remember that natural foliage may die after a day or so, and will have to be replaced.

• Clues of Presence

When extracting from the OP ensure that you take everything with you when you leave. This includes all rubbish, string, camouflage nets, human waste and so on. You should endeavour to hide the fact that you were ever there, as you may want to use the same location again in the future and so you have to protect its security.

Others Fault

• Accidental Finding

On occasions, an OP may be walked upon purely by accident which is why camouflage and concealment is such an important factor.

Be aware of children playing

A couple of years ago, a colleague was in a Standing OP in a ditch on some bare moorland in North Yorkshire, were he had to observe a gateway in order to identify the driver of a vehicle when he stopped to open the gate. He had been in the position for little over two hours when he came up on the radio to say that he had been compromised by two horse riders. They had seen him and asked what he was doing.

This was a total fluke and bad luck as the operator had kept well away from paths or tracks and the moor covered such a large expanse. The riders just happened to pass the same spot by coincidence.

• Purpose Finding

A very aware target may be on the look out for observation positions and make an effort to 'patrol' his local area and look for signs of your presence.

• Children

Playing children can stumble across your position but usually you will have plenty of warning by the noise that they make. So you can either burrow yourself in deeper or have a reason for being there if discovered. After a compromise by children it is always best to extract as it will not be long before they tell someone who also comes for a look.

• Dogs and Farm Animals

A dog will react and bark at something it is unsure about and there are various reasons why it will react to you: your smell, any noise from the OP and even inaudible sounds from your video camera or night vision equipment will be heard by them.

Sheep scatter, cows are curious

Horses, sheep and S attract their attention and the last thing you want is a herd of cows surrounding your OP on the edge of a field.

What to do in the event of a compromise

• Be absolutely certain that you have been compromised, you do not want to leave the position unnecessarily

• Wake those who are sleeping, if necessary

• Inform your Back Up straight away. They may need to extract you, cause a diversion or intercept those who have spotted you

• Pack items of equipment (only the essentials should be out anyway)

• Move out, decide if should be covert or overt (silently or at the 'crash')

• Move to the Emergency RV for pick up

• Move clear of the area

• Consider sending an operator on a drive past to monitor any activity at the OP site

The Rural Observation Post (OP)

When conducting a pre-surveillance, if you decide that the only way to conduct static observations would be from a rural point of view, (from a hedgerow running alongside a perimeter fence or from a small wood adjacent to the target) then there are many factors to consider. [1]

Remember, that these types of OP require much personal discipline. The operator has to work for long periods, often lying down, motionless, in poor weather and in uncomfortable conditions. Your personal camouflage and the concealment of the hide has to remain paramount to avoid detection. You may not always have the advantage of having natural cover immediately available and therefore may have to create your own in the form of a hide.

Planning and Logistics

The length of stay in your OP will decide on what comforts or necessities to take with you.

Considerations are:

All equipment should go in a small rucksack

- Food and water, you will need enough for the duration and do you eat hot or cold? Is it tactically safe to use a camping stove, or self heating foods such as 'Hotcan'. Take enough to drink and a flask is essential

- Toilet paper and something to defecate in should be considered. Ziplock type polythene bags are ideal. If the OP position is to be used over a period of time, it is unwise to relieve yourself in the position. Take all waste with you when you leave

- Should you be in the OP for a considerable amount of time, you may require a re-supply of food and batteries. In addition, you may have to pass on surveillance logs and films to be processed. A system should be planned for re-supply, whereby you may have to leave the OP to collect/leave equipment from a pre-arranged location

- Take enough batteries to supply radios and cameras. When used in the cold they have a shorter lifespan

- Use a sleeping bag, one between two

The Recce

Carry out a day and night time recce if necessary. If you have to walk about during the daytime in unusual surroundings then adopt an identity to suit. Walking dogs is ideal cover or wear running clothes as if you are orienteering/jogging. Wear a fluorescent jacket as if carrying out a road survey. All circumstances differ so use your imagination but make it realistic.

Prior to going out on the ground, obtain any relevant information from maps, aerial photographs or any previous reports in order to help you.

You have to pick your point of observation carefully, taking the following into consideration:

• What is the awareness level of your target and are others in the locality likely to be aware or notice anything out of the ordinary. Remember third party.

• From the OP do you have a good view of the target area. There is no point in having an excellent OP position if you cannot see your target. You do not necessarily have to be right on top of the target, the further away the better in some circumstances.

• Do you have a good view of the targets approaches. This is important if the target goes mobile as it gives you those extra seconds you may need to have your camera up and running or to radio your team.

• Is the position obvious or are you overlooked? Do not choose a position where you stick out like a sore thumb, always be aware of being overlooked by buildings or from hillsides. In addition you should have a clear view of the approach to the OP in the event passers-by become too close.

• Is your route in and out covered from view? This avoids casual observers wondering where you are going to and from. Choose your route tactically, keep to hedgerows, banks, ditches and railway tracks and avoid crossing open spaces.

• How will you insert and extract from the OP, will you walk in or be dropped off by vehicle? Is there a suitable spot to do this?

• Consider your concealment as you may have to construct a hide. Is there any natural cover about, will you have to dig down and what construction materials will be needed such as camouflage nets, shovels, sandbags and wire netting.

• Where can you RV in case of compromise and where can your back up be positioned? Should the OP be discovered and the OP party have to split up, then you need an emergency rendezvous where you can meet up again or be picked up.

• Your back up needs to be positioned where he can get to you quickly, with his position also being safe from suspicion.

• Is there provision for a rest area in the location? If you are in a two man OP. It may be practical to have a rest area to the rear where one man can sleep and eat whilst the other is observing.

The view from an OP into a quarry

• Allow for any special equipment that may be required (for example, spotting telescope or night vision aids). You may find yourself in a confined space so take only the equipment that is necessary for the task.

• How long will it take to move into position and to establish the OP? Consider if you are moving at night, add plenty of time to move in and establish the OP before your task should begin. Establish what time the sun rises and sets (a GPS can often give you this detail).

• Note any particular hazards. The possibility of dog walkers or farmers in the vicinity, also wildlife and farm animals, cows are very curious and will crowd you, whilst sheep will scatter. Familiarise yourself with landmarks and features on the route in, to aid navigation at night.

• Carry out a radio check to your back up location, you must have comms.

The Insertion

In some ways, once you are settled in your OP all you have to do is lie there. You should be able to carry out your task and you should not be compromised unless you are literally walked on top of. Therefore the most risky and vulnerable part of using OPs is the insertion and extraction when there his a high risk of compromise.

To minimise this risk consider the following:

• Move in and out at night

• If during the day, have a reason for being there if challenged

• Move in bounds keeping to public paths as much as possible, it looks more natural than walking blatantly across fields

• Be dropped close by using a vehicle

About one year ago we put a two man OP team into a very rural area in order to observe an industrial waste site. We could drive to within 1.5 miles of the target and then we had to walk the remainder. The insertion route took us about a mile along a canal tow path and we walked this quite openly as any other hikers would. Once at the spot where we would leave the path, we would check for any observers and then quickly disappear into the adjacent wood. We would then lie in wait for 15 minutes in the event that we had been seen. After it was clear, we changed into our camouflage clothing and moved off to our lie up position (LUP) just short of the OP.

Vehicle Drop Off Points (DOP's)

Quite often the OP team or individual will have to be dropped off by vehicle as the distance to the target area will be either to difficult to cross, or take too long to walk, especially if you are carrying equipment. The last thing you want to be is tired and wet after walking for a number of hours in the dark and then have to establish an OP and remain alert for the next day or so.

Therefore the various methods of transport and the procedure for the drop off and pick up is important.

The drop off can be carried out by car, van or boat but obviously the type of task will dictate the method of transport used. However the procedure for the actual drop off remains more or less the same for each type of transport.

Pre-Deployment Checks

• The transport should be reliable and checked for serviceability, there should be no rattles or unnecessary noises, all lights should be working properly

• The vehicle should suit the area in which you are operating. A four door car is better than one with two, use a van if necessary

• The driver should carry out a map study and be fully briefed on his routes in and out and what to do in the event of a compromise, have a cover story ready

This cut tree makes an ideal marker for drop offs and pick ups

• A secondary drop off point should be decided in the event you cannot use the primary one

• The driver should note any 'markers' such as gates or telegraph posts, in order to count him down to the drop off point

• All equipment in the vehicle must be close at hand to enable quick de-bussing

The driver of the vehicle is responsible for the actual vehicle and for getting you there at the right place at the right time. He should consider the following:

• **Drive Past**

Carry out a drive past recce of the drop off point but only make one pass as driving up and down could soon attract attention. This should be done the day before or a number of hours prior to the actual drop off, note any count down markers.

• **Speed**

Do not drive too slow or too fast at speeds that would draw attention to yourselves. Keep to your road sense and do not forget to check your mirrors for third parties. When stopping, do not brake violently or screech to a halt, you will only draw attention to yourself.

• Noise

When getting out of the vehicle ensure that there is no talking or unnecessary noise from equipment being dropped or knocked about. Do not slam doors or drop tail gates but slowly push the doors closed, if need be, use your body weight such as your backside for the final push to snap it closed. The drop off should be silent. Ensure that your mobile phone is switched off or in silent mode.

• Vehicle Lights

You may have to make the drop off in total darkness when you will have to 'kill' all of the lights but be aware of your rear brake lights illuminating the area. It may be practical to have a cut off switch fitted in order to use the brakes without the lights glowing as you apply them.

Disable interior lights if working at night

Remove the bulbs from the interior courtesy lights to prevent illumination when opening doors and also check that there are no lights fitted into the door skins as a safety feature.

The Drop Off

• The Approach

On approach, the vehicle begins to slow down, the driver gives warning and the operators prepare to de-bus by ensuring they have all equipment necessary, do not leave anything behind.

The Vehicle Stops

If at all possible the vehicle should stop on the side of the road on which the operators intend to move off in, they should not have to cross the road. A layby is a natural place to stop a vehicle, so use one if you can. If not, try to carry out the drop off at a point where the vehicle would naturally slow down such as approaching a junction. A natural dip in the road may provide 'dead ground' which cannot be seen into by any nearby observers.

The team should de-bus, whist doing so, the driver remains in his seat and keeps the engine running, he should also act as a look out. They should de-bus in silence from the rear of the vehicle just closing their doors on the first click. If the vehicle headlights lights are still on, ensure that you do not cross in front of them as this would alert any onlookers, have the same regard for the tail lights.

Once you are happy, you can let the driver move away. You should move a short distance away and wait for about 15 minutes in order for your senses to get used to the dark and your new surroundings before moving off. Carry out a radio check to your back up and keep them up-dated with your progress.

The Route In

Allow plenty of time to move into your OP position. If you have to be in position before first light, allow enough time to set up and establish the OP and check its concealment.

Do not cross infront of car headlights

Select your route with care and consider that an ideal route is one that provides:

• Places to observe without being seen

• There is cover from view

• There are no or very few obstacles en-route

• You avoid farms and wildlife

Move in with caution, at all times you must:

> • Remain alert, stop frequently to look and listen. Do not cross open spaces but keep to hedgerows and wood perimeters to give cover. Move slowly, thus creating less noise. Should you have no option but to cross a field, move singly, keeping your body as low as possible and crawl if necessary. Remember, your silhouette will betray you.

> • Move in bounds from one location to another, After each bound, confirm your direction from distant landmarks such as hills, pylons, urban lights, the position of the sun and stars, or use a compass or a GPS.

Use different types of cover such as:

• Dead Ground

Dead ground is the ground, which cannot be seen into from the target's location such as low ground, hollows, small valleys and re-entrants.

• Ditches

These provide cover from the target's view but they can be obvious approaches.

• Trees and Bushes

These provide cover from view but remember that isolated bushes and trees are obvious places to hide and should therefore be avoided if possible.

• Plantations and Tree Lines

These provide cover from observation and man made plantations can be very difficult to move through so keep to the perimeter if you have to.

• Habitation and Farms

If possible avoid going near farmland and habitation as animals can be inquisitive and thus give away your presence.

Personal camouflage is essential

• Make use of surrounding noise (such as cars passing) which will give you cover and distraction when moving. Be extra cautious when crossing obstacles such as roads, bridges, gates or fences. Crawl under gates and fences and do not vault over them. If crossing walls, assist each other and keep flat, do not drop rucksacks over the other side.

• Do not take risks, have a plan ready if compromised and keep your back up informed of your progress. Take note of where you can take cover and hide if necessary along your route.

• Enter the OP from behind keeping the position between you and the target and be aware of creating tracks that lead to it.

Moving at Night

At night we hear more than we see and so silence is vital in order not to be compromised. To move at night silently, requires very slow deliberate movement and so your route has to be selected carefully.

When moving consider:

• Stop at frequent intervals, scan the area and listen. If you have night vision scopes then use them

• When stopping, keep as low to the ground as possible and turn your ears towards the direction of sound. An open mouth will help pick up the direction of the sound

• If you hear any suspicious noises en route, stop, scan and listen until you are happy to move on

• Keep checking your direction regularly with use of the stars, distance landmarks or a compass/GPS. If you have to stop to look at a map, get into some cover and keep low to the ground as possible. Do not let torchlight give away your presence

At one time in the military, it was taught and practised to have a red filter over the end of your torch in order to preserve your 'night vision'. This can be good practice but if the torchlight is seen by a casual onlooker, all they will see is a red light in the distance and may become suspicious of it. There are more 'white' lights seen at night than red lights and so the point could be argued that a small amount of white light is preferable.

Establishing the OP

Move into the OP position keeping low to the ground. Once there, remain silent and motionless for a 5 to 10 minute period. Listen and observe in case you have been seen or followed into the OP and get accustomed to the local noises and area.

Attempt to hollow out the foliage by pushing back brambles and foliage. If necessary use secateurs to snip at the foliage to make a comfortable observation position. A viewing position may have to be constructed using 'chicken wire' and then suitably camouflaged. If necessary add extra foliage to the outside of your cover. Remember if you intend using the same position over a period of time, you will have to replace the foliage as it dies off.

Do not forget to cover the rear of the OP. A camouflage net draped inside the OP at the rear will prevent you from being silhouetted by light shining in from the rear.

At first light, (if you are able), crawl forward of your position and look back to identify any gaps in your camouflage. If you are unable to do this, radio your back-up and ask him to make a pass and check it for you.

Establish radio check with your back up as soon as possible. If comms are difficult, remember that there will be little that you can do about it and so it is your back up that will have to move to a better position. If necessary, erect a 'dipole' or a mag mount antenna. It may not be necessary to report by radio every time you see something and so battery power can be preserved by going on air at pre-set times of the day such as on the hour, every two hours.

When camouflaged, the di-pole antenna will ensure good comms

Some OPs provide enough room to be able to sleep in when you are not observing. If this is not possible, then an area to the side or rear of the OP will have to be used as a lie up position (LUP) where you can sleep or rest away from the 'business end' of the OP. The LUP has to be camouflaged and the route in and out of the OP has to be safe and secure.

OP Routine

Once settled in the OP you should adjust your camouflage and make a comfortable viewing area where you are able to clearly see your target without having to move position.

You should unpack the items that you require to use such as radio, camera, small tripod and a note book & pen. All other equipment should be stored away in your rucksack at all times in the event that you have a compromise.

Any food and drink should be pre-prepared, you do not want a mountain of rubbish and wrappings, nor do you want to use a camping stove for obvious reasons. If you have to go to the toilet, you may have to do this within the confine of the OP.

On a recent OP that we carried out in a very rural area, the final approach was via a lake as one of the OPs was conducted from the waters edge and the banking undergrowth. Dressed in a divers dry suit and camouflage clothing a short distance was swum in order to get into a position. This OP was maintained all day during the daylight hours and I had to keep the dry suit on for my extraction as it was not practical or possible to take it off. At first, having a pee was a joy of warmth but after a few minutes the novelty wore off with the cold. All day we spent there.

Care of Equipment

You may be using sensitive equipment such as video cameras and radios in the OP, therefore it is important that they are taken care of and not damaged by the elements. Rain, sand and dust can get into the smallest of places and so do not put equipment down on the ground and keep it covered. If you are operating in a dry environment, consider wrapping your radio in 'cling film' to keep the dust out but be aware of morning dew that will penetrate and remain trapped inside.

Camouflage Equipment

Any piece of equipment, especially binoculars, scopes or cameras, will possibly require some form of camouflage as they will be forefront in the OP.

Lenses should be covered with some form of fine netting. A green 'cam scarf' obtained from ex Army stores is ideal. Cut a piece to size and retain over the front lens with an elastic band. Also use this material to wrap around equipment or drape over a tripod. A piece of black stocking stretched over the lens reduces lens flare and reflections when shooting into the sun without any considerable loss of light.

Vehicle camouflage nets cut down to small sizes (6ft square) are ideal for quick camouflage when covered with some natural foliage. Items to assist putting up camouflage nets are cord and string, clothes pegs, elastic bungees and extendable fishing rod rests to act as supports.

On completion of a task, give all equipment a thorough clean. If it has been damp, air the equipment to dry out, then test it to make sure that it still works. Replace batteries or recharge them if necessary.

Ensure that all equpiment at the front of the OP is also camouflaged

Suggested OP Equipment

Green waterproof sheet, cameras, radios, trowel, small saw, chicken wire, mag mount antenna, insect repellent, camouflage netting, secateurs, green string, food, water, sleeping bag (one between two), spare batteries, refuse bags.

The Extraction

At the end of the surveillance, you will need to prepare to leave the OP which we call the extraction, or withdrawal phase.

You will be required to:

• Pack away all equipment that will not be needed

• Inform your back up when you intend to leave, he can then assist by picking you up or by observing the area to give you warnings of third parties. At this time you can confirm the time and place of your pick up point

• Dismantle all camouflage and bring natural foliage inside the OP to die. Leave the position as you found it, taking with you all refuse, including all human waste

• Move out one at a time and never in haste, be as cautious during the extraction as you would during the insertion

• Inform your back up of your progress along the way out

• If necessary remove cam cream and camouflage clothing before appearing out in the open. This may be done just prior to the Pick Up

The Pick Up

Once you have arrived at your pick up point, you may have to wait a short period before your vehicle arrives. Do not become complacent at this time and remain concealed and out of view. Your pick up vehicle should inform you of his progress to your position and it may be necessary to guide him to the right spot or put out a 'cats eye' marker peg if at night.

A cats eye marker is made up from the glass element that you would get in a 'cats eye' (right) found in the centre of the road is secured to a tent peg to make the shape of a 'T'. When you have arrived at your pick up point, it is placed in the ground at the edge of the road. When your pick up vehicle arrives, he should be able to see the reflected light from his headlights and know where to stop for you.

On the vehicles arrival, all equipment should be placed into the vehicle and do not forget to leave anything behind. This is a vulnerable part of the extraction and so noise must be kept to a minimum and the driver fully briefed and informed. Do not slam car doors but pull them to, to engage the first catch. When on the move you can then close them fully.

Field Craft

Soldiers are taught field craft during their basic training in order to help them observe, and identify friendly or enemy positions. They are also taught how to judge distances in the event that they have to report where targets are and more importantly set their weapon sights. Below are a few disciplines that are of use to the surveillance operator whilst operating in OPs.

> **PETE'S TIP:** *Keep one eye closed if your vision is going to be ruined by approaching car head lights.*

Observation Skills

If we recall the reasons why things are seen: Shape, Shine, Surface, Sudden Movement, Spacing, Silhouette, we should be able to use this to our advantage when we are looking and observing an area, a target or piece of ground from our OP.

We can observe in a number of different ways, primarily by Scanning and Searching.

• Scanning

Scanning is a general and systematic search of an area of ground to detect any unusual or significant object or movement. You may scan an area by dividing the ground into the foreground, middle distance and far distance. By looking at the far distance sweep your eyes from side to side and slowly move closer to cover the middle and then the near distance. Scan each area horizontally and move the eyes in short overlapping movements so not to leave any gaps, this way you should not miss anything.

• Searching

Whilst scanning, your eyes may 'lock' onto a building or something that has attracted your attention. You should now give this a thorough examination and search paying as much attention to it as possible, using binoculars if necessary.

If your position is overlooked by any high ground, buildings or risky areas where third parties may see you, these should be scanned first.

Scan from side to side, far to near

Judging Distance

If we recall in Chapter Three on evidence we discussed the pneumonic ADVOKATE and the fact that we may have to judge the distance that we were from the target. Therefore we have to be able to judge distance accurately and with practice you can become quite proficient.

There are several methods to judging distance and there are certain aids that can also be used.

Methods of Judging Distance

- **By Unit of Measure**

- **Appearance Method**

• Unit of Measure

Provided that all the ground between you and the target is visible, you can use any unit of measure that is familiar to you such as length of a football pitch, or the length of your garden.

It is used by estimating how many units of the familiar length (a football pitch), can be fitted in between the position and the object to which the distance is required. A quick calculation should give a figure, which can be used as an estimate of the distance.

• Appearance Method

The appearance method of judging distance is based on what an object looks like compared to its local surroundings. The amount of visible detail of a person at various distances, gives a good indication of how far he is away.

At **100 metres,** all details are clear

At **200 metres,** clear in all detail, colour of skin and clothes are identifiable

At **300 metres,** clear body outline, see colour of skin, remaining detail is blurred

At **400 metres,** body outline clear, remaining detail is blurred

At **500 metres,** body begins to taper, head becomes indistinct

At **600 metres.** body now appears wedge shaped

Conditions Effecting Judging Distance

Certain circumstances and environmental conditions can make your target appear closer or further away than you actually realise.

Objects seem closer than they are when:

- The light is bright or the sun is shining from behind you.

• They are bigger than the other objects around them.

• There is dead ground (valley or re-entrant) between you and the observer.

• They are higher up than you.

Objects seem further away when:

• The light is bad or the sun is in your eyes.

The use of image intensifiers is essential at night

• They are smaller than the other objects around them.

• Looking down a street.

• You are lying down.

• You are looking the wrong way into your binoculars! (joke)

Aids to Judging Distance

There are various aids that we can use to assist us in judging distance in order to become more accurate.

• Bracketing

The bracketing technique is a useful aid at most times. Quite simply estimate the maximum possible distance to the target and then the minimum possible distance. An accurate estimate of the actual distance should be set midway between the two distances.

• Halving

For long distances, estimate what the midway distance is and then simply double it.

• **Team Average**

When in a group, get each person to judge the distance, add them together and then divide by the number of people in order to get an average distance.

The Close Target Recce (CTR)

A Close Target Reconnaissance or Recce (CTR) is effectively a stealthy patrol conducted to collect information about a specific location and detailed information at that location in order to gather intelligence. The operators may have to enter a yard, farm, business premises, garden or whatever to conduct their search and so stealth and slow movement is vital. The CTR has to be carefully planned and executed using all your field craft skills.

A daylight recce of the area should always be carried out to establish your routes in and out and establish the layout of the target area and so identifying any difficulties.

A covert search using night vision goggles

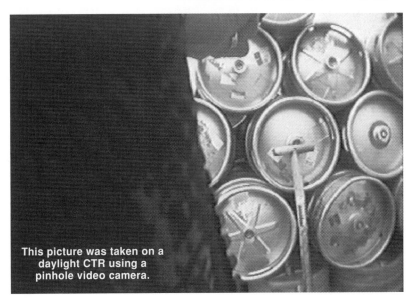

This picture was taken on a daylight CTR using a pinhole video camera.

The CTR team should always cover each others movements by moving one at a time and using as much cover as possible. You should always have a back up ready to cause a diversion or to have them extract you should you become compromised.

Make the most of covert equipment such as Night Vision Devices. If you have to obtain photographs and use infra-red film and flash, or use 'Zero Light' video cameras.

A couple of years ago we had to enter a commercial property that was located on an industrial estate in the bottom of a large disused and converted quarry. The aim was to identify and photograph the chemicals that were stored in the yard contained in 40 gallon chemical drums.

Two of us had set up an OP during the day and kept watch of the premises and yard area. From our vantage point at the top of the quarry we are able to observe all deliveries made during the day and were also able to plan our route in for the night time CTR.

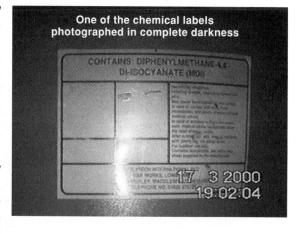

One of the chemical labels photographed in complete darkness

After the premises were locked up and all the day shift had left, we were able to establish that there were still approximately five members of staff left during the night. After dusk fell we moved from our OP to a closer vantage point which overlooked the drum storage area. It was intended that my partner, Ray, would enter the premises and I would keep an eye out for any staff members. Ray carried his personal radio with a covert ear piece and a video camera with an infra red (night shot) capability.

After an hours waiting in our LUP, all appeared quiet and Ray moved silently forward, balaclava pulled over his face and entered the premises. From above, I could monitor his progress through a night vision scope and also warn of anyone entering the storage area.

Every now and then I would give him a radio check and receive 'three clicks' in response to say that he was okay. After a while I received 'four clicks' (ask me a question). I asked him he had located the 'obvious' and then received three clicks in response, he had located the chemicals.

Through the intensified night scope, I could just make out Ray in the shadows, his video camera up to his eye and I could see the infra red beam from the camera illuminating the labels on the barrels. After twenty minutes or so, Ray started to move back to my location, slowly and deliberately just as he had done when entering. Once back, we moved slowly back to our OP then waited for a while in the event we had been seen. When satisfied, we checked the video tape (we did not want to leave if the shots had not come out okay) then gathered our rucksacks and left the area to where we had parked the car.

CTR Basic Procedures

The CTR in some ways is an extension of your observation post and so the same meticulous planning should be considered. You should have an aim and a plan of how you are going to achieve it.

Cache Equipment

It may be necessary to leave a rucksack in a safe area hidden from anyone finding it. If you do this, ensure that it is properly camouflaged and easily located on your return. Use a gate post, telegraph post or another fixed object nearby to use as a reference point to help you find it again later in the dark. A GPS (global positioning system) is ideal for locating a cache as they can be accurate to within 10 square feet.

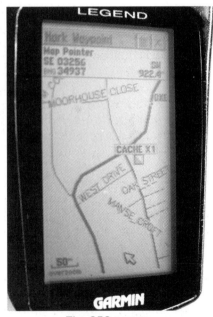

The GPS screen, accurate to 10 feet

Probing

You will be moving at night, carrying very little equipment. If you are suspicious of a noise or movement, then go to ground, look and listen until you are satisfied that it is safe to move on. Do not push yourself and go any closer to the target than is necessary, you do not want to risk compromise.

You may not want to go directly into the target area and so we want to examine it by 'probing' and there are two ways that we can do this:

- **Satellite Method**
- **Probe Method**

• Satellite Method

This is simply done by selecting a route around your target, which allows you to walk 360 degrees, giving you a view from all sides. How close you get (the radial range) depends on the ground and also the targets awareness level and how much intelligence you need.

• Probe Method

This method is similar to the Satellite Method but at a number of points along the route, for example North, East, South and West, you close in on the centre of the target for a closer look. You then withdraw back onto the satellite route and move round to the next probe point. This is a very effective method but can be very tiring and time consuming.

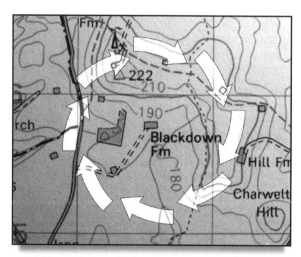

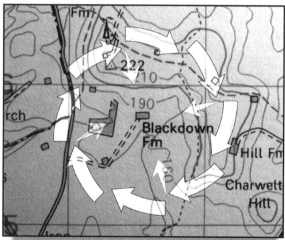

Conclusion

Rural surveillance is a very specialised skill, which requires the proper training and experience in order to carry out properly and achieve results.

We have carried out many static rural OPs over the past few years, not just in rural areas but also in urban areas where at first view an unskilled investigator would comment that the job was impossible to do. There is a time and place for everything and so keep an open mind and think about all the possibilities.

Chapter Nine
Technical
Surveillance

Technical surveillance is a means where we rely on electronic surveillance devices to assist in gathering audio or video information. Should the device be installed in the best possible place, it can be used to maximum effect. They are only an aid to an investigation and at times can be unreliable. In the UK there are particular laws relating to their use and ownership, in a nutshell, we can quite freely purchase much of this equipment off the shelf but there are grave restrictions when using it.

There are many '*Spy Shops*' in Britain and many suppliers can be found on the internet. Type in the words 'surveillance equipment' or 'spy shop' into a search engine and see what you come up with.

Technical surveillance methods and types of equipment are constantly changing due to technological advancement but essentially we can say that Technical Surveillance can fall into the following categories:

- **Room Audio**

- **Telephone Audio**

- **Covert Video**

- **Tracking/Locating/ Triggering**

- **Computer Monitoring**

ROOM AUDIO

Conversations taking place in a room or specific area can be listened to by the following methods

- **Hard Wired Systems**

- **Transmitted Radio Signals**

Hard Wired Systems

• Hard Wired Devices

A microphone placed in the target area can be concealed almost anywhere. A cable must be run from the microphone to an amplifier (which gives the signal clarity, especially over long distances) or directly into a tape recorder. Headphones or a tape recorder can then be connected to the amplifier in order to monitor the conversation.

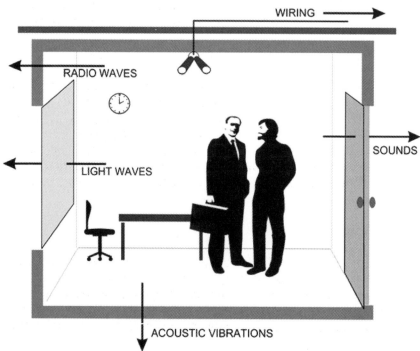

THE TARGET AREA
Information Pathways

WIRING

RADIO WAVES

LIGHT WAVES

SOUNDS

ACOUSTIC VIBRATIONS

Obviously concealment of the cable is the most important factor when using this method. Redundant cables that are already in situ (such as unused telephone/computer cables or mains wiring) that are often found in offices can be used to carry the signals from the microphone to the amplifier.

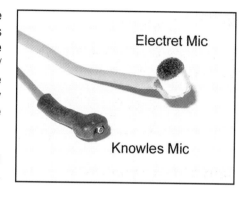

Electret Mic

Knowles Mic

Hard wired microphones can be located in the target area, buried in wall cavities or even listened to through the wall fabric. A microphone connected to a fine tube becomes a 'probe mic' and can be used to listen through small holes and cracks in walls.

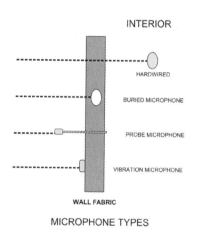

INTERIOR

HARDWIRED

BURIED MICROPHONE

PROBE MICROPHONE

VIBRATION MICROPHONE

WALL FABRIC

MICROPHONE TYPES

A simple microphone connected to a tape recorder will provide you with a reasonable and simple hard wired recording system. An 'electret' microphone can be obtained easily and for little cost, a more expensive microphone such as a 'Knowles mic' will provide you with studio quality sound but you can expect to pay up to one hundred pounds for it.

Types of Microphones

The very latest type of microphone manufactured by a company in Israel, and has no metallic, magnetic parts or wires making them extremely difficult to detect. The microphone relies on fibre optics as a beam of light is sent through an optical fibre to a sound sensitive membrane. Sound causes the membrane to vibrate and 'modulated', the light which is reflected back down the cable is translated into audio.

• Recording Briefcases

A popular recording device on the market is the recording briefcase, where a tape recorder and amplifier are built into the case for it to be taken into a meeting. Quite often the switching mechanism to operate the recorder is built into the handle or can be operated remotely by radio switch. In a similar fashion, microphones can be built into any everyday objects such as a wristwatch or a pen.

Recording Systems

• Analogue Tape Recorders

Conversations, whether they are room audio or telephone are more likely to be recorded so that they can be listened to at a later time. There are many different types of tape recorders available and some that can record for six hours or more on a single side of cassette.

A standard C90 tape will record for 45-minutes on one side, a C120 for 60-minutes each side. A standard recorder will not be sufficient in most cases and so the recording time has to be extended and this can be done by various means. If you are consulting suppliers catalogues, ensure that you know the 'exact' recording time. Some suppliers will state that a recorder has a recording time of eight hours but will omit to inform you that it is really four hours before you have to turn the cassette tape over.

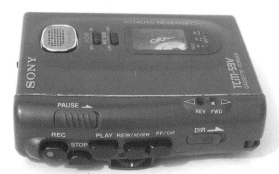

The smaller 'memo' or dictaphone type recorders are small when it comes to concealment but the size of the cassette tape can limit the length of recording time and also the quality and are not always recommended.

The Sony TCH-59V is a reliable auto-reverse recorder

• Dual Speed Recording

Some machines have two recording speeds, Standard and Slow so that you would get 120-minutes of recording on one side of a C120 tape when on 'slow' mode. The slowed down machines if used, should be purpose factory built (Sony are a good manufacturer). These are very reliable recorders but you may lose slight sound quality when slowed down.

The disadvantage of using these machines is that you also require a 'slowed down' machine to replay the tapes. A tape recorded on slow speed will not be able to be played back on your car tape player for example, as the conversation will be played back at high speed and sound like *Mickey Mouse.*

Be aware of inexpensive long play recorders that are on the market. It is possible that the internal drive wheels have been tampered with in order to alter the gears to make them run slower. These machines can be unreliable for professional use and should be avoided.

• Auto Reverse Recording

A tape recorder with 'Auto-reverse recording' will double your recording time by recording on one side of the tape and then recording on the other. These machines are very reliable, virtually silent and are recommended for most surveillance purposes.

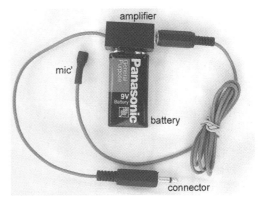

Microphone and mini amplifier

• Combined Operation Recording

There are a few tape recorders available which not only have a dual speed but also have an auto reverse facility. With this, on a standard C120 tape you can achieve four hours of recording without touching the tape to turn it over.

• Voice Activation

Many recorders have a voice activation facility or 'VOX' as it is often called. This enables you to set the level of noise to be recorded and therefore the recorder will remain dormant until a sound such as a voice is heard, and then start recording. In surveillance this can be very unreliable (except for telephone tapping) as the VOX system will pick up every other external sound. If you wish to record conversation in an office for example, the voice activation will also switch on if it hears a telephone ring, a radio playing in the background or a door slam and so on. This system will not work in vehicles as the engine noise, road noise and car stereo/radio will all activate the recorder.

• Cascading Recorders

A number of tape recorders can be connected to each other with cables and all set to record, but only one will record at any one time. Once the tape finishes on the first machine, it trips the second one into record and so on. Recordings can be obtained for an infinite time period, depending on how many machines you use.

External power pack connected to tape recorder for longer recordings

• **Video Cassette Recorders**

If a domestic video recorder is set to Long Play (LP) it will record on a C240 tape for eight hours. Using the Audio input (which all video recorders have) you will be able to attach a suitable microphone and record for this amount of time. Obviously you will have to play back the tape on a VCR through a monitor or TV in order to listen to it.

Switching Devices

If the length of battery life is a concern, there are various methods that we can use to switch recorders on and off in order to conserve energy. The systems below are concerned with switching tape recorders but the same systems can also be used in conjunction with radio transmitters (bugs), making them very difficult to locate.

REMOTE CONTROLLED TRANSMITTERS

TARGET AREA

SURVEILLANCE TRANSMITTER

SWITCHING RECEIVER

SURVEILLANCE RECEIVER

CONTROL TRANSMITTER

• **Radio Controlled Switch**

A remote switching receiver can be connected to the recorder and thus be operated from a distance of 100 metres or so. The remote transmitter (similar to the key fob switch for a car alarm) will activate the switch. When pressed, the coded signal is picked up by the receiver and subsequently switches on the recorder.

• **Timers**

A small timer powered by a lithium cell can last for months. When connected to the power supply for a recorder it can be programmed to switch on and off at set times of the day or week.

• **Pressure Pads, Light Sensors & Tilt Switches**

Various switches can be connected to a tape recorder in order for them to be activated. If the wire that runs from the battery pack is cut, you will cut off the power, touch the wires back together again and the machine will continue recording. If a switch of some kind is spliced into the battery pack wiring, the recorder can be operated at will by carrying out a physical action.

A small pressure pad placed under a carpet can be used to activate a recorder when walked upon. Light sensors can also be used to switch on a device when daylight (or darkness) arrives or when a light is turned on. In a similar manner, the use of a tilt switch can activate a recorder when an object is moved or a physical action is carried out.

• Infinity Switch

A simple yet very effective switch that can be operated from the other side of the world can be constructed with limited technical knowledge. This switch can be used to activate tape recorders and camera systems. The switch comes in two parts; the first being a standard radio pager with the facility to vibrate when receiving a message (which most models have). The second part is a switching device that activates by using a vibration or trembler switch and thus connected to your recorder or camera. The way the system operates is simple, the two units are held together (by Velcro or elastic). When you want the recording to start, you send a message to the radio pager. This receives the message and vibrates, the switching unit picks up these vibrations and activates the switching relay.

Digital Recorders

Digital recorders are becoming more common as the technology makes them easier to use and also makes them much more affordable. These digital recorders store the recorded information differently than the conventional method of using audio tapes.

The recorders store audio in their 'computer memory' and may have to be transferred to tape if needed. The audio reproduction is very high quality and easily out-classes audio tapes. The use of these devices have their 'pros and cons' but their main advantages are:

- They are small, lightweight and easy to conceal
- Exceptional audio quality
- Very power efficient
- They can record for over 30 hours
- Have the ability to be connected to external microphones
- They can be used for telephone monitoring
- They can be connected to conventional tape recorders
- The recording can be downloaded to a computer and sent as an attachment by email

These devices are approximately 3x1x9cm in size, weigh about 50g and can easily be concealed in a shirt pocket, some of them even look like fountain pens.

A number of models are available and cost in the region of £250.00. At the top of the range is a recorder that can record continuously for 30 hours and is ideal where space for concealment is a problem or there is a requirement for longer term telephone monitoring.

The disadvantage of these devices is that the recording has to be stored on a separate medium in order to store it indefinitely, otherwise you run the risk of erasing it from the memory.

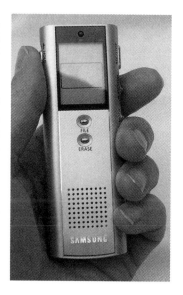

• Mini-Disk

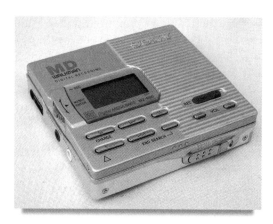

Mini-disk, as their name implies, records audio on a small floppy disk. The recorders are approximately 8cms square, are very slim and very easily concealed. The mini-disk combined together with a 'Knowles' microphone is probably the best surveillance recording medium that you will get.

At the moment the maximum recording time that mini-disks permits is about 90-minutes but the quality is outstanding.

Electronic Stethoscopes

A surveillance device often referred to as a 'Through Wall Microphone' consists of a ceramic contact microphone that is placed onto the wall adjacent to the room you wish to monitor. The microphone picks up the audio vibrations that travel through the wall like a large eardrum. The microphone is connected to a high gain amplifier to which headphones or a

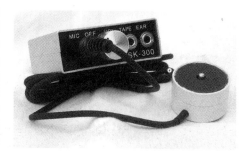

recorder can be connected, it can also be used to listen to the floor above or below you. A transmitting contact microphone is also available for surveillance purposes.

Mains Carrier Systems

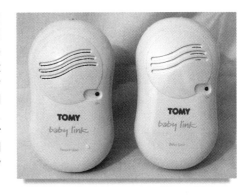

This system comprises of a special microphone unit that draws its power and also transmits its signals through the electrical ring main in a building. It operates very similar to a domestic 'Baby Alarm' whereby a listening unit is plugged into the mains socket of the baby's room. In another part of the house, a similar receiving unit is also plugged into the wall and can listen to the sounds of the baby crying.

The audio is not transmitted through 'the air' but the signal is 'carried' along the mains wiring system in the house. Purpose built eavesdropping devices can be covertly installed in the mains system to operate in this way or for the sake of spending about £20.00, this device can be improvised and is still effective.

Inside the 'baby monitor'

PETE'S TIP: If wearing a body-worn microphone, ensure that it is securely taped to you skin or clothing to prevent unwanted recordings of 'rustle'.

Radio Transmitting Microphones (Bugs)

• Transmitted Radio Signals

Radio Transmitters (Bugs) are small devices that can be left concealed in the target area. They will pick up conversations via a microphone and then transmit the signal to a receiving unit located nearby. This receiver can be monitored with headphones or be connected to a tape recorder.

Transmitters can be manufactured and supplied as 'stand alone' units or disguised in everyday objects such as calculators, pens, mains power sockets or built into briefcases.

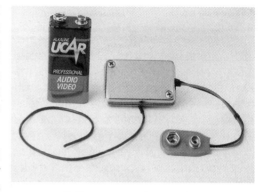

Battery powered transmitter

Transmitters require an electrical supply in order for them to operate. They can be Battery powered, Mains powered, Telephone Line powered, Solar powered, or a combination of all four.

• Battery Operated

Battery operated devices are very easily installed and can operate for a number of days without the need to change the batteries. Battery operated devices should only be used for short term operations or you may risk compromise every time you change the batteries. A high-powered battery pack (concealment permitting) could power a transmitter for months.

• Mains Powered

Mains powered devices can be more time consuming and trickier to install and you may have to isolate the power supply to avoid an electric shock. Once installed, these devices will operate indefinitely, so long as there is a power supply. Some mains powered devices may have a battery connected to them to act as a back up in the event of a mains failure. Be aware that computers, electric motors or fluorescent lighting, which operate on the same ring

main can adversely affect some mains powered transmitters. These devices can be wired into an appliance or be purchased built into mains sockets and adapters.

• Solar Powered

Some devices rely on solar power to operate such as a calculator transmitter. The transmitting range of solar powered devices will not be very far due to the small amount of power generated.

• Telephone Line Powered

A special room transmitter can be powered by drawing its power from the line voltage found in telephone cables as they have approximately 49 volts running through.

• Combined Room and Telephone Transmitters

This device is also powered from the voltage found in telephone cables and is able to transmit room audio via a microphone. However, when the telephone is used, the microphone is cut off and the telephone conversation is now transmitted. When the telephone handset is replaced, it switches back to monitor the room.

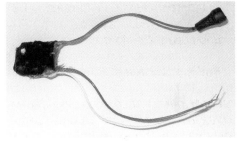

Combined room and telephone transmitter

• Power Switching for Transmitters

Some transmitters will be operated by a battery which will last for a number of days. Without the use of extra high-powered batteries, normal batteries will go flat within a limited time period when in constant use. If a transmitter were to be used only during office hours, we would be wasting valuable battery life during the night, when no conversations are taking place. In order to conserve the battery life, there are a number of options open to us which have been described above about switches.

All of these transmitting devices can easily be found and located with counter measures equipment such as Radio Frequency (RF) detectors but only when they are transmitting. Be aware when carrying out 'Counter-Surveillance' sweeps using RF detectors such as the 'Scanlock' or 'OSCAR'. A transmitter that is switched off during an electronic search or sweep will not be located easily as it will not be emitting radio signals, another good reason to use a remotely switched transmitter.

• Voice Activated Transmitters

Voice activated transmitters (or VOX as they are commonly known), although using up very little power whilst 'asleep' they will power themselves up and start transmitting when a certain audio level is picked up by the microphone such as voices and conversation.

These devices can be unreliable as any noise apart from voice can trigger the transmitter such as ringing phones, passing traffic, radios or TV sets. If you were carrying out an electronic sweep it would be advisable to play music from a cassette recorder in the room that is being searched. This would activate any voice-activated devices, that will otherwise will go undetected.

Types of Transmitter

There are two common ways in which the devices transmit signals, they are Free Oscillating or Crystal Controlled.

The Free Oscillating transmitter is normally a cheaper device to buy and should not be relied upon for professional purposes as the signals tend to 'drift'. They normally operate within the 'air band' frequencies of 108-138Mhz. The transmitted signal is propagated in a similar manner to water leaving a hose pipe that is being swayed from side to side, the water spray will cover a wide arc and will not always land directly into a bucket (the radio receiver). This signal is not 'locked' and can drift, the receiver therefore has to be continually tuned in and therefore unmanned monitoring would not be advisable.

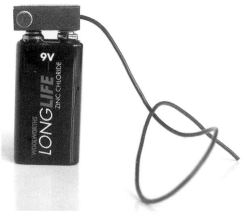

The Crystal Controlled signal is locked and is propagated in a similar manner to a fast steady jet of water leaving a hose pipe and falling directly into a bucket (the radio receiver). These signals are transmitted on a very narrow band to a dedicated receiver. They are very reliable as no tuning is required and the audio clarity is excellent. They are also much more energy efficient than their free oscillating counterparts.

Transmitting Frequencies

The crystal controlled devices sold in the United Kingdom normally operate in the UHF band (318-490Mhz) or the VHF band (169-174Mhz).

Free oscillating devices often operate in the VHF band only and may use the frequency bands for commercial radio (88-108Mhz) or the Air Band (108-138Mhz).

Transmission Range

All devices have different transmission ranges, range is dependent on the power output of the battery, the power output of the antenna (normally stated in watts or milli-watts) and the antenna used to transmit and receive the signals. A standard hand held radio transceiver may push out 3-5 watts, whereas an average eavesdropping transmitter may only push out 10mw-50mw.

The transmitter antenna should ideally be vertical and has to be the correct length to correspond with the frequency used. For example, a transmitter using a frequency of 174Mhz requires an antenna that is .43 of a metre long (or 43cms / 17- inches) and this is quite important.

To obtain this length we can make a calculation by dividing the number 300 (a constant) by the frequency. Then we divide the answer by 4 to give the length of the antenna in metres.

For Example:

$$\frac{300.00}{174.00\text{Mhz}} = 1.724 \quad \text{then} \quad \frac{1.724}{4} = 0.43 \text{ m} = 43\text{cms}$$

This rule is also prevalent for the radio receiver and also if you are calculating the length of a mag' mount antenna for your vehicle radios.

If the transmitter has 'line of sight' to the receiver, you should achieve maximum transmitting range. When objects such as buildings, trees or hills become between them, the range will be drastically reduced.

• Yagi Antennas

The use of a high gain Yagi antenna will greatly increase your radio reception range. The Yagi antenna is similar in appearance to a TV aerial and should be pointed towards the transmitter to obtain maximum reception.

Yagi Antenna

Long Range Transmission

At times, we may have to monitor a transmitter from a considerable distance away. Transmitters bought from the run of the mill 'spy shops' will not be able to transmit for more than 300 metres for the reasons mentioned above.

It would be difficult for these same devices to be installed in a vehicle to monitor conversations due to the shielding of the metal car body. If the engine is running, you will also encounter interference.

• High Power Transmitters

A cheap way of providing a powerful transmitter (with 500mw output) is with the use of two way radio. Currently on the market are many small pairs of 'walkie-talkies' costing about £100.00. These radios operate on what is called the PMR446 Service (Public Mobile Radio 446Mhz) and this frequency is licence exempt.

They are a good, small and robust radio with a range of up to 2km in open terrain. A radio of this type with a socket for an external microphone and earpiece can be easily adapted for covert requirements.

On some models, when a microphone is plugged into the set it automatically starts transmitting (a switch could be added if required). You would then be able to monitor the conversations on the other matching receiver or a scanner.

A device similar to this has been used with success in the past when it was installed in the cab of a lorry. It was wired up to the vehicles power and the microphone concealed within the cab. We were able to listen in to conversations taking place inside the cab from a distance of 600 metres away.

• Re-Broadcasting (Repeaters)

Some RF detectors scan the airwaves for the nearest and strongest signal in their search for transmitting devices. Due to this, some transmitters are manufactured to transmit at a very low output in order to defeat them. However, a 'repeater' located nearby, assists to transmit the very weak signals over a much greater distance. In theory the principle is very simple; the repeater receives the signals from the bug, amplifies them and then re-transmits it at higher power on a different frequency to be received some miles away.

• Encrypted Transmitters

There are a number of suppliers that produce encrypted transmitters. The radio signal is 'scrambled', so it cannot be intercepted and listened into like your standard device. However, RF locator/detectors can find signals transmitted from these devices just as easily as any other.

• Spread Spectrum Transmitters

Rather than transmit on the traditional 'narrow' band, these devices transmit over a very wide frequency band making them difficult to detect with an RF detector.

• RAFT

A covert system such as the 'RAFT' enables audio to be recorded and stored digitally on a device similar to a digital recorder. However, the data will remain stored in the device until it is remotely activated, this could be by a person walking nearby with a special receiver in a briefcase. When the device is activated when walking past, it burst transmits all the data to the receiver, which can then be taken away and analysed. This type of system is not readily available to the general public.

The Stage Microphone

One of the most effective audio transmitters available is actually a transmitting stage microphone used by performers on stage. The small system comprises of a small transmitter (UHF or VHF) which is connected to a high gain microphone. This transmits to a dedicated nearby receiver with two antennas (to ensure positive reception). The range is limited but the audio clarity is superb and far outshines any surveillance device on the market today and in some cases at a fraction of the cost.

The Infinity Device

This device monitors room audio, and as its name implies can be monitored from anywhere in the world. It is installed into the telephone wiring of a property and draws its power from the line. From a telephone (anywhere in the world) you can dial into the target's telephone using the normal telephone number but add an additional digit (preset by the manufacturer). This prevents the target telephone from ringing and 'opens' up the microphone in the device. You are then able to monitor conversations in that room over the phone network. If someone picks up the phone, the device is automatically cut off.

Radio Receivers

• Crystal Controlled Receivers

UHF Receiver

Crystal controlled transmitters normally come packaged with a dedicated receiver, the audio clarity received is excellent quality. Some receivers are only the size of a cigarette packet and can be connected to a recorder. Others can be larger 'desk top' size and can be built into the same module as a recorder. As with all devices, they require a power supply. Be aware of the small receivers that use tiny six volt batteries, they will not last very long and can be expensive to replace. Not many of them can be plugged into a mains adapter, however, they can easily be modified to operate from a larger power pack so they can operate indefinitely without any attention.

The antenna has to be the correct length to match the frequency and be as vertical as possible. A directional antenna (one that points towards the transmitter such as a Yagi) will greatly effect the transmission/reception range.

• Tuneable Receivers

Tuneable receivers are normally used to receive 'free-oscillating' signals that operate in the 'Air Band' frequency range (108-140Mhz) and special receivers are available for this. These free oscillating devices tend to suffer from 'signal drift' and so constant fine-tuning is necessary to keep the signal clear. Overall they are not very reliable and would not be recommended for professional use.

• Scanners

Radio scanners are receivers that are able to receive signals over a very wide frequency range. Individual frequencies can be stored into the scanner and then selected at random. If many devices are used on different frequencies, only one scanner will be needed rather than many dedicated receivers.

TELEPHONE MONITORING

Intercepting telephone conversations is probably the most effective way of technically gathering information and can be gathered in the following manner:

• Hard Wired Telephone Tap

• Transmitted Signals

• Induction Telephone Tap

Telephone systems can be divided into two categories. Analogue or Digital. Analogue is the system normally used for domestic (home) systems and small businesses. The signals carried through the system cabling have not been processed and could effectively be listened to by attaching a pair of headphones. Digital systems are more likely to be found in offices and businesses.

With digital systems, the signals are converted into digital code before they are sent through the system. Due to this, the signals are unable to be intercepted by conventional methods. We will later look at the methods of intercepting digital systems but first we will look at analogue telephone systems.

PETE'S TIP: As a rule of thumb, if a supplier states that a device will transmit for 300 metres, halve it in order to get a realistic transmission range. If there is a wall between you and the transmitter, then halve it again.

Analogue Systems

• Hard Wired Telephone Tap

A tape recorder can be connected by various means to the telephone system and can intercept conversations taking place over one particular target telephone, or from any other telephone extension that is being used on the same circuit.

The recorder has to be physically connected to the telephone line and the signals pass through an interfacing-switching device that stops and starts the recorder as the telephone handset is lifted. These switches can operate by 'voice activation' (VOX) or by voltage 'relay' switches. This system is very effective and the recorder can be located in another part of the building some distance away from the target telephone. If you are unable to use the existing wiring, you may have to lay a separate cable that looks part of the system and run it to a safe concealed area.

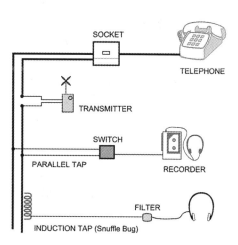

TELEPHONE MONITORING

The switching device or tape recorder may be manufactured with a standard BT plug fitted. If this is plugged into an unused socket it should record any of the telephones on the same circuit. If it is not feasible or covert to plug it into the wall socket, the plug can easily be removed, the two 'outside' wires made bare and then connected into the junction box or spliced into the two correct wires. These devices are normally to be connected in 'parallel' to the wires numbered '2' and '5' in a conventional socket in the UK. This will enable all the telephones on the same circuit to be recorded and the recorder can be located in a safe place.

A digital recorder can also be used to record the conversation if concealment and recording time is a major factor. A hard wired recording system will not be located by RF detectors.

• Hard Wired to a Computer

You do not necessarily require a tape recorder as there are interfaces available that allow telephone conversations to be recorded on a personal computer. In addition to the conversations, you will be able to tell the date, time and duration of any calls received or made.

Domestic Telephone Intercepts

A cable has been laid in the house to look normal but leads to the loft where the recorder is 'hard wired' into it.

Loft

Recorder

Intercept with a transmitter here, to monitor all phones.

1: Master Socket

Intercept with a transmitter here, to monitor phones 2 & 3 only.

Additional Line

Parallel Conection Inside Socket

2

3

Parallel Conection Spilced Into Cable

Cellar

Recorder

A 'hard wired' recorder connected in parallel can be installed anywere along the line to monitor all phones. Additional lines can be laid to ' secure areas' such as a loft, cellar or cupboard where the recorder can be concealed.

Transmitters have to be placed with care if there is more than one telephone on the same circuit. To monitor all telephones the device has to be located between the first socket (Master) and the pole.

Telephone Transmitters

In a manner similar to that of room transmitters, telephone transmitting devices can send conversations over the air to a nearby receiver. The transmitters have to be connected to the line (by splicing) at a point between the telegraph pole and the target telephone, or inside the telephone itself.

Depending on how and where the device is actually installed will reflect on whether one telephone or many extensions will be intercepted.

There are various telephone devices available: the more common types rely on the telephone line voltage to operate them. Some have a rechargeable battery

Simple Telephone Transmitter

This telephone transmitter is fitted in 'series' by splicing it into the wire that leads to terminal 5 in the telephone socket. Terminal 2 could also be used.

Exposed Wires

Cable Sheath

Splice

Telephone Socket

1 2 3 4 5 6

To Pole
Phone Cable

Floorboards

Drilled Hole

Cable Sheath

Transmitter

Transmitter

built into them to provide extra transmitting power. Telephone transmitters can be supplied as 'stand alone' units or come ready- made built into telephone sockets and adapters. In an analogue system, the wires connected to terminals 2 and 5 carry the voice transmissions and it is one of these that the device is connected to.

When carrying out electronic searches ensure that the telephone handset is removed from its cradle and a dial tone obtained. Otherwise no signal will be transmitting for the RF detector to lock onto. In addition, do not assume that transmitters will be connected to the lines or junction boxes that you can see. Double check to see if any cables spur away, where transmitters may be 'remoted' to avoid detection.

• Induction Telephone Tap

This device often referred to as a 'Snuffle Bug', can be used in

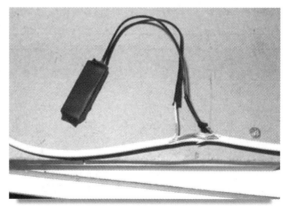

A transmiter fitted in series to a single wire

conjunction with a transmitter or hard wired into a recorder. The snuffle bug is placed on the outside of the telephone wiring and picks up signals by 'induction'. Every wire that has a current running through it (such as a phone line) radiates a magnetic field. This device is able to read the signals carried along this magnetic field. The advantage to this device is the fact that the telephone line does not have to be 'broken into' making it very difficult to detect and leaves no trace of tampering with the lines.

Telephone pick up coil

A cheap common device that works by induction is called a 'telephone pick-up coil'. It is a small device that is connected to a recorder, at the other end is a small black device housing a coil with a rubber sucker on the outside. The sucker is connected to the telephone receiver (next to the earpiece) and picks up the signals. Although not covert, it is a suitable cheap device if you need to record telephone conversations. To a degree, it will also work if you place it close to the telephone cabling.

Mobile Telephones

Without very sophisticated equipment mobile phones cannot be generally intercepted. However, at times you may want to record a conversation that you are making or receiving on a mobile. To attach a conventional microphone to your mobiles earpiece should work in theory but you will find that you will hear interference from the phones radio transmissions. A special microphone is available that is 'shielded' from your mobile which you fit into is possible.

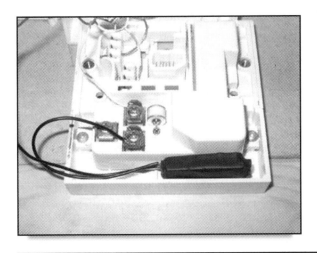

A telephone transmitter installed
in a 'primary' junction box

Digital Telephone Systems

Telephone conversations on digital systems can be difficult to intercept as the signals are 'coded' or processed.

In order to monitor and transmit these signals, we have to intercept them before they are digitised. This means that a transmitter has to be installed to catch the signal as it leaves the 'curly' lead from the handset and before (or where) it enters the printed circuit board and becomes digitised.

Once the correct pair of wires that lead to the handset ear-piece are identified we should be able to connect our transmitter. In digital systems, the power through the system is very low, therefore any transmitter will require its own power source and switch.

• Fibre Optic Switch

One switching system incorporates two light sensors which 'see' the ambient light from two short fibre optic cables. Two tiny holes are drilled into the telephone body (one in the handset cradle, the other on the top surface of the phone), the fibre optics 'see' the light levels and activate a switch. The sensor that is set into the handset cradle will be in darkness when the handset is resting, the sensor on the surface of the phone will be in the light. This difference in light from each sensor sets the switch in the 'off' position.

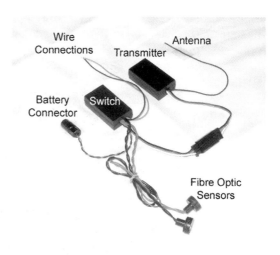

When the handset is lifted from the cradle, the two sensors now pick up equal amounts of light that activates the switch and causes a transmission. This system is very clever but over sophisticated when there are easier methods of carrying out the same task.

• Handset Tilt Switch

Another and much far simpler system of monitoring digital systems comprises of a normal room transmitter, but it is installed into the actual handset and has its own power supply which lasts for about one month. The microphone is able to pick up the voice of the person holding the receiver and also the person on the other end. In some devices, two wires are also connected to the telephone earpiece in order to hear the other side of the conversation. As it is battery operated, you would not want the batteries to go flat within a number of hours and so a small 'tilt' switch is used in order to power and activate the device. When the handset is resting in the cradle, the device is dormant, when lifted up to the ear, the tilt switch activates the device and transmits.

Interception of Digital Telephones

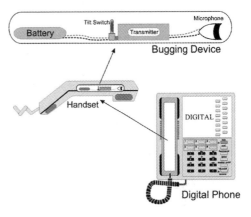

If the target's telephone has to be taken apart, try and practice on a telephone of the same model (not the target's). That way you will not leave any suspicious scratches or marks on the target phone.

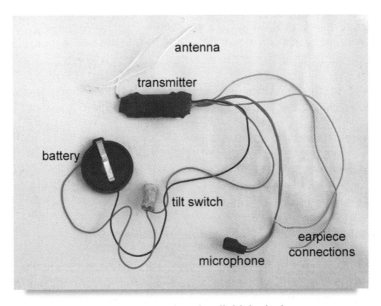

Tilt switch transmitter for digitial telephones

• Hard Wired Recorders

Recorders can be hardwired into digital systems but they are expensive. As with analogue systems, a device is available that can be attached directly to the telephone cabling but in this instance it converts digital signals to analogue prior to being recorded.

Miscellaneous Monitoring Systems

• Mobile Telephones

This device, for all intents and purposes is a standard mobile telephone but it then becomes a covert listening device with an infinite range. You can dial this mobile telephone from anywhere in the world and be able to monitor conversations picked up by the telephone's built in microphone or a microphone attached to it as part of a hands free kit.

These devices can be purchased from 'spy shops' and many will be adapted to use a better quality microphone, however, you can improvise and do it yourself with good results. A *'Pay-as-You-Go'* phone will not cost you line rental and a £10.00 card will last indefinitely. The majority of Ericsson phones can be adapted and some Nokia models.

The phone is not modified in any way except for alterations to the phone's 'Settings Menu'. Make the following settings via the Menu to adapt the telephone:

- Turn the Ringer Tone OFF (to make it covert)

- Turn off the Display Light (to preserve power)

- Set the phone to Auto Answer (so it answers itself)

- Connect the hands free kit (to remote the microphone)

When you dial into the phone it will not ring as you have turned the ringer off. After the second 'ring' the phone will 'auto answer' and open up the microphone in order for you to listen in (only with the hands free kit connected). The 'life' of the device is reliant on the battery standby time, unless the battery is connected to the mains via the battery charger, in which case it will operate indefinitely.

If you require to monitor conversations taking place in a vehicle, this is probably one of the most effective ways of doing so and the power supply can be obtained from the car's battery.

• Spike Microphone

A Spike Mic is what the name implies and is a microphone attached to a spike that can be pushed and embedded into wooden window frames and walls. Operating very similar to the 'Listen Through Wall' device, the Spike Mic picks up vibrations when access to the area to be monitored is not possible. It can be connected directly to a tape recorder or to a transmitter.

• Optical (Infra Red) Transmitters

These devices are not freely available to the general public and can be effective in the correct conditions. The audio transmitter does not send its signals by conventional radio signals but by pulses of infra red light. A small infra red emitting diode (bulb) has to be in direct line of sight to the optical receiver and operates in a fashion similar to that of a set of wireless headphones or the TV remote control unit.

The receiver, normally utilising a telescope, 'sees' these invisible infra red emissions and converts them back into audio signals in order to be heard. These devices will not be found by conventional sweeping/scanning RF equipment.

OPTICAL (Infra Red) TRANSMITTER

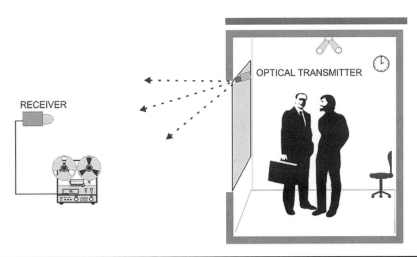

RECEIVER

OPTICAL TRANSMITTER

• Laser Reflective Microphone

This device can be unreliable and requires accurate operating conditions in order for it to operate. It is used to monitor room conversations when access is not possible to install a device. In simplistic terms, a laser is 'fired' at the target window, which vibrates due to the sound waves made from within like a gigantic eardrum. The laser is reflected and now carries with it the vibrations from the window (or modulated). The received or bounced laser signals are captured and converted back into audio.

Any external audio such as a vehicle passing the target window or heavy winds can effect the system, hence the conditions need to be ideal.

LASER MICROPHONE

• Fax Intercepts

Equipment is available that can be used to intercept fax messages. These devices are not cheap due to the technology involved. They are able to be 'hardwired' into a phone/fax line or a transmitter can be used in order to intercept and transmit fax data.

• Passive Microwave Flooding

In the famous 'Bug *in the Great Seal'* case during the early 1950s, the Soviets concealed a listening device in a replica of the Great Seal of the United States and presented it to the US Ambassador. The seal hung on his office wall for the

The 'Bug in the Seal' being made public in the United Nations on 26th May 1960

next six years monitoring conversations until it was discovered. What was unique about this device and what actually prevented it from being detected for so long, was the fact that it did not require a power supply, it had no wires and it did not actively transmit. Quite simply, an ultra-high radio frequency signal was beamed at the office containing the device from a van parked nearby. These radio waves were then reflected back after being modulated by sound waves from conversations hitting the bug's diaphragm. At this time during the cold war, this device was technically very advanced but also simple in its design thus managing to avoid detection for so long.

These devices (transponders) are still used today and can lie dormant for many months before being activated but their range is very limited.

Computer Monitoring

Over the past few years, with more and more people using computers, I found myself being asked to investigate and establish what individuals are doing on a computer, in particular what they were doing on the Internet. The clients' initial request was to hide a video camera in the vicinity and record what was on the screen. Technically this is quite difficult for a few reasons; you have to site the camera very close to the screen, (which is not always possible), and even if you do get close, the recorded picture can be obscured by TV flicker.

There are now a number of ways to achieve this aim, which need only a minimum knowledge of using a computer.

• Keyboard Logger

Some 18 months ago, we were contacted by a client who asked us if we could access one of his office computers which was protected by a password. The client strongly suspected that the user (a sales team manager) was setting up his own business in company time. The client wanted to examine his word processing files and emails for any evidence. We supplied our client with a small device called a 'Keykatch' and within the first day of operation the client had the computer password and access to the machine.

A very small device called the 'Keykatch', is freely available and is able to record all the keystrokes made on a computer keyboard. This identifies what a target is typing into a computer, obtain his passwords and ID codes and also identify what websites are being visited.

The device connects into the back of the computer into the socket where the keyboard normally plugs in, the keyboard is then plugged into the device. Any keystroke then made on the target computer will be stored on the device, different storage capacities are available and the 64Kb model will store up to 64,000 keystrokes, which equates to 40 pages of A4 typescript.

The KeyKatch Device

The device, which requires no batteries can be interrogated whilst still connected to the target computer or be removed and interrogated elsewhere. All that you need to read the device is a word processing package such as Windows Notebook or Microsoft Word. After a password is entered into the keyboard, it is recognised by the device and a short menu appears on the screen giving you various options to view the data or erase it.

If you choose 'view', the stored data suddenly appears on the screen and can be read as a normal document full of information. The data can then be saved on a floppy disk and device 'emptied' of all data ready to start again.

How much does this device cost? You should not expect to have to pay more than about £140.00.

Automatically Record Everything your Spouse, Children & Employees Do Online

Spector

Computer Monitoring Software

• Spector Software

Another simple and very effective method of viewing the activity on a computer monitor is with a nifty software programme called 'Spector', produced in the USA by Spectorsoft. If you can imagine a camera inside your computer which takes a snapshot of the screen every five seconds and then stores the pictures in a hidden file for you to look at later on, then this is what 'Spector' is capable of doing.

The software, on floppy disc or CD, takes about 3 minutes to install and is immediately in use with no fuss. By accessing the hidden file with a password, the screen shots can then be reviewed using the on screen buttons similar to a video recorder which has Play, Rewind and Fast Forward which help you scan through the snapshots.

It is an amazing piece of software and anything that appears on the screen will be recorded.

- All applications and programmes
- Typed letters
- All web sites visited
- Email activity
- All keystrokes typed
- Screen snapshots

If you need to know what someone is looking at on a computer, this programme is first class.

• Remote Computer Monitoring

There are numerous computer software packages on the market that enables a person to monitor the activity taking place on a target computer from a remote location. One common package similar to Spector is called 'eBlaster'.

This programme carries out the same monitoring activities as Spector but you do not need access to the machine in order to examine the information or screen shots. With eBlaster, whenever the target computer goes on-line, it will secretly email you (to a designated email address) all the computer activity and screen shots. It will do this every 30 minutes or once a day, depending on how you program the software. This software is not expensive and can be bought for as little as £65.00 over the internet.

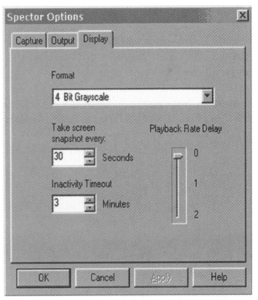

One of the programmes menus used to alter the memory settings

A special feature of the programme is that every time the target receives or sends an email, you also receive a covert copy of it in your designated email post box. Going further into the depths of cyber spying, you can also tell eBlaster that you only wish to receive emails with a selected word in it. So if you only want emails mentioning 'theft', you tell eBlaster, so it filters them out and sends them on.

This is a very powerful monitoring tool indeed. Imagine, if you have an employee located in one part of the country and you want to monitor him from your office elsewhere and all for £65.00. Spectorsoft also produce a Spector Professional Edition, which is a combination of eBlaster and Spector.

• R.A.I.D.

R.A.I.D. stands for Rapid Action Imaging Device and was designed to be used by computer forensic investigators. It is a small hand held unit designed for copying computer hard drives easily and quickly. Remember that not all computers are connected to the internet and so conventional hacking will not give a cyber spy access to the machine. A R.A.I.D. device in the hands of an industrial spy, can copy computer files at an astounding high-speed of nearly one gigabyte of data a minute.

• VDU Monitoring

When we look at a computer monitor (screen) we see the picture, what we do not realise is that it actually emits radio waves. It is possible to place a special bugging device in the vicinity of the monitor, which transmits these signals to a nearby receiver, which then converts them back into readable video pictures. This system is not normally available to the general public but used at government level and is commonly known as 'Tempest'.

INTERCEPTING VDU EMMISSIONS

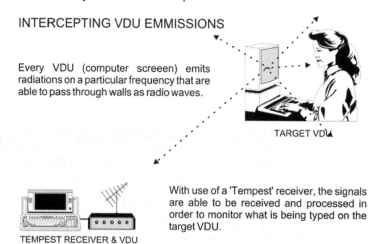

Every VDU (computer screeen) emits radiations on a particular frequency that are able to pass through walls as radio waves.

TARGET VDU

With use of a 'Tempest' receiver, the signals are able to be received and processed in order to monitor what is being typed on the target VDU.

TEMPEST RECEIVER & VDU

• D.I.R.T.

D.I.R.T. stands for Data Interception by Remote Transmission and is a software programme very similar to Spector Pro and eBlaster. However, this is different as you do not need access the target computer in order to load the programme. With D.I.R.T., the programme can be emailed to the target computer riding on the back of an innocent looking email with an attachment (commonly known as a Trojan). This is why it is advisable not to open any unsolicited emails that arrive with attachments. The attachment may be opened and appear to look all innocent, but behind the scenes, the Trojan is unleashed and embeds itself in a dark corner of your computer.

Once installed, it will monitor all computer activity and send reports back to a pre-programmed host computer. In addition, the cyber spy will be able to browse around the inside of the target hard drive and files for anything of interest to them.

The software was designed for US government, law enforcement and military use and may not be freely obtained to be used by the general public.

PETE'S TIP: Ensure that your computer has anti-virus software and a 'firewall' installed to prevent unauthorised access by hackers. Never open any attachments sent to you from someone you do not know.

Technical Surveillance Counter Measures (TSCM)

> **"...In order to defeat the buggist, we need to know how he operates... know thine enemy"**

Electronic surveillance counter measures is a very technical complex subject which cannot be covered in half a chapter. There are many people out there who advertise a search and sweep service but in my opinion, the majority are just going through the motions without really knowing what they are doing, what they are looking for and without sufficient equipment or any training.

The telegraph pole is vulnerable to transmitters

If you spend thousands of pounds on purchasing an RF detector such as Audiotel's 'Scanlock', without having the training to use it or understand its capabilities then it is of no use to you. The Scanlock is a first class RF detector/locator (and mains carrier detector) but it will not locate a hard-wired recording device such as a buried microphone or a transmitter that has no power source. If you have to use or hire a counter measures team, do not be afraid to quiz them about their qualifications and do not be impressed by the cost of the equipment. Anyone can have a Rolls Royce if he has the money, but not everyone can drive properly.

A private investigator offering his TSCM services very recently stated, 'You don't need the brains of an astronaut in order to look for bugs'. Well, I don't have afternoon tea with Neil Armstrong, nor do I drive a rocket but I know one or two things about Electronic Surveillance. De-bugging equipment is very sophisticated; it is very easy to operate and is very user friendly. However, unless you know exactly what you are looking for, how devices are connected, concealed and operated, you may miss them in your search.

Threat Assessment

We have often received telephone calls from clients stating, 'I think that our office or telephones are being bugged'. 'Okay', I reply, 'Where are you telephoning me from? 'Why, the office of course!' is often the reply, and then the client suddenly realises how stupid he feels as he has just informed the 'buggist' that he is on to them.

If you have a client that claims that he may be the victim of electronic surveillance it is very important to carry out an initial threat assessment in order to establish the level of the threat and the likelihood of an electronic attack.

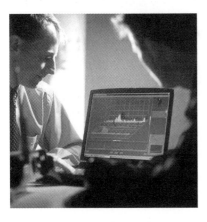

They should be asked:

• **Why would anyone wish to carry out an electronic attack on you and what would they be interested in?**

If your client were to be monitored, ask by who? If they have a genuine reason for being attacked in this way then you can judge whether there is a genuine threat and possibly the expense and effort that the threat would go through, in order to attack your client.

If it is a private client who suspects that their partner is tapping the phone due to suspicions of a matrimonial affair, you would not expect to see a high degree of sophistication or high cost equipment which has possibly been installed by a private investigator. Alternatively, a commercial client who has high value confidential information that would be of use to competitors could be attacked at a higher level of sophistication and cost.

If the client states, 'I don't really know why or who would want to attack us', then you must get to the bottom of why you have been called in the first place. Do not forget that there are people about who suffer from paranoia, but do not become complacent, there may be a real threat.

• Who do you suspect of attacking you in this way?

There could be one potential threat, there could be many for various reasons. If they are under attack, how was the device planted, by an employee, a visitor or by unauthorised access such as a mock break in.

• What are your reasons for suspecting that you are being monitored

If the client is convinced that information is being 'leaked' or confidential information has got back to them via a circuitous route, there is obviously a breach of security. Many clients automatically suspect that they are being 'bugged', but check to establish if the 'leaked' information could have got out by any other means and consider:

- Loose talk by staff
- Disgruntled employee
- A confidence being broken
- Confidential waste and refuse being examined
- Documents left on desks
- Unauthorised access to computers and files
- Dictaphone tapes left out on desks
- A 'mole' in the company

The Knowles Microphone

• Who has leaked the confidential information?

If the details of a confidential conversation have got back to the client, he should recall the place and circumstances when the conversation took place. If it was in an office or boardroom, you can suspect that these may be vulnerable target areas. If the conversation took place over the telephone, this is obviously a prime area to check and search.

• If a device is found, what are you to do?

- **Remove the it**
- **Leave it in situ**
- **Disable the it**

If a device is found there are a few options that are open to discussion with the client. Remember if you locate one device do not pack you bags and go home. Continue your search for other devices, some may have been planted to act as decoys.

• Remove the device

If we remove the device, there will no longer be a threat but the buggist will know that his operation has been compromised. This will either make him go to ground or attempt a further attack.

• Leave it in situ

You could leave the device in place and then provide false information (dis-information) to the buggist. If this is done, you should be careful as the buggist may have heard your attempts to locate the device.

• Disable the device

If the device is left in situ but disabled, the buggist may be tempted to return and service it. In this event, a covert camera system could be installed to cover it in order to identify when the buggist returns.

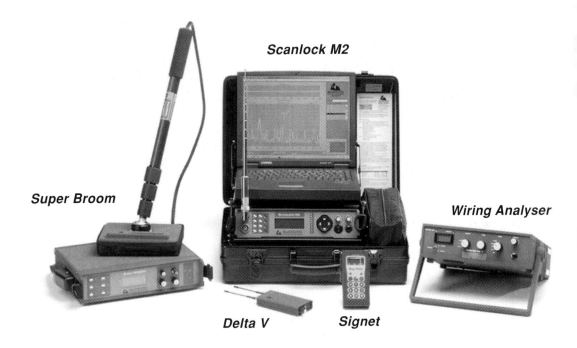

Scanlock M2

Super Broom

Wiring Analyser

Delta V *Signet*

The range of TSCM equipment supplied by Audiotel Ltd

If your client suspects that he has been bugged, tell him:

• Not to panic.

• Continue to use the telephones in a normal manner but avoid discussing sensitive issues. To stop using the phones altogether may alert the buggist.

• To contact a search team as soon as possible using a 'secure means'. He should prepare for them a 'threat assessment'.

• Not to employ a local private investigator to carry out the search as he may have installed the device. Look for someone out of the area and check their qualifications.

• Do not use the suspected phone for confidential matters.

• Use a mobile cell phone in a 'clean' area to discuss counter-measures or sensitive information.

• Do not try to locate any devices themselves. Do not telephone the police or phone company as they will not be able to help them.

• Secure any suspected areas in the event the buggist attempts to retrieve any devices before a search team arrives.

After this has been discussed, you should arrange for a professional and qualified person to carry out the sweep/search. It is strongly recommended to use only those practitioners that do this solely for a living. A private investigator may advertise a sweep service but he will also carry out accident enquiries, tracing missing persons, process serving and debt collection. The phrase, 'Jack of all trades but a master of none' comes to mind. There are qualified people out there who have many skills but would you expect your plumber to be able to fix your roof, tarmac your drive, re-point the walls and re-wire you house? I think not.

Counter Electronic Surveillance Equipment

Listed below are a number of types of equipment and devices that a counter surveillance team would be expected to use in an electronic search. These devices all have limited use but should tell you that a device is present. An electronic search should be backed up by a physical inspection as it is only the eyes that will find a device or any evidence of tampering.

Radio Frequency Detectors/Receivers

Counter surveillance receivers such as Audiotel's 'Scanlock' are able to pick up signals from active transmitters and are

The Scanlock M2

then used to locate them to within a few inches. They are also able to detect 'mains carrier' transmitting systems and radio telephone taps.

What they do not identify, are any devices that are switched off (such as remote controlled) or devices that have flat batteries. In addition, they are unable to pick up or identify hard wired microphones, recorders or hard wired telephone taps. However, the new Scanlock M2 can run 24 hours a day logging all signals onto a laptop computer which comes supplied with the receiver, this will monitor and note any out of hours transmissions.

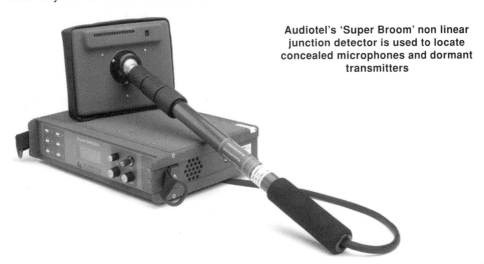

Audiotel's 'Super Broom' non linear junction detector is used to locate concealed microphones and dormant transmitters

Non-Linear Junction Detectors

The 'NLJD' or Harmonic Radar is often referred to as 'The Broom' which is actually a trade name. They are used to identify and locate printed circuit boards, cables and microphones that may be buried in walls, cavities or furniture. The NLJD will locate any inactive transmitters or devices.

Hand Held RF Detectors

Smaller portable, hand held RF detectors are cheaper alternatives and often used by close protection teams. I would not recommend using one for a major search and be aware of the 'cheap and nasty' ones that sell for about £150.00 as they are virtually useless. Audiotel's Delta V is a hand held device, that is portable and very effective in locating transmitters.

The Sig-Net is also a hand held receiver, which identifies and locates mobile phone bugs and GSM transmitters. This receiver can be left in an office whilst a meeting is taking place in order to protect 'real time' in the event anyone activates a GSM device.

The Delta V

Spectrum Analysers

These devices allow you to see a visual display of the radio signals in the locality on an oscilloscope. To a trained person, these signals can be interpreted and establish if a transmitting device is present. Modern counter measures receivers use PC based spectral analysis software for faster response and location.

Time Domain Reflectometer

This device is used to detect breaks and splices in cables. Quite often it is not possible to follow a cable along its length and so a TDR will identify where a cable has been broken and repaired or a device attached. An experienced operator should be able to tell where the 'break' has occurred in order to examine it physically.

The 'Signet' which identifies and locates GSM (mobile phone) transmissions

Multi-Meter

This is used to measure line voltages and other current measurements especially within telephone wiring. A measurement taken across the line (at terminals 2 and 5) should give you a reading of 49 volts when the handset is in the cradle (on hook). When removed (off hook), the voltage drops to about 9 volts.

If a device is installed in series on the line, the voltage measurement when off hook should increase from 9 volts up to 25 volts due to extra resistance. If a device is installed in parallel on the line, both the on hook and off hook voltages would be less than normal (below 9 and 49 volts respectively). This amount will differ according to the type of device used.

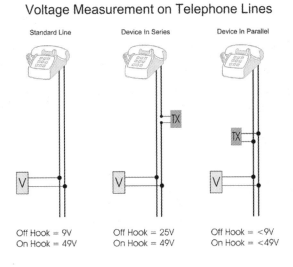

Voltage Measurement on Telephone Lines

Standard Line	Device In Series	Device In Parallel
Off Hook = 9V On Hook = 49V	Off Hook = 25V On Hook = 49V	Off Hook = <9V On Hook = <49V

Example of a TSCM Report

Report

After our threat assessment taken with the co-operation or Mr Webb, we attended at the offices of Webbo Ltd in High Wycombe, on Monday 10th June 2002.

We carried out a complete electronic sweep of the executive offices and board-room for any active or voice activated transmitters. Special emphasis was placed on the electrical mains and telephone system.

The electrical power system was inspected and tested for mains carrier transmitters and mains operated transmitters.

The telephone system was electronically inspected which included all handsets and wall junction boxes, they were also subject to an internal physical search. The fax systems were also tested for radio transmissions.

All ancillary electrical equipment was inspected and tested, these included: table lamps, calculators, lap tops, coffee machines, mobile phone chargers, and PIR detectors.

A physical search was also carried out of the lowered ceiling and wall cavities for hard wired microphones, tape recorders and inactive transmitters.

Findings

No surveillance equipment or evidence of such was found within the suite. The telephone system was found to be clean of all interception devices.

The electrical system in the office suite was found to be clean of active transmitting devices and mains borne carrier devices. The fax machines were clear of radio transmissions.

The ceiling voids and partition walls were electronically and physically inspected and again no evidence was found of any transmitters.

Conclusion

No specific evidence was found to associate concern over the loss of information with the use of electronic surveillance devices. However, certain lacks in general security were noted:

- The photocopier was not secure and open to misuse.

- There was no 'clear desk' routine and important files were left insecure.

- The waste (including confidential) was not shredded but placed in a open skip at the end of each evening by the cleaners.

Should you have any comments regarding the above please do not hesitate to contact us.

This report is correct to the best of our knowledge and belief dated the 9th September 2003.

Legal Issues

In the United Kingdom, there is a belief within the investigative industry and those that sell surveillance products that there is a 'grey' area regarding the use and legalities of electronic surveillance equipment. There is in fact no grey area but law, which clearly defines black from white when it comes to using this equipment.

There are various Acts, which govern electronic surveillance in the UK, these include:

- Regulation of Investigatory Powers Act 2000
- Interception of Telecommunications Act 1985
- Intelligence Services Act 1994
- Security Service Act 1989
- Police Act 1997
- Wireless and Telegraphy Act 1949
- Human Rights Act 1998
- Data Protection Act 1998

Public Authorities

For 'Public Authorities' such as the Police, Customs and Excise, the Security Service (MI5). to carry out a technical surveillance, they have to have a signed authority and warrant from the Secretary of State. This authority is given under the terms of the Interception of Communications Act 1985 where warrants will only be issued if the warrant is deemed necessary in the interests of national security, or for the purposes of safeguarding the economic well being of the UK. This is normally against threats from overseas in order to prevent or detect serious crime. This type of surveillance is classed as 'intrusive' under the Regulation of Investigatory Powers Act 2000.

The crest of MI5

In order to install these devices, the authorities will require permission (again from the Home Secretary) to enter premises to do so. Authority would be granted on the grounds that the information it is likely to be of substantial value to the authorities and that it is being used as a last resort when all other avenues have failed.

Scanning and Listening

Under Section 5(b) of the Wireless Telegraphy Act 1949 it is an offence to use radio equipment with intent to obtain information as to the contents, sender or addressee of any messages, whether or not the information is passed on, which the user has not been authorised to receive.

If you listen to anything other than 'licensed broadcasting' or Amateur Radio (including CB) you are breaking the law. You are also breaking the law if you pass on any information heard on the radio. Even having a private frequency stored in a receiver's memory channel (such as a scanner) is considered to be proof of intercepting messages that are not intended for you. Penalties can include heavy fines and/or imprisonment, or both.

This basically states that it is illegal to listen in to any transmission, which is not intended directly for you or the public audience.

It is agreed that scanners can be freely obtained on any high street but to use and monitor frequencies outside the commercial and licensed bands is illegal.

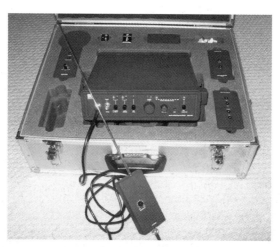

Radio Transmitters

Using **ANY** radio transmitting equipment without a licence in the UK is an offence under the 1949 Wireless & Telegraphy Act. You could also be liable to confiscation of any other related equipment used at the unlicensed station or premises and/or a fine of up to £5,000 and up to six months imprisonment. Therefore using any transmitting bugs (whether used on private property or not) is an offence. This includes the improper 'normal' use of transmitting equipment such as Public Mobile Radio (PMR) or walkie-talkies.

Interception of Telecommunications (Telephones)

It is an offence under the Telecommunications Act 1985 to attach a device or telephone instrument to a British Telecom line/system which has not been authorised by B.T. regardless of whether it is on private property or not. In addition, the recording of a person without their knowledge of the fact is also illegal under the Data Protection Act, hence why some recorders emit a bleep. In addition, you may have noticed that sometimes when dialling certain companies and call centres, they have a warning message at the start of the call informing you that all calls are being monitored for training purposes. This message is really a 'get out' clause in order for them to legally monitor and record offensive customers.

PROHIBITED from direct or indirect connection to public telecommunication system. Action may be taken against anyone so connecting this apparatus.

APPROVED for connection to telecommunication systems specified in the instructions for use subject to the conditions set out in them.

British Telecom approval stickers

Some telephone recording machines have a 'green circle of approval' and therefore can be connected to your phone system. However, if it has been modified in anyway (by cutting off the connector plug) or is not used according to the instructions, this invalidates the approval.

This junction box on the outside wall on a modern house is one of the most vulnerable places for a telephone technical attack

Audio Recordings Not Using Transmitters

A recording made with tape recorders and hardwired microphones is perfectly legal in the United Kingdom and can be used in evidence so long as the integrity of the tapes (evidence) is preserved.

Trespass

There are many forms of trespass but we are concerned here with Trespass to Land. In the UK this is defined as:

A wrongful direct interference with another Person or with his possession of Land or Goods.

Or

Unjustifiable, direct and immediate interference (of an intentional or negligent nature) with another persons land, for example, by unauthorised walking on it.

Trespass To Land, usually takes the form of entering it without the owners' permission. It is no defence to show that the trespass was innocent.

This exterior telephone junction box, found on the walls of many modern homes is very vulnerable to telephone transmitters.

Conclusion

Technical surveillance can be a very complex subject but due to the many devices available on the open market today, they are made very user friendly. The majority of the devices mentioned above all had a genuine commercial use before being adapted for surveillance use and many can be improvised with a little thought.

Counter surveillance is very complex and should be left to a qualified expert. If you carry out a search, remember that you have to leave the premises with your hand on your heart and be able to say, 'Yes, that office is clean'. If a client later finds a device and can prove that it was present when you carried out your search, and has lost information as a result, he is likely to sue you. Be careful.

Chapter Ten
Anti and Counter
Surveillance

10

Having read this book you should now have the knowledge to understand how a surveillance is carried out and the fundamental principles involved. This chapter deals with anti-surveillance and counter surveillance measures that you or the target of a surveillance could carry out in order to identify a surveillance team. Now that you know how to do it, you should know how to counter it and know what to look out for.

Firstly let us define the difference between the two disciplines.

• Anti-Surveillance

Anti-Surveillance is defined as the actions or manoeuvres that a person carries out in order to

> • **Confirm that he is under surveillance and by whom**
> • **Evade and lose the surveillance team**

Anti-surveillance manoeuvres will be the actions of a target who suspects that he is being followed in order to expose the team and confirm that he is being followed, and also to draw the team into a position where they can be identified. Anti-surveillance measures can be carried out **Covertly** or **Overtly**. Covertly, where the target is aware of the surveillance teams' presence but does not let on to the fact. Or overtly where the target lets the surveillance team know that he is aware of their presence.

• Counter Surveillance

Counter Surveillance is defined as the actions that a third party (person or team) carries out in order to:

    • Identify any presence of a surveillance team
    • Prevent that a person (the Principal) is under surveillance

A close protection (bodyguard) team would carry out counter surveillance in order to establish whether their 'Principal' is under surveillance in the event that he may be attacked or kidnapped. These actions are normally pre-planned and rehearsed by a team or an individual.

Hardened, experienced criminals and terrorists will also use a form of counter surveillance team, in order search and identify Police surveillance operators.

Surveillance Awareness Levels

In an earlier chapter we discussed the various awareness levels of the target, which can be listed as:

    • Aware

The aware target disciplines and trains himself to look for 'watchers' and 'followers' and who may carry out anti-surveillance tactics as a matter of course every time he appears in the open.

    • Semi-Aware

This Target would expect to be followed or watched as they have a reason for doing so (i.e. they are up to no good). They may adopt some anti-surveillance tactics to identify whether they are being followed but may not really know what to look out for.

    • Unaware

This Target does not consider or think about being watched or followed. This type of target can be very complacent about his activities and is easily caught out.

    • Hidden

The target we consider 'hidden' would more likely to be the hardened criminal such as the drug trafficker of terrorist who rarely carries out his activities in the open.

There is also one other person that we have to be aware of when we are talking about anti-surveillance and that is the 'Lost Driver'. We will discuss this person towards the end of this chapter.

ANTI-SURVEILLANCE MEASURES

As we have defined, anti-surveillance is described as the actions or manoeuvres that a person carries out in order to get a reaction, and therefore confirm that he is under surveillance and then to possibly evade and lose the surveillance team.

Imagine that you are at home and intend leaving for work, you will drive to a car park and then walk a short distance to your destination. What noticeable things would draw your attention to the fact that you were being followed. What actions would you carry out to confirm that you were being followed and what would you do to lose the followers.

Ensure that all maps, radio parts and cameras are covered up at all times

The Plot Up Phase or Stake Out

• Observe from upper storey window for unusual vehicles or persons in the street/area especially small vans. Unusual vehicles, although they may appear to be unoccupied, may be fitted with video transmitting equipment.

• Look for one or two persons in parked vehicles. In poor or cold weather, look to see if the windscreen wipers are being used or the heaters to prevent the windows from misting up.

• Do not just concentrate within the close proximity of your home/office. A surveillance could be triggered from some distance away by a surveillance operator parked in a 'safe' place using binoculars.

• Walk or drive around the block returning home shortly afterwards, looking out for the unusual or for anyone pulling out directly behind you. If you carry out this action, give yourself a reason for doing so, such as visiting a nearby neighbour or a local shop. You should not alert the watchers to the reason for your actions, a 'dummy' run will always confuse any watchers.

• Do not be afraid to challenge any suspicious persons. Any challenges will put the surveillance operators on their guard, which may cause them to 'lift off' or make their job even more difficult for them.

• If you see a suspicious vehicle, take a good look at it and note the details. Ask the owner of the property who's house it is parked outside if they know the owner.

• Alter your routines, do not leave home at the same time. Consider using the front door and rear door at irregular intervals.

• Leave the house in a vehicle that is being driven by someone else whilst you are out of sight in the rear.

• Enquire with friendly neighbours about anything suspicious. In addition, send someone else out such as a friendly neighbour to look for the unusual.

The Follow Phase Whilst Driving

• Note if anyone pulls out immediately behind you. This is unprofessional. Make note of the vehicle behind you as you encounter the first or second junction/turning after departure.

Loosing The Tail

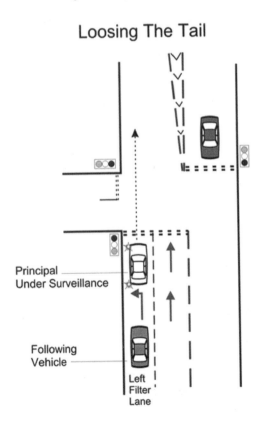

Principal
Under Surveillance

Following
Vehicle

Left
Filter
Lane

• As you depart, continue on your original direction for a short distance and then do a 'U' turn taking you back past the spot you have just left, looking at the other vehicles as they pass you.

• Stop frequently and suddenly, observing the vehicles behind you, noting their details and actions.

• Drive around a roundabout several times to throw watchers into chaos.

• Jump a red light to see if you are followed across.

• Frequently alter your speed by slowing down then speeding up, note if following cars overtake you or keep to the same speed.

• Stop immediately after taking a left hand turn and note the vehicles that pass you.

• If held in traffic, closely examine the car and person behind you, look for signs of talking into a radio or the driver that 'creeps up' behind you.

• Pull into a petrol station and observe the area whilst out of the car and filling up.

• Pull into a large car park with multiple exits.

• Drive on a motorway changing speed frequently from high to slow. Come off at an exit and then rejoin the carriageway.

• Pretend to break down on a motorway to see if anyone stops behind you.

• Drive into the country using narrow lanes whilst observing the vehicles behind you.

• Enter a cul-de-sac or multi storey car park to see if you are followed in and observe the drivers actions.

• At a junction or crossroads, indicate to turn and then move off in a different direction or go straight across. Observe if the watchers indicate to turn also, but then follow your actions.

Follow Phase Whilst on Foot

Foot surveillance can mean that you are in close proximity with the target and so the risk of being noticed by an aware target is much greater. If you were being followed you could carry out the following anti-surveillance measures:

• Frequently look directly behind you.

• Drop a piece of paper and see whether it is picked up and examined.

• Enter a telephone box and use it to observe your surroundings from. You can stand there for a couple of minutes and observe on three sides.

• When leaving the phone box, keep a close eye on it in the event a surveillance operator is 'clearing' the box for any information.

• Enter a shop or large store or café and observe the doorway to see if you are followed in.

• Frequently turn about and change direction.

• Walk into areas where there is little pedestrian activity such as a quiet housing estate.

• Use large department stores with many exits and levels.

• Remove or add different types of clothing such as a hat or coat.

• Establish eye contact with suspected watchers, you do not necessarily have to challenge them in order to put them off.

• Square the box.

• Rather than look directly behind you, use street furniture such as a bus stop where you can stand for some time looking up and down the street for watchers. In addition, frequently cross the road, this gives you the opportunity to look up and down the street whilst waiting for passing traffic.

• Use different modes of transport; bus, train or a taxi. If on a bus, sit at the rear and observe those also getting on.

• Challenge anyone suspected of following you, consider taking their photograph which will really put them off.

• Move about by bicycle, it is too fast for those on foot to keep up with and too slow for vehicles to keep track of you.

Public Transport

Utilising public transport can cause confusion and create anxiety in the team, especially if you are changing from one type of transport to another. Some tactics could be:

• Wait at a bus stop and then don't get on but let the others.

• Stay on the bus to the terminal, notice who else is on, then get on another bus.

• Stand on a train platform and attempt to be the last person to board it, noticing if anyone else is hanging around on the platform.

Using public transport is a good way of identifying and losing followers

• Get a train but then get off prior to your stated destination.

• Get onto a train or a 'tube' and then get off before it moves away. This tactic became a classic manoeuvre in the film *The French Connection*.

The Housing Phase

• Just before entering, stop and take a good look around you for anything unusual.

• Enter a 'denied' area such as a private car park or office block that may have a reception or security guards, 'watchers' will only be able to enter if they 'blag' their way in and may feel uncomfortable like a fish out of water.

A target may leave his home totally unaware but remember the two most important things that will get you noticed; Multiple Sightings and Unusual Behaviour. The first time you notice someone, you are none the wiser. The second time could just be coincidence but the third time is a positive identification.

The Lost Driver

We briefly mentioned above the 'lost driver'. When carrying out a mobile surveillance, your target will at times enter areas that will be unfamiliar to him and he may become lost. If this happens we need to identify at an early stage whether he is in fact lost, or carrying out anti-surveillance manoeuvres as his actions will appear very similar. Think to yourself, what actions will a lost driver carry out, he will:

• Suddenly stop at the side of the road
• Frequently change direction
• Goes twice around a roundabout
• Enters a dead end or one way street
• Goes twice around the block
• Indicate to go one way and then suddenly change his mind

All of which are classic signs of someone who is carrying out anti-surveillance. Therefore we should establish at an early stage whether the target is lost or on to you and the team. This cannot be easy, but try to think back to the way the surveillance was going before any manoeuvres were carried out. If you are convinced that you have done nothing to alert the target then you should be reasonably safe to assume that he is lost. If he is carrying out these manoeuvres in his 'home' area, he is possibly carrying out counter surveillance.

COUNTER SURVEILLANCE

As we defined earlier, counter surveillance is defined as the actions that a person or team carries out in order to prevent a person from being under surveillance and, to identify any presence of a surveillance team.

These actions are normally pre-planned and rehearsed by a team or an individual and can be carried out either covertly or overtly. Or in other words, we let the watchers know you know of their presence or by letting them appear to carry on undetected. Close protection teams that are responsible for their 'Principals' safety, often carry out counter surveillance, especially when there is a high threat level. Anyone who is a serious threat and intends to carry out an attack or kidnap will most probably do his homework and carry out some reconnaissance and surveillance beforehand.

American Secret Service bodyguard

The counter surveillance team (CST) will carry out various checks and observations in order to establish whether there is a surveillance presence in the area where the Principal is housed, and also when the Principal is on the move. The CS team should be very alert, very observant and fully understand the principles of surveillance.

Having looked at the different phases of a surveillance; the Plot Up (or stake out), the Pick Up, the Follow and the Housing, there are procedures that we can use at each phase in order to identify and detect watchers. The counter surveillance team have to think 'surveillance' and if they were to carry out a surveillance on their Principal, how would they do it.

The Plot Up (or Stake Out) Phase

• Make use of a scanner, which constantly scans the VHF and UHF commercial wavelengths in order to pick up close transmissions, which may be used by surveillance teams.

• Use encrypted communications amongst the close protection team in the event a surveillance team is monitoring for your transmissions.

• Carry out a foot patrol and a mobile patrol of the Principal's home in order to look for likely trigger positions that a surveillance team may use. Remember the various means that a trigger can be performed and the trigger locations open to them.

• Search for anything unusual such as people sat about in vehicles or on motorbikes. Make a note of empty vehicles and their contents, things to look out for are:

- Brief sheets
- Radios or radio parts
- Maps
- Fast food wrappings
- Old newspapers

• Approach and confront anyone you find suspicious.

• Widen your search area and check along known and frequent routes, especially 'choke points' for trigger locations away from the starting point.

Pick Up Phase

• Have a member of the CS team depart in the Principal's vehicle as a decoy in order to draw watchers from their lie up positions and to listen in for any scanned radio activity.

• Utilise one of several vehicles with tinted glass in order to transport your Principal. The watchers will be unable to identify which one contains him.

• Vary the times of departure, do not set a routine.

• Watch for vehicles pulling out directly behind you. Only an amateur will do this.

• Watch out for the first, second and third car to leave behind you.

Follow Phase

• During the follow phase, a CS team should throw a protective cordon around the Principal's vehicle. These operators should be looking out for anything unusual or frequent sightings of the same vehicles.

• The Principal or his driver, should carry out those manoeuvres as previously described concerning anti-surveillance.

• The route the Principal takes should be varied as should the times of departure.

• Drive a circuitous route making at least three turns in direction to the left or right so that you 'box' three sides to a square. Anyone also seen taking this same route should be treated with suspicion.

Housing Phase

• The CS team should arrive at the destination prior to the Principal and check for watchers who may already be present and for those that may have followed the Principal.

• If the Principal proceeds on foot so must the protection team. Therefore, the CS team should also follow, observing from a distance for any watchers.

• Take the Principal into a controlled area where the principal has easy access and would be difficult for a surveillance team to enter, such as a place of work.

Boxing The Square

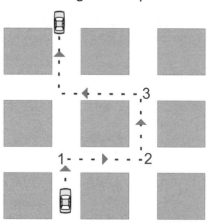

What to do if you find yourself being followed

Whether the target of surveillance turns on you or you just happen to find yourself in a position where you suspect that you are the target of a surveillance, carry out some of the anti-surveillance measures listed above in order to initially confirm that you are being followed.

Travelling by bicycle is very hard to follow - too slow for cars and too fast for foot teams

Then:

- Stay calm and do not panic

- Inform your team, the police or a friend who may be able to help you by mobile phone

- Decide, do you want to identify the followers or just evade them

- Make a note of the descriptions of any vehicles including registrations or personnel

• Do not try to out race them, you will make the situation worse and possibly cause an accident

• Keep driving until you are in a safe area or a police station

• Do not lead followers to your destination or home address, this is a must, they may achieve their aim

• Do not stop and confront them, they could be dangerous.

• Try to detach yourself from the followers by putting other vehicles between you and them and then making turns where they are likely to be held, such as traffic lights.

Conclusion

Having learnt most tactics relating to surveillance, you should be able to think to yourself, 'If I were to be put under surveillance, what would I do in order to identify the watchers and what would I do to draw them out into the open?'

If the target travels about by bicycle, he could be quite protected from any observation team as this is one of the most difficult ways of mounting a surveillance operation. The target is too fast for foot surveillance and too slow for mobile surveillance so if you have something to hide, buy a bicycle.

An unprofessional team is easily spotted and very easily caught out. An experienced surveillance team is more likely to carry out tactics to ensure that they are not spotted, and if they suspect that they are being drawn into a compromise, they are more likely to 'lift off' from the surveillance and let the target run. It is better to let the target run rather than suffer a compromise, a target left to run can be picked up another day. One that has noticed you, will be on his guard for a very long time.

Chapter Eleven Surveillance Photography

11

This chapter deals with the aspects of still and video photography in relation to surveillance. It is not intended for the reader to become a professional photographer but deals with the various aspects that will enable you to produce a quality photograph which has been taken in not so ideal conditions, poor light and with telephoto lenses.

If you are watching an individual or premises for a long period of time to obtain photographic evidence, it is imperative that you know your photographic equipment and it's abilities. It can be embarrassing having to report back to a client after twenty hours of observations with a photograph, which is either blurred, out of focus or under exposed.

After you have read this chapter it would be wise to go out and experiment on a roll of film or get out your video camera and practice some of the techniques that have been described. Use your camera's manual to assist you or obtain a photographic book from the local library, that will provide you with more detail. It is said that 'practice makes perfect' and during a surveillance the situation changes constantly so familiarise yourself with your equipment.

In today's world of investigation the video camera is being used more and more than the SLR stills camera. Although an SLR camera will produce excellent results, a video camera can be used by anybody after only a few minutes of handling and practice.

There are many cameras available and choosing one can be difficult. At the end of this chapter there is a check list of features to help you decide, but principally a 35mm SLR (single lens reflex) camera is ideal. Ultimately the quality of your photographs will be a combination of factors; your ability to use the camera correctly, the quality of the equipment, your personal judgement, the quality, type of film and lens that you use. Digital cameras are coming into play now more often than before. Technology now enables us to be able to take a photograph and within minutes it can be sent from a lap top computer by email to a client for his perusal.

Video Photography

Video cameras (camcorders) are now used more often in investigative work than SLR cameras. Personally, I prefer still photography to video as a medium but clients now prefer video and if you are investigating 'personal injury' type claims, then video is essential in order to record physical activity and movement.

Over the years we have seen video evidence presented by various investigation agencies in many different styles, especially for the ever-increasing personal injury investigations.

We have often carried out investigations second time around after another agency has had the first shot. Alarmingly, some of the tapes we have witnessed have been shocking and embarrassing as a member of our profession has actually submitted these in to a solicitor or client.

A recent tape that was reviewed, opened up with a superb animated introduction to the 'Agency' that warranted an Oscar. It was followed by 12 seconds of terrible film showing a

Digital Camcorder

female putting her handbag into a car, getting into it herself and driving away. This shot involved 'violent' zooming in and out, it was mostly out of focus, the camera shake was of earthquake proportions and added to the video was the investigators voice exclaiming, 'Yes, Yes, get in that f***ing car...!' Not very professional really, especially when the agency concerned charged £35.00 per hour.

To this end, if you are watching an individual or premises for a long period of time to obtain video evidence, it is imperative that you know your photographic equipment inside out, its abilities and limitations. A professional photographer once told me that to use an SLR camera takes skill and experience. To use a video camera you only have to know how to read, the first five pages of the instruction book! This is true to some extent but we need to discuss a number of topics that should enhance your video technique.

So in this section, we look at video photography using camcorders and also how to set up a fixed and portable CCTV system.

Types of Video Cameras

Essentially we have two types of camcorder:

- **Analogue**

- **Digital**

Analogue video cameras are very popular and are still in use especially the 'Hi8' types that offer a very good reproduction and quality. The recordings are stored on the tape in an 'analogue' format.

Most models available have pretty much the same features and will vary in price due to their size and the amount of extra features

Analogue Camcorder

they have. There are certain features to look for in a video camera when using it for surveillance. A good brand name such as Sony, Canon or JVC should give you a quality camera, personally I use Sony equipment, as their cameras have the majority of features that I require. Listed below are certain features to look out for.

- **Minimum of a 12 x Zoom Lens (Optical)**

All cameras have a zoom facility in order for you to view through a wide angle picture or zoom in to a close up. If you can, obtain the highest number of optical zoom that you can, this enables us to film from a distance without losing any picture quality.

What happens during 'optical' zoom, is that when you move the zoom control, the actual lens inside the camera moves and thus brings the picture closer (or further away). Cameras that state that they have a 'digital zoom' actually zoom in electronically by enhancing it to appear closer. This has a big drawback as you lose picture quality by making the picture full of pixels.

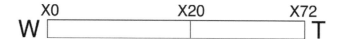

If we take a camera that has a **x20** optical and **x72** digital zoom, we would expect to get clear pictures up to **x20**. After that, as the picture gets closer, the quality will also deteriorate. Do not be fooled that a camera of **x400** zoom will give you the option of filming from two kilometres away because it won't. It is recommended that you set the zoom facility on your camera to 'optical' only, to prevent using the digital zoom.

Try not to over use the digital zoom as the picture will become 'pixelated'

Focal Length Conversion

If you are familiar with still photography, you will be used to focal length (or the length of the lens) given in millimetres, such as a wide angle lens would be 28mm, a standard lens being 50mm and a telephoto lens of being 210mm and upwards. In video photography (and digital still cameras) they tend to use a 'times' ratio (for example x 6) rather than a measurement. The table below describes the corresponding times (x) scale with the focal length of a stills camera.

The formula used is:

times x divided by 0.03125 = focal length in millimetres

For example:

x 6 on a video divided by 0.03125 = 192 which equals a 192mm lens

• Anti-Shake Feature

The majority of camcorders have an 'anti-shake' feature built in, as camera shake is more apparent when using video, especially when filming at the top end of your zoom. These features do work and are not included as a sales gimmick.

Times	Focal Length	Lens Size approx'
X 1	32mm	50mm
X2	64mm	50mm
X4	128mm	130mm
X6	192mm	200mm
X12	384mm	400mm
X18	576mm	600mm
X24	768mm	800mm
X40	1280mm	1200mm
X62.5	2000mm	2000mm

• Ability to playback through the viewfinder or screen

The majority of cameras have this facility. Some view finders are monochrome (black and white) only whilst you will pay more for a colour viewfinder and is more favourable if having to record and give descriptions at the same time.

• Manual Focus as well as Auto Focus

Not all cameras can be focused manually, but I consider this essential in surveillance photography as one of the main problems seen with video evidence is the fact that the picture is out of focus. Most camcorders utilise an 'auto-focus' lens but they also have the facility to be disabled manually. Whilst 'auto-focus' is okay for the family wedding shot, it can make legal evidence look very unprofessional.

• Time and Date Facility

All cameras have this facility which is an important factor when marrying up your surveillance logs to the video tape.

• Standard and Slow recording speeds

Cameras have the facility to record at Standard Play (SP) or Long Play (LP). This is a good feature but try to use SP whenever possible to obtain a better picture quality. You may consider using LP if you are going to place a camera on constant record. In this mode, the most you may get is up to three hours continuous recording on one tape.

• Back Light Compensator

If your target is stood in front of a white or bright background, the cameras aperture will close down and make your picture appear very dark. By simply altering the exposure you can override this and brighten up the whole picture, this is useful when shooting into the sun.

• Night Shot Capability

Many of today's camcorders incorporate a 'Night Shot' facility, enabling you to record pictures in total darkness (or zero lux). The camera can be switched from daylight mode to night mode quite simply and only infra red light (which is invisible to the naked eye) will be recorded. This feature is useful during dawn and dusk as well as at night time.

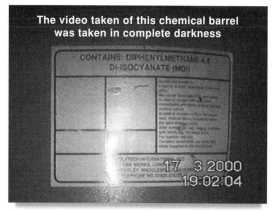

The video taken of this chemical barrel was taken in complete darkness

As with all cameras and electronics take very good care of them as they do not take much abuse and knocking about.

One of the biggest dangers to the camcorder is probably the damp air.

Video Techniques

It is worthwhile obtaining a text book on video photography from your local library. Video photography is not always easy and your films can be greatly improved just by learning a few simple techniques concerning panning, zooming and composition. All of which enhance your film, making it look more professional. The best way to improve your technique is to actually watch the tapes after you have shot them and learn by your mistakes.

Zooming

An irritating and popular pastime seen on videotapes is overuse of the 'zoom' control. Because it is there, we feel that we have to use it and it can make very frustrating viewing to the point of inducing seasickness! When watching TV programmes, take note of the lack of zoom used by photographers, you will be surprised.

Some camcorders boast a high magnification in order to bring the picture closer but remember picture quality. In addition, the more zoom (or close up) that you use, the more camera shake you will encounter. Think to yourself, 'Do I really have to zoom in that close?'

By going through the camera's menu, switch off the facility to use the digital zoom so that you will only be able to zoom optically

Focusing

I would suggest that you use manual focus for the majority of your filming as you are in total control. An example: Quite often you would be filming your subject who is walking down a street or getting in or out of a vehicle. You lift your camera up and start recording. A pedestrian or vehicle passes between you and the subject and what happens? The lens now auto focuses on the 'passer-by' whilst turning your subject into a fuzzy blob. Once the obstruction has passed, the camera starts to refocus on the subject but then locks onto the dead fly or dirty windscreen and remains focused there until the subject has disappeared out of shot.

Camera Shake

Camera shake is very noticeable when using video, especially when filming at the top end of your zoom. The way you hold your camera will greatly affect your picture taking and make all the difference. The following should assist in taking a steady film:

> • Grip the camera firmly with the right hand, thumb positioned on the button with your forefinger on the zoom control. The left hand should be placed under the body to steady it. Held like this, you should be able to remove either hand and still have a tight grip of the camera

> • Stand or sit in a position where you will not sway about, use a support to lean against, keep your elbows tucked into your body for support

PETE'S TIP: If you are concerned that you will knock the camera out of focus whilst in manual mode, then place a piece of sticky tape against the lens focusing ring in order to stop it from moving. Alternatively, put the camera onto 'infinity focus'. This should keep the whole picture in focus provided that you are not zoomed in too close.

• Hold your breath or use shallow breathing

• If filming from a vehicle, turn the engine off

• Ensure that your camera has an 'Anti-Shake' feature

• Use a mono-pod or tripod for support

Camera shake is the main fault when using video and is very distracting to watch

Sound / Audio

Much video evidence does not require sound on the tape unless voices or certain sounds need to be heard as part of that evidence. As a rule, many colleagues and I always have a dummy plug (2.5mm jack plug) pushed into the external microphone socket. This disables the built in microphone and avoids recording any unwanted sounds whilst you are filming. Radio voice procedure, background noises/voices and even the odd piece of bad language do not want to be

recorded. Remember, your original tape may be played back in open Court.

I have seen tapes in the past where the investigator actually adds a running commentary on to the tape whilst filming. This is a personal preference but be careful if you are not very fluent and articulate. You can also trip yourself up if you're not too careful. On one film, I saw a taxi drive past with only the driver in it (the subject in his vehicle) only to be told by the added commentary that '*The subject driver is now leaving Cherry Close having picked up another fare.*' Again, something that a smart barrister could use to discredit you.

Don't Forget to Synchronise...

A very important factor and so much overlooked is the synchronising of the camera's clocks. If you are using two or more cameras on the same investigation, ensure that all the timers are synchronised (preferably to the 'pips'). This should be a professional habit carried out on every morning of the surveillance by all of the team. It greatly assists when editing the tapes and more importantly it does not leave you open to unwanted criticism and cross-examination by those smart barristers.

> *Don't Forget*
>
> *In the UK do not forget to alter the camera's timer for British Summer Time (BST) and Greenwich Mean Time (GMT)*

Going Covert

Quite often, you will have to get out on foot and take your camera with you. Obviously you will not want to walk around the streets with a camera in your hand (unless the situation permits it) and so there are various methods in which it can be concealed. The crudest way is to put your camcorder in a bag with a hole cut in it for the lens to see through, commonly known as a 'Bag Fit'. This is a good photographic aid as you do not always have to be 'face on' to the target. You can be to the side, in front or behind them to get your film. In some instances, the bag can be put into a shopping trolley if you had to follow someone around a supermarket.

The Bag Fit

This sports bag has been fitted with a wooden cradle inside, in order to hold and steady the camera without it rattling around. The camera can be pushed into it knowing that a clear picture will be obtained.

The hole is cut in the correct place and then camouflaged by gluing a piece of wire mesh over the hole on the inside of the bag. Other types of camouflage I have seen, is to use a baggage tag that appears to hang over the lens hole or a pair of sunglasses for the camera to see

though. The view through the lens is very clear and the wire mesh does not show if the camera is set correctly.

If you are going to make a bag fit, there are certain techniques that you can use in order to get a better picture:

• Set the focus to infinity

Do not use auto-focus as the lens will constantly be re-focusing as people move between you and the target. If you set the focus to 'Infinity' anyone from the camera to a far distance should remain in focus.

• Wide angle

Pull the zoom right back so that you are at the widest possible angle. This ensures that your target is captured in the frame and assists the picture being in focus when set to infinity.

• Use 'Sports' mode

Most cameras have various exposure modes for different conditions. If you have a sports setting, set it to this and the wire mesh camouflage should disappear.

Technique

Using a bag fit takes practice, it has to be held steady and pointed in the right direction, not at the sky or the floor. It also has to be carried naturally down by your side. On training courses, we have seen people that are unused to camera bags, walk around with their arm stretched out, bag in hand as if there is a time bomb in it!

Transferring to Analogue Video to VHS Format

Most of our films, once taken on 8mm or Hi8 film will need to be transferred to a larger format such as VHS in order for the client to view it. This is a simple case of connecting the camera to your VHS recorder with the supplied leads. It is possible that on modern recorders there is a 'scart' socket at the rear. A cable needs to be run from your cameras 'Video Out' socket to the 'Video In' on the scart plug. If you require sound (Audio) to be transferred, you have to make similar connections via the Audio socket/plugs.

Set your VCR to either Channel 0, LINE IN or AV mode (depending on the model), this is normally done with the remote control in order to accept a signal from an outside source (your camera). Now play the tape from your camcorder, which should now appear on your TV screen. If the picture appears, we are all set for recording.

All you have to do now is to rewind the tape in the camcorder or set it to where you want to start. Insert a VHS tape into the VCR and press record, after a few seconds press play on your camcorder and the film will be transferred.

If you need to edit out bad footage, all you have to do is press PAUSE on the VCR, move the original tape to your next sequence, press play on the camcorder and take the PAUSE off the VCR to carry on recording.

Portable Covert Video Systems

If you want to be more covert, then a smaller lens and camera can be used when you have to go in close or when concealment is a major factor. Using a small video recorder such as the Sony Walkman and a connecting pinhole lens, the system is small and portable enough for you to enable covert video recordings.

These camera systems can be purchased ready built or be put together yourself with a little technological know how. The unit can be housed in carriers such as a briefcase, a handbag, jacket, rucksack or a sports bag to suit.

The recorder shown in the photograph has had its bulky lid removed to help

concealment and when set to long play it will record continuously for three hours if necessary. The camera is a pinhole board camera, which can be obtained from many electrical outlets such as Maplins or security firms for as little as £30.00 and are easy to set up. The more you pay, the better quality you will achieve and ideally you could do with a camera that has a resolution of about 380 TV Lines or more. The majority of these cameras are powered by 12 volts but make sure you use the correct battery for the correct camera.

When handling the camera board, be careful not to touch the printed circuit at the back of the lens or you may damage it. It may be wise to house the lens in a plastic case or special heat shrink material in order to protect it. Some cameras come hermetically sealed already, which is a great help.

There should normally be four wires coming from the camera. Two are for the power supply (positive and negative) and are likely to be coloured red and black. The other two wires are for the video signal leaving the camera to be plugged into the recorder and are likely to be coloured yellow and black (Video and Ground).

If there is a white wire, this is probably for a microphone if you have an audio facility on the camera, but we will ignore that just for now.

The camera requires power to make it work and it is suggested to use a 12 volt rechargeable battery which will power your camera for about three hours and it would be wise to fit a switch to turn it on and off when required. The video cables should terminate with a 'phono'

This film was taken through a pinhole lens in a hairdressers salon

plug which is connected to the 'video in' socket on the recorder. The yellow cable should be attached (preferable soldered) to the centre pin on the phono plug and the black lead to the outer ring or shield.

Digital Video Cameras

Technology is advancing at a fast pace, especially in the video camera market. Although not old fashioned by any means, the analogue camera is very good but is slowly being replaced by their digital counterparts. Essentially the cameras are the same but the recorded information is stored on the tape in a digital format.

You will notice that these cameras are smaller in size but this is not always a good thing as some of them can be quite tricky to hold before getting used to

This rucksack has a pinhole lens in the shoulder strap. The recorder is concealed in the base

Board Camera Wiring

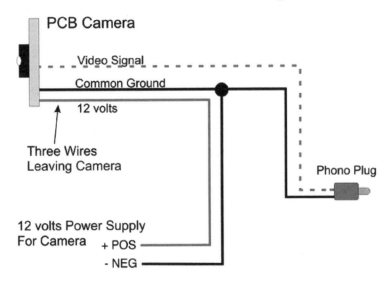

them. In addition to being used as a video camera as we have discussed above, the digital camera also boasts a number of other features depending on what you pay for.

Smaller Size

The cameras are fairly small and if you have large hands you may find them tricky to use at first. For concealability, they are very good especially when incorporated with a separate camera lens as mentioned below.

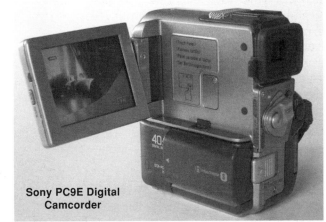

Sony PC9E Digital Camcorder

Memory Sticks

Many of these camcorders have a 'Memory stick' which is a small device which slides into the camera rather like a floppy disk and stores still photographs. With a digital camera you can also use it as a stills camera but the picture quality is not that magnificent but adequate for general purposes. In addition, you can also take still pictures from the videotape as you watch it, and store them on the memory stick as JPEG files.

You can then attach your video camera to a computer and download the photographs from the stick into the machine. You can then process them on a package such as 'Adobe Photoshop', to print them off, or insert them into a word processing file.

Sony Memory Stick

Email

The Sony IP5 and IP7 cameras have a facility where the camera can transmit and receive emails via a mobile phone. This gives you the ability to take a piece of video film, take a still shot from it and then email it to a client whilst you are still on the ground, all without getting out of the car!

Analogue Video Input

One of the beauties about some of these digital cameras is the fact they are able to accept a video input signal (AV in), the Sony PC 100e is a favourite or the Canon ZR-45/50 models. What this means is that we can take our pinhole board camera as previously described, hook it up to a battery and then connect it to the digital camera. Other cameras with an AV input are the Sony PC9e, PC100e and the PC120e.

Due to the small size, it can easily be concealed almost anywhere from being body worn, to fitting it inside a bum bag or hand bag.

Digital Tape Editing

The editing of tapes on to VHS can be carried out in the manner previously described but it is far easier by doing it on a computer. By hooking up the camera to a PC or AppleMac computer you are able to control the camera with the computer mouse. You can play the original tape and view it on the computer monitor and select the start/finish points of your 'cuts'. Once done, you then bring all the cuts into a 'time

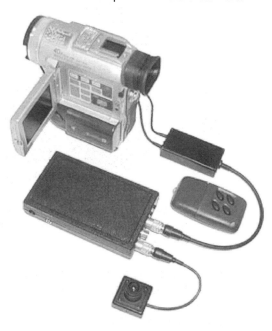
This digital video camera has been adapted to accept video in, from an external source such as the small pinhole lens

line' in the order that you want. When you are happy with your finished recording, you can then transfer the edited version back onto a digital tape by 'squirting' it back to the camera, onto a VHS tape or even save it to a CD ROM to be viewed on another computer. There are various software programmes used for video editing but I find that 'I Movie' which comes as standard on an AppleMac to be very effective and very simple to use.

'Dazzle' Device

Tape editing on a computer can only be carried out if the data is digital. However, there is a device on the market called a 'Dazzle' which lets you convert analogue video to digital video and vice versa. This is handy if you shoot film with an analogue camera and wish to edit the tape digitally on a computer and then store the finished film on a CD, DVD or send it to a VHS video tape. A Dazzle will cost about £150.00 and they certainly have their uses.

Covert Closed Circuit TV Cameras

Covert Closed Circuit TV (CCTV) and video has an important role in covert evidence gathering. By means of a video camera linked to a video recorder and monitor you will be able to unobtrusively watch events taking place at the time they happen or you can view them at a later time.

Many cameras have been installed and supplied in the past which have achieved excellent results, especially where theft and unauthorised access to premises have been suspect. If covert cameras can resolve the problem it saves much manpower, time and unnecessary expense having to provide a manned observation team. In addition a covert camera may be the only option available to you, if the target area is impossible to watch.

Miniature covert video camera

A recent call to use a covert camera involved installing a miniature camera in the store room of a newsagents shop. Packets of cigarettes were going missing (cartons of 200 at a time) and it was suspected that one of the older 'paperboys' was the thief. A camera like the one shown here was installed in the storeroom above head height and a cable was led to a room upstairs (after drilling through the floorboards) to a video recorder and TV monitor.

One of the shopkeepers would be at the front of the shop serving and the other was upstairs watching the monitor. The culprit was allowed to enter the storeroom and he was seen on the monitor to hide a carton of 200 cigarettes down the sleeve of his jacket. The shopkeeper upstairs telephoned the person downstairs and the culprit was stopped as he left the shop.

Hardware

Video cameras are now available on the security market that are as small as a matchbox and are as thin as a wafer. A camera such as this can be concealed in almost any object and placed in a position to view the target area. The camera may be able to be fitted with various lenses that will give you a choice of wide angle or telephoto views. Many cameras come ready built into objects such as smoke detectors, PIR detectors and wall clocks.

Cameras are either colour or black and white (monochrome). Colour cameras are more expensive but I find that monochrome cameras have a better picture quality and suit for most purposes. The quality of the image is made up of TV Lines (TVL) rather like the pixel quality of a digital image on a computer screen, the more TV Lines the camera supports, the better the resolution. A camera of 380 TVL and above should be sufficient for professional use.

Cameras also have a different threshold to the amount of light they will operate in, and this is measured in 'Lux'. Zero lux is total darkness. A 0.3 lux camera will operate quite well in low light situations whilst a camera with a 1 lux would not be so good as it needs plenty of light.

 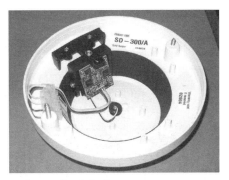

A camera concealed in a domestic smoke detector

Infra Red

Monochrome cameras also have the ability to see infra red (invisible) light. Therefore if you have a situation where you need to record in total darkness, a monochrome camera together with an IR light source should suffice. Some cameras come with an array of infra red emitters for this reason but they are not always very powerful or efficient.

Picture obtained from the smoke detector camera

13- 1-02
10:38:14

Some time ago we installed a camera in an office where the thief would remove a desk drawer key from a filing cabinet and then steal cash from the drawer. The prime suspect worked on the night shift and it was suspected that the thefts were taking place during dark hours. We installed a covert camera in the office observing the filing cabinet but we had the problem that we could not leave the lights on, as it would alert the thief. We used a camera with built in infra red emitters but the range from camera to cabinet was slightly out of range to get a quality picture.

With a bit of improvisation, we purchased a couple of infra red light emitting diodes (LED's) from an electronics store and a battery pack. The LED's were wired up and then taped to a pencil to act as a holder.

The LED arrangement (which lasted for 18 hours) was concealed in a dried flower arrangement placed on top of the filing cabinet and worked a treat. The thief was caught as he approached the filing cabinet and as he reached into the top drawer,

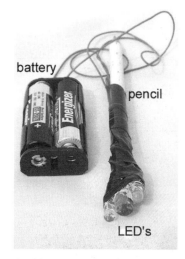

battery

pencil

LED's

unbeknown to him his face was completely flood lit with infra red light from the LED's and captured on film.

In the wiring diagram you will note that the camera requires power to make it work (12v positive and negative) which takes up two wires. We also have to get the video signal back to the recorder (positive video and ground/or negative) which takes up another two wires, therefore, four wires in total. Quite often 4 core telephone cable is used to link a camera to the recorder which is ideal for short runs up to about 100 metres. Some cameras already come supplied with cable and connectors, which make installation a very simple process. The hardest task and the most time consuming when installing cameras is actually laying and concealing the cable.

Time Lapse Video Recorders (VCR)

A standard domestic video recorder will provide you with a maximum of eight hours recording time when set at long play (LP) speed. Any longer recording time required will mean having to resort to a Time Lapse Recorder. These recorders are more expensive than the standard machines but can record for periods of anything from 3 to 960+ hours on a standard VHS tape. In addition the time lapse VCR will print the time and date onto the recording. When recording, always set the minimum amount of recording time on your VCR to ensure the best quality in playback. A 24 hour time lapse VCR will possibly also record at speeds of 3, 6, 12 and 24 hours. If your time period to be recorded is 8 hours, you will need to set the record speed to 12hr mode in order to cover it as 6 hours is not long enough. If you were to set it a 24hr mode, you will lose picture quality as the longer the time set, the less frames are taken and the poorer the quality and any movement will appear to be staccato.

Why are the 'Crime Watch' videos always poor quality?

Video tapes shown on TV of thefts taking place in shops often show that the picture quality is rather poor. This is due to various reasons:

- Camera is sited in the wrong position
- Poor resolution camera
- The lens is out of focus
- The lens not cleaned regularly

Camera System Wiring

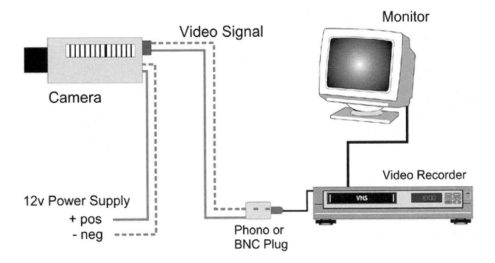

- Old tapes used in the recorder, they stretch and become magnetised after a short period and is one of the main problems
- Poor wiring
- A tape recording speed that is too slow
- Cheap, inexpensive equipment

More often that not, it is the tape that produces a bad picture because the user has used the same tape over and over again. Tapes should be changed for new on a weekly basis.

Recording Audio

Time Lapse VCR's will also record sound (audio) via the audio input or a microphone socket. However, if you need to do this, It would not be expected to get a good quality sound recording if the recorder is set to anything over 12 hours. As the time lapse feature takes so many 'snapshots' per second, this also applies to the sound, leaving gaps in the recording.

TV Monitor

You will require a monitor connected to the VCR, to watch the recording and the cameras view. A good basic system comprising of a miniature camera, 24 hour time lapse video recorder and a monochrome monitor together with cables can cost as little as £450.00 if bought from specialist wholesalers.

Real Time VCR's

Also on the market are what is termed as 'Real Time' VCR's. These recorders operate in a similar manner to time lapse for 24 hours but they record in real time onto the tape. This gives a smoother picture rather than the staccato characteristic of a time lapse VCR.

Digital VCR's

Analogue time lapse VCR's although still in demand, are now becoming superseded by their digital counterparts. The recordings are not stored on standard video tape but on special data tape or a 'hard drive' and then can be transferred to conventional video tape or a CD ROM. The quality of these machines is very good and can record for a very long time depending on the amount of memory. In a few years time it is possible that all recorders will be digital.

Radio Transmitting Cameras

If you are unable to physically link the camera to your video recorder by cable, it is possible to transmit the video signal by radio waves to a receiver, which in turn is connected to your VCR. The camera and video transmitter will still require a power supply (mains or battery) but no other cables would be necessary.

There are many video transmitters on the market and you really get what you pay for. Radio frequencies used for these transmitters in the UK are normally either 1.394GHz or 2.4GHz which do not require a licence. Some transmitters can provide a range of 1000 metres line of sight with a decent antenna such as a Yagi.

The camera pictured is a combined camera and transmitter and is very small indeed. The small unit together with a power supply is concealed in an empty video cassette case.

PETE'S LINK: www.dataprotection.gov.uk/dpr/dpdoc.nsf

Camera Trigger Systems

If it were not possible to get into a position to trigger a surveillance, it would be viable to put a transmitting camera in the locality to enable you to sit away and monitor the activity on a small TV monitor. The camera and transmitter, if fitted in a vehicle can be powered by batteries concealed in the boot. The vehicle can then be driven into a position to cover the target and left there.

For short-term measures, especially in rural areas, the covert 'tree log' has its uses. Quite simply, this section of a tree trunk has been hollowed out and fitted inside is a camera, video transmitter and a battery power pack, all weatherproof. Placed on the ground and covered with a small amount of natural foliage it will transmit pictures back to the operator, located nearby.

If you need to record some pre-surveillance activity, for example, you need to know at roughly what time a person leaves home and in which direction. A camcorder can be left in the log recording on long play with a 90 minute tape (giving you three hours recording time). After that time, you can then retrieve the camera (and log) and review the tapes to give you the information.

Transmitting Camera System

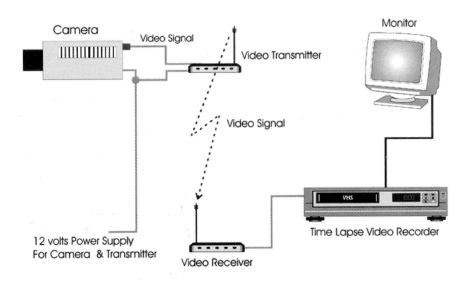

Remote Surveillance Modules

Cameras can now send their pictures via a special transmitter down a standard (PTSN) or digital (ISDN) telephone line, a good example would be a 'webcam' used over the internet. The camera, hooked up to the transmitter/modem is connected to the telephone socket at the location to be monitored. At the receiving station, a receiver is plugged into the telephone system and connected to a recorder and monitor. This enables video monitoring over great distances.

Miniature transmitting camera

Cameras used in this instance are often 'dormant' but transmit when an alarm is activated so that security personnel can verify whether there are intruders in the area.

Date Time Generators

Not all video recorders or monitors have the facility to add the date and time to a video recording, especially domestic VCR's. With the aid of a small device called

a 'date time generator', a camera can be connected to it where it electronically overlays the information before being sent to the recorder. They are not expensive and cost around £60.00.

Multiple Cameras

Sometimes it is necessary to utilise two or more cameras at once. Rather than have a separate recorder for each, we can make use of a device called a 'Quad' or 'multiplexer' which has inputs for a number of cameras. The device then sends the signals from all of the cameras to one video tape. All of the cameras can be viewed simultaneously on one monitor.

Data Protection Act 1986

There are strict guidelines within the Data Protection Act in relation to CCTV. The requirements of the DPA is quite heavy reading in respect of CCTV and the law, and it is advised to become familiar with the process, especially regarding the security of recorded material. Anyone using CCTV should be registered with the DPA.

STILL PHOTOGRAPHY

Still photography is a great medium but it is now becoming to be used less in surveillance or investigation work. The reasons are many, more clients prefer to see their evidence on video tape and many investigators/surveillance operators find video cameras far much easier to use without having any technical know how. In addition, technology has introduced the digital stills camera, which some people are now switching over to, but these cameras are not always suited to our type of work.

Digital Stills Cameras

Digital cameras operate in the same as conventional photography (shutter speeds and apertures) but the difference is that instead of capturing the image on a film, it is read by a series of light sensors which is then converted into signals and then stored on a memory card.

This card can then be read on a computer and the image downloaded for printing or manipulating with a suitable computer programme. A photograph taken with a digital camera can be quickly and simply downloaded into a lap top computer and sent by email to anywhere in the world within minutes. The price of a digital camera can range from £50.00 to £3,000 and you literally get what you pay for.

This camera was used to take many of the pictures used in this book

Image Resolution

One of the most important features to look for when choosing a digital camera is the amount of memory that it has, normally measured or described as mega pixels. A camera with a memory of 6 million pixels (the amount of dots within the picture) is very high resolution and will provide extremely clear pictures as opposed to a camera with only a memory of 1.2 million pixels. Many of the photographs used in the technical surveillance chapter were taken with a camera resolution of 3.3 million pixels.

Memory Sticks and Compact Flash Cards

The pictures are stored on memory cards and like floppy disks, there is only a certain amount of information that can be stored on it. If you alter the cameras settings to shoot at a lower resolution and picture size, you will cram more pictures onto the card. Pictures taken at very high resolution will limit the number of pictures stored, for example, on a 64mb card, it will store approximately 40 pictures taken at 3.3m pixels.

Surveillance Use

Whilst digital cameras are good for all round photography so that the pictures can be included in reports, I would not yet use one for surveillance. Many digital cameras have a habit of taking a few seconds to 'warm up' and after pressing the shutter release there tends to be a slight delay before the picture is actually taken. Due to this reason, many reporters are sticking to conventional cameras in order to catch the action. If you decide to pay over £1,000 for a digital camera, this problem should not be apparent as much. Digital cameras also like plenty of bright light and therefore tend to suffer in poor lighting conditions.

Power

Most digital cameras require a substantial power source (batteries) and they get eaten up at a terrific rate. Re-chargeable batteries last three times as long but it is always advisable to carry a spare set.

Manipulating Digital Photographs

Most of the digital photographs taken in this book were processed with 'Adobe Photoshop' software. This package lets you do all manner of things to your pictures from altering the brightness/contrast, the depth of colours, cropping, re-touching and manipulating them beyond recognition.

Single Lens Reflex (SLR) Cameras

Manual or Auto Focus?

The majority of cameras now being produced are auto focus, which offers speed and accuracy when focusing on your subject. It is personal preference, which type of camera to use, if you are happy with a manual focus camera then why change, but they are becoming less common.

PETE'S TIP: If buying a digital camera, ask a regular user for their advice; some shopkeepers may try to sell you one that is unsuitable and far too pricey.

Having used both systems, the auto focus camera is used for the majority of surveillance work. Manual cameras are more robust and durable whilst the auto focus are more fragile but offer additional features such as built-in auto-winders, more accurate metering and more compact telephoto lenses. Not only can they focus more quickly than a manual camera but they can also adjust to keep a moving subject in constant focus.

How a Camera Works

A camera is a light proof box with a piece of film at one end and a lens at the other which focuses the light onto the film.

The amount of light that enters the camera is controlled by two things:

> • **The size of the hole (aperture)**

> • **The length of time the aperture is held open (shutter speed)**

Different combinations of these two factors give different effects on film which are very important and are described below.

Correct Exposure is a combination of aperture setting and shutter speed

Aperture

As stated the aperture is the size of the hole that allows light to reach the film. The size of the aperture can be altered and is given a value which represents the size. These values are called '**f**' numbers or '**f stops**' and follow in sequence:

> **f:2   2.8   4   5.6   8   11   16   22**

> **f2** being the widest aperture and **f22** the smallest.

The series as a whole is arranged so that each **f** number lets in twice as much light as the previous number.

So why is aperture so important to the surveillance photographer?

A wide aperture such as a f2.8 will allow in plenty of light and this is what is required in a low light situation, which is common in surveillance photography, especially early morning or evening time.

Shutter Speed

Shutter speed is the amount of time the shutter is held open to allow sufficient light to fall on the film.

Shutter speed is calibrated and measured in fractions of a second, such as:

1/15   1/30   1/60   1/125   1/250   1/500   1/1000   1/2000

They are similar to the aperture **'f'** numbers in that each speed either doubles or halves the one next to it.

As we said at the start of this chapter, a correct exposure is a combination of aperture setting and shutter speed. On average a setting of 125/250th of a second is the norm.

Exposure Modes

Many cameras have different exposure modes and your cameras manual should explain what modes are available.

- **Automatic Exposure (also called Program)**

- **Aperture Priority**

- **Shutter Priority**

- **Manual**

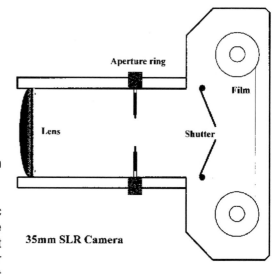

35mm SLR Camera

- **Automatic Exposure (Program Mode)**

Most SLR cameras have an Automatic or Program mode. When in this mode all that is required is for you to point the camera which takes its own meter reading. The camera reads the amount of available light and automatically sets the cameras aperture setting and shutter speed to obtain a correct exposure. This is good for the novice but not always ideal in surveillance photography where more control over the camera is required in differing situations, therefore shutter priority and aperture priority are discussed at some length.

Let's imagine you've just taken a meter reading and your camera suggests an exposure of **1/125** sec at **f8**.

To achieve the same exposure you could use any of the following aperture and shutter speed combinations:

2.8	4	5.6	8	11	16
1/1000	1/500	1/250	1/125	1/60	1/30

The combination you choose depends on the subject being photographed as the settings are relative but the resulting picture can alter.

• Aperture Priority

When in this mode, the camera takes a meter reading and then adjusts the shutter speed according to which f number is manually set.

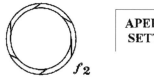

APERTURE SETTINGS

For example:

If aperture **f16** is selected, camera may automatically choose **1/15 sec**

If aperture is set to **f2.8** the camera may then choose **1/1000 sec**

In surveillance photography, this mode should rarely be used except when Depth of Field is important when taking pictures such as:

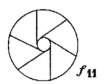

- Landscapes, large areas
- Buildings, pre-surveillance
- Aerial photography
- When you need to place a subject in its surroundings

Depth of field is explained later in the chapter, but we tend to use this mode in poor light so that the widest aperture can be set on the camera. In turn this will automatically set the fastest shutter speed.

• Shutter Priority

When in this mode, a desired shutter speed is selected and set on the camera (for example 1/250 sec). The camera meter then automatically sets the correct aperture, to match.

Your choice of shutter speeds affects how moving subjects will appear in the picture. Slow shutter speeds such as 1/30 or 1/15 of a second, will blur moving subjects. Fast shutter speeds such as 1/250, 1/500 or 1/1000 of a second, can be used to freeze the action of a moving subject. Fast shutter speeds are required when using telephoto lenses to prevent camera shake.

• Manual Mode

This mode is used when you require full control over exposure. Photography in this mode would only be recommended in surveillance circumstances to the experienced photographer.

Depth of Field

Depth of field (sometimes referred to as Depth of Focus) describes the extent of the picture that will be in focus when set at a given f number.

F No.	22	16	11	8	5.6	4	2.8	2	1.4
Units of light	.5	1	2	4	8	11	32	64	128

In theory, only the subject on which you focus is completely sharp but an area of acceptable sharpness lies in front of and behind it. This area is called the 'Depth Of Field'.

As the size of the aperture decreases, the depth of field lengthens bringing more of the picture in front and behind the subject into focus. The size of this depth of field area varies and depends upon three factors.

- The focal length of the lens

- The aperture the lens is set to

- The camera to subject distance

Depth of field can be used when you require to photograph a person when the background is important and also requires to be in focus, so use a small aperture.

Conversely, if you require a photograph of a person but need to keep the back/foreground out of focus. Such as taking a picture of a figure through a wire fence, you do not want the fence appearing in the photo and obscuring the subject. Therefore use a large aperture which will limit the depth of field making the fence invisible.

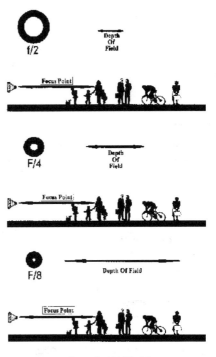

Depth Of Field

Shutter Speed and Telephoto Lenses

When using telephoto lenses, fast shutter speeds should be used to prevent image blur caused by camera shake. Camera shake is much more apparent with long lenses, in addition to the picture being magnified, camera shake is also exaggerated. Whenever using telephoto lenses try to use a support or tripod. If the camera has to be hand held, use the following table as a guide to selecting minimum shutter speed to prevent blur.

Correct use of depth of field will eliminate obstacles such as the fence shown here

For every mm of focal length lens used, use a like shutter speed, for example:

In poor lighting conditions, you will not always be able to obtain an ideal shutter speed, for example, if the weather is very dull and you have a 300mm lens fitted to the camera, the camera's exposure meter may tell you that a speed of 1/125 sec is required. If this is so, either use a support or try to hold the camera as steady as you can.

Keeping Your Camera Steady

The way you hold your camera will greatly affect your picture taking and make the difference between a pin sharp picture and a blur caused by camera shake.

The following will you help take sharp pictures:

Camera shake is the cause of many poor pictures

• Grip the camera firmly with the right hand, with your finger on the button. The left hand should be placed under the lens barrel to focus and zoom. Held like this you should be able to remove either hand and still have a tight grip of the camera

• Stand or sit in a position where you will not sway about, use a support to lean against especially when using slow shutter speeds. Keep your elbows tucked into your body for support

• Breathe out, hold your breath, squeeze the shutter gently, do not snatch it

• Use a faster shutter speed when practically possible

• If you are in a vehicle, switch off the engine

Lens	Minimum shutter speed
35mm	1/30 sec
50mm	1/60 sec
100mm	1/125 sec
210mm	1/250 sec
300mm	1/250 sec or faster
500mm	1/500 sec

Metering

We have discussed how the camera's meter is able to read the amount of light and adjust the settings accordingly to obtain the correct exposure. Metering systems vary from camera to camera but most modern cameras work on 'multi-pattern' metering. The camera's 'eye' is split into separate individual 'cells', the camera's computer then averages the amount of light read in each of these cells to give a correct reading. Many cameras have a Spot Metering area which helps when shooting in difficult situations.

Spot Metering

If your camera has a spot metering facility you will find this may be one of the most important features when taking covert photographs to obtain a correct exposure. This meter is very precise where only the light at the centre of the lens is measured.

When the 'spot' button is pressed, the metering system restricts its measurement to the circular area marked in the viewfinder frame. Therefore any light outside this area is ignored, so why is this of use to surveillance photography?

- When your subject is surrounded by bright features

- When your subject is surrounded by dark features

• Surroundings too Bright

If we have to take a photograph of a man who is stood in front of a white garage door loading a white van, the camera's meter would normally read all this 'whiteness' and close down the aperture to obtain an average exposure.

In doing so, the man will turn out very dark and under exposed. With spot metering, the spot is placed over the image of the man and the photo taken. The meter reads only the light from the man, ensuring a correct exposure. A similar situation would occur when your subject is stood in front of a bright window, in a snowy location or when the sun is behind him, giving him a silhouette.

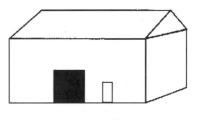

SPOT METERING

• Surroundings too Dark

Additionally if you are shooting into a garage in poor light but the inside of the garage is illuminated, a normal exposure would read all the dark areas and open the aperture to obtain an average exposure. In doing this, the man would appear bright and over exposed. Again, the spot would be placed over the subject and the photo taken ensuring that the subject is correctly exposed.

A meter reading should be taken from the inside of the shutter doors

If your camera does not have a spot metering facility and you find yourself taking photographs in similar conditions, you may be able to adjust your camera manually by over-exposing or under-exposing the picture by 1 or 2 stops (f numbers). Care should be used when using the exposure override control so that you do not compensate the wrong way. If the surroundings are too bright, over expose, if they are too dark, under expose.

Camera Lenses

The lens is the device which focuses the light on to the film to form an image, unless that image is sharp you will not produce clear pictures.

Focal Length

The amount of view seen through any lens is governed by its focal length (usually measured in millimetres), which is the distance from the lens to the film. On a 35mm camera, a standard lens is 50mm and has roughly the same view as the human eye. To photograph more of an area or to bring an area closer you will need lenses of a different focal length.

Range of Lenses

There are a wide range of lenses available and to the surveillance photographer, lenses of 300mm are normally adequate to bring your subject in close enough. Zoom lenses (lenses with varying focal length such as

28-70mm, 70-210mm or 100-300m) are ideal which enable you to frame the picture.

Lens Speed

As previously mentioned, a large aperture will let in more light than a smaller aperture. Lens size is relative to how large that aperture may be. For example an average 50mm lens will have an aperture range of f1.4 to f16 whereas an average 300mm lens will have an aperture of f4.5 to f22. This 'f' number is referred to as the 'speed' of the lens, dictating how fast it is.

200mm, f2.8 lens

This tells us that the 300mm lens will not be able to cope with poor light conditions only having its widest aperture of f4.5 instead of f1.4. Fast 300mm f2.8 lenses are available as are 800mm f2.8 lenses but they are very expensive and costs run into thousands of pounds. Fast telephoto lenses are used by many sport and press photographers to obtain fast shutter speeds. Depth of field is normally very shallow with these lenses especially using wider apertures and therefore focusing has to be very exact.

Tele-Converters

Tele-converters offer a cheap way of extending your lens by increasing the focal length of the lens that you already have. A tele-converter is a small cylindrical tube that is fitted between the camera and the lens.

A 2x converter doubles the focal length so that a 200mm telephoto becomes a powerful 400mm.

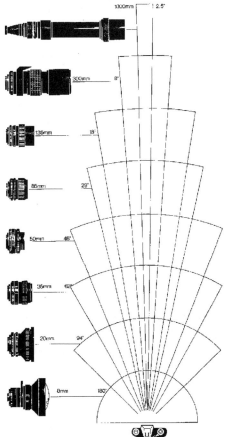

Focul length and angle of view

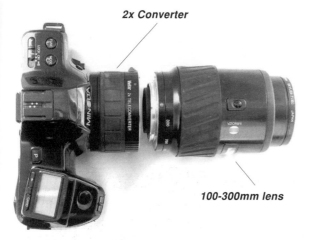

2x Converter

100-300mm lens

The main disadvantages of tele-converters is that your aperture settings will be reduced by 2 'f' stops, for instance, if your 200mm lens is an f4 it now becomes f8 and so photographing in low light may be difficult. A mirror lens is a tele photo, usually with a focal length of 500mm. They utilise internal mirrors to fold light to enable the lens to be as short and as lightweight as possible (approx' five inches long) The only drawback is that they usually have a fixed aperture (normally f8) which can be very limited in poor light.

Focusing

There is nothing worse than having a photograph that is out of focus. Auto-focus cameras are now more common as manual focus cameras. They offer speed and ease of handling and also have the facility to be operated manually. They also offer continuous auto-focusing which will 'track' an approaching car for example.

Various techniques can be used when manual focusing is required:

• **Predictive Focusing**

If you know that your subject is going to pass a certain point (such as walking through a gate), focus on that point and wait for your subject to appear.

• **Follow Focusing**

If your subject is moving then you will have to continually adjust the focus with your free hand as the subject moves. This technique can be tricky and requires practice. Maximum depth of field should be used if possible.

Film

Using the correct film for the correct situation can make all the difference between a good and a bad picture. It is therefore vitally important to know the full range of films available.

There are many brands of film available and vary in price. If you keep to brand names such as Fuji, Kodak or Ilford, you should not experience any problems of quality, experience will help you decide which is the best to use.

When choosing a film decide on:

- Colour or Monochrome
- Film Speed
- Number of Exposures (24 or 36)
- Print or transparency (slides)

• Monochrome Film

Black and white pictures, if taken properly, provide a good medium. If you carry out your own processing, it is possible to take photographs even when your exposure meter tells you that it is too dark. By using a technique called 'Uprating', with a 400 ASA (ISO) film you manually set the film speed to 800 ASA, (this gives you an extra f stop or lets you double your shutter speed), an important factor in low light situations.

When the film is processed the development time is slightly increased to compensate for being under-exposed. Your processor should be informed of any uprating to make adjustments in developing.

Monochrome film can often take over a week to process but *Ilford XP2* film can be processed at any high street processors in an hour. The only disadvantage is that the prints turn out with a slight blue or red tinge but the quality is still very good.

• Colour Film

Colour print film is probably what you would use on most occasions. It comes in many different speeds (explained below) and can be processed within an hour at many high street photo shops.

• Infra Red - High Speed Film

Infra red film is available and enables photographs to be taken in total darkness and is explained later in the chapter.

Care of Film

The following points should be noted:

• Film Date   When you buy film, check it is not out of date

- **Avoid Heat**   Film deteriorates in warm conditions. If you keep a stock, the refrigerator shelf is ideal or somewhere cool

- **Loading**   Always load and unload film in dull or dark conditions. Make sure the film and internal parts of the camera are free from dust and dirt

- **Jammed Film**   If your film is jammed and will not wind on, open the camera's back in a darkened room and try to rectify the problem

- **Used Film**   Always wind the film right back into the cassette to prevent accidental re-loading. Have it processed as soon as possible

Film Speed

The term 'Film Speed' describes how 'light sensitive' a film is. A 'fast' film reacts very fast to light, a 'slow' film is less sensitive and reacts slower, therefore requires brighter light or a longer exposure.

Grainy Photographs

Film is made up of light sensitive crystals. It is the size and number of these crystals which determine the film speed. The crystals, or grains, on fast film are much larger than those on slow film which is why fast film produces 'grainier' pictures.

Speed Ratings

Film is usually marked with the speed ratings as ISO/ASA (International/American).

• Slow Speed Film

Slow film gives sharp detail and a grain free image. It is an ideal film for static subjects such as landscapes, buildings or still life. It requires longer exposure times and therefore has little use in surveillance photography.

• Medium Speed Film

This is the best for general purpose photography and gives a compromise between speed and grain. You may get away with using medium film if the light is good or you are using a 'fast' lens.

• Fast and High Speed Film

These films are a must for surveillance photography, especially speeds of ASA 800 or 1000 ASA.

In low light they give you the ability to shoot at faster shutter speeds (avoiding camera shake with long lenses). In bright light they perform equally as well. As previously mentioned, high speed film means that pictures look grainy, but with speeds of 800 and 1000 the results are acceptable.

The faster the film, the granier the picture

Manufacturers are continually improving film and so perhaps in a couple of years 800 ASA will have the clarity of 100 ASA film.

Setting Film Speed

Once you have loaded your film, the film speed should be set on the camera's dial. Whenever you load a new film, always check this dial. A wrong setting may cause your pictures to be incorrectly exposed.

DX Films

Just about all films are now 'DX coded'. This is a type of bar code found on the film cassette. Most new cameras have a DX reading facility, with this facility, the camera automatically sets the film speed rather than having to do it manually with a dial. The above table shows the different film speeds and their applications.

DX code on side of film cannister

Removing a Film For Later Use

Should you only take eight pictures on one roll of film and then wish to remove it to be reloaded at a later date, this can be easily done. Make note of how many exposures you have made and rewind the film into it's cartridge leaving out an inch or so of the 'leader'. Write on this leader how many pictures have been taken to act as a reminder.

Reload the same film as you would normally. Put a lens cap on and keep the camera in darkness in the event the cap is loose fitting. Set the shutter speed to a fast setting and fire off the required number of frames to get you back to the

Speed	ASA/ISO	Use
SLOW	(25)	Static subject requiring detail,
	(50)	landscapes, buildings etc.
	(64)	
MEDIUM	(100)	General use.
	(125)	
	(200)	
FAST	(400)	Sports, Action, Low light.
	(800)	Surveillance in good visibility
HIGH SPEED	(1000)	General purpose surveillance.
	(1600)	Very low light
	(3200)	

right place (8 in this case) and then add another two frames in the event the frames overlap. Should you have a Data Back fitted, make sure this is switched off otherwise a time/date will appear on each on the eight photographs.

Photographic Composition

Far to often photographers do not maximise the picture frame to film their subject. Attempt to cram in as much of the scene as possible and use the whole frame. Professional photographers use what is called the 'Rule of thirds' when composing a picture. Divide your frame into thirds both horizontally and vertically so that you have nine equal parts. It is said that at the four points where the lines intersect are the strongest points in which to place the most important feature of your picture.

ADVANCED PHOTOGRAPHIC TECHNIQUES

Panoramic Photographs

Quite often you may require to take a panoramic photograph if the subject covers a wide area or you need to record detail using a telephoto lens, such as photographing a large area such as a farm.

This is done by taking a series of photographs and then panning the camera slightly to one side after each shot is taken. The resulting photographs are then joined together to form an overall picture.

It is important to hold the camera so that it pans horizontally. A tripod is ideal and if necessary a purpose made spirit level will aid horizontal panning. Take the series of pictures from left to right, each one just overlapping the last. This overlap assists in lining them up and joining them together.

Aerial Photography

There may be occasions when you will be required to take an aerial photograph giving you a birds-eye view of your subject, particularly when carrying out a reconnaissance.

To hire a photographer who specialises in aerial work can be quite costly, these photographers are normally pilots who have an interest in photography and use this combination to earn a living by providing commercial and private clients with pictures.

If you already know a pilot you are halfway to obtaining your photographs, a pilot at a local airfield may be approached and asked to take you up. Although pilots are not allowed to accept payment for flying passengers, an offer of paying for the fuel and hire of aircraft may tempt him. After all, he will be logging flying hours at your expense.

Photographs should be taken from as low as the pilot and law will allow and the geography will dictate, taking into consideration that you may not want to alert the subject.

View of new GCHQ building

The following should be considered:

• Brief your pilot in advance, he may require weather reports and flight clearance for certain areas. He will want to know estimates of flying time and fuel consumption which affects costs

• Use a medium speed film to provide picture quality unless the light is poor or if you use a telephoto lens

• Use a fast shutter speed of 1/500 second or more

• Try to support the camera to avoid camera shake, do not brace the camera against the aircraft frame

• Use a lens hood to prevent 'flare' from the sun

• Set focus to Infinity

• If the light is bright, use an Ultra Violet (U.V.) filter

• Use a motordrive, take as many shots as possible, it could be costly to make a second flight

• Avoid shooting early or late in the day, if the sun is bright this will cause long shadows

• Use an aeroplane as opposed to a helicopter. They are quieter, cheaper, plentiful and less observed from the ground

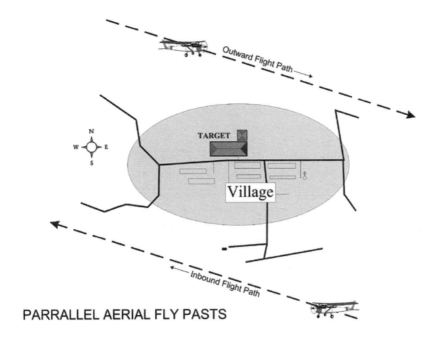

PARRALLEL AERIAL FLY PASTS

Photographing Television Screens

You may need to obtain hard copies of a scene that has been shot on video. This can be done with the aid of a video printer especially designed for the purpose or by using special software on a personal computer. Alternatively you can photograph the screen yourself and this can easily be done if carried out properly.

Set your camera on a tripod fitted with a lens of about 100mm in front of your TV or monitor and fill the frame with the screen. A shutter release cable should ideally be used to avoid any camera shake.

Darken the room as much as possible, this enables the correct exposure to be read from the screen and avoids reflections off the screen from windows. Adjust the picture controls for sharpness and contrast.

The TV picture you see on the screen is made up of ever-changing tiny lines and dots which replace each other every 1/30th of a second and so create a moving picture. Should the screen be photographed at a fast shutter speed, a dark band may appear across the photograph and ruin the picture. For this reason a slow shutter speed is required so set the shutter to either 1/15th or even better, an 1/8th of a second and let your camera's meter select the correct aperture. Should the TV screen be curved, try to make use of depth of field so that the edges of the screen are not out of focus, and focus on the centre of the screen.

Infra-red Photography

Infra red photography is seldom used now in surveillance due to the advent of 'Night Shot' video cameras making it far more simple.

When there is a requirement to take photographs in total darkness you would normally use a conventional flash to provide the light source. For covert reasons this may not always be possible as the light from the flash will alert others of your presence. The power of flash, even though for a fraction of a second is very powerful and can be seen over great distances.

The use of infra red film combined with an infra red light source such as flash will enable you to take photographs in complete darkness undetected.

Infra Red Film

Infra red film is available from most good photographic dealers, Kodak or Konica film is the easiest to obtain. The film comes in either colour slide, or monochrome print format, I would recommend the use of monochrome print film as the colour film can produce odd colours (this film is mainly used for scientific purposes).

This picture was taken in complete darkness with IR film and flash

The film should be handled with care and be removed from its container and loaded into the camera in **complete** darkness. Likewise when the film is removed and sent for processing.

Many major film processors can process the exposed film, although it may take a week to be returned. For the home dark-room enthusiast, the film is developed in D76 chemicals and then printed as normal. As with any black and white negatives you are able to have prints made from them at any High Street processors. The results will not be a true monochrome but will have a light blue or sepia tint to them.

The film costs about £8.00 for a roll of 36 exposures and processing not more than £12.00.

Once the film is loaded, set your cameras ASA/ISO setting to 100. The film is not speed rated and so any setting could be used but 100 should suffice.

Now your camera is loaded with infra red film, all that is required now is an infra red light source. This can be obtained by fitting a piece of infra red filter glass over your flash head. Infra red glass is sold in sheets from security specialists to be fitted over lamps used for CCTV cameras. The glass is actually strong plastic, which is dark red in colour and can be cut with a hacksaw and filed to shape.

Some flash heads have a recess at the front to accommodate special effects filters. If your flash is of similar design you can shape your IR filter to fit in this space. It should then be held in place with black insulating tape to cut out any escaping light through possible gaps.

When the flash is fired in darkness you will not see any light but it is there, in an invisible form as it is infra red. What may be seen though, is a pink flash if you look directly into the flash head.

When fitted to your camera you will need to operate it in manual mode so that the correct settings are obtained. As a guide, a shutter speed of 1/60th at an aperture of f5.6 or f8 will be needed. I would recommend that you experiment with this film if you have not used it before and 'bracket' the exposures, for example, speed of 1/90th but aperture set to f5.6, f8, or f11.

Focusing for Infra Red

Infra red light focuses differently to that of normal light. On some lenses for manual cameras, you will find a red dot that is used for this purpose. The distance from your subject should be set to this red dot rather than to the scale centre line at the top of the lens barrel as you would normally do.

If your lens is not fitted with a dot then it would be wise to focus on a spot which is slightly behind the subject to be photographed.

A wide angle lens such as a 20mm or 28mm is preferred with Infra red photography to provide a maximum depth of field and also enables you to photograph objects close up to obtain detail such as writing on documents.

Photographic Accessories

Tripods

The best way to prevent camera shake is by the use of some support, especially in OPs or the van. Either obtain a small tripod or other alternatives are:

- **Monopod,**   One legged tripod

- **'G' Clamp**   Which attaches to almost any surface with a screw for the camera

- **Bean Bag**   This soft cushion will support and mould a camera in the correct position

Support the camera whenever possible

When using a tripod, a cable release should ideally be used to prevent touching the camera, causing it to shake. If using video, set the camera's remote control to operate the camera.

Camera Data Backs

The back door of most SLR cameras can be replaced with a Data Back. This enables the date and time to be printed onto your photograph as it is taken.

If using a Data Back ensure that the clock is synchronised correctly to your watch and other cameras. A photograph with an incorrect time on it could be disadvantageous if it is to be used in legal proceedings. It should be noted that the time recorded on the photograph does not necessarily mean that it was taken at that

time and could be argued in a court of law. It does however assist when matching up photographs with your surveillance logs, making reading and collation of reports more simple.

Lens Filters

Special effect filters have no real purpose in surveillance photography. However, it is recommended to fit a skylight 1B filter to each of your lenses. This will give a slightly better colour rendition to your photographs but more importantly it will protect the front of your lens from scratches. It is far easier to replace a scratched or cracked filter than it is to replace a lens.

Motor Drives and Auto Winders

Non auto focus cameras can be fitted with a Motor Drive and this will enable you to take up to 5 frames per second which is useful if your subject is in view for only a short period.

In addition they also give you the opportunity to take a series of photographs without having to move the camera away from your eye whilst winding on the film. This not only enables you to view your subject constantly but minimises camera shake. Most modern cameras available have built in auto winders.

Compact Cameras

There are many compact cameras available and these are handy for their small size and simplicity of use. Although their lenses may not be interchanged but some have a built-in zoom lens of 35-110mm. They are auto-focus and can be fitted with a Data Back. These cameras can easily be concealed in a pocket and can be produced quickly to take a no fuss photograph.

Points When Choosing a Camera

• Ask an experienced user for of their advice and recommendations. Do not rely on a Camera Sales persons' advice, all they want to do is close a sale

• Choose a camera that will withstand knocks and rough handling

• Choose lenses with focal length and speed in mind, 100-300mm is ideal

• Make sure the camera feels comfortable and balanced in your hands

• Are the controls simple and quick to use?

• Operating the camera may appear complicated at first, after a few days handling, you will become accustomed

• Ensure that it has a Spot Metering facility

• Does it have automatic or shutter priority exposure modes?

Photographic Tips

• Hold the camera steady, use a support if necessary

• Use a fast shutter speed when shooting hand held to prevent camera shake

• Use a high speed film in low light

• Use spot metering or adjust exposure if necessary in contrasting light

• Maximise depth of field whenever possible

Switch off the engine if filming from your car

Conclusion

Photography can become complicated but it does not necessarily need to be so. I have seen many an investigator spend hundreds of pounds on photographic equipment and then not learnt how to use it properly to great waste and shame. If you learn a few basic rules such as choosing the right film speed and the correct shutter speed you should be able to produce clear pictures that are not blurred by camera shake or out of focus.

If you buy a new camera, read the instruction book and experiment with it. After a few days, read the book again and I am sure that you will learn twice as much. Why spend many hours on surveillance when at the crucial time your evidence is lost because you did not understand how to use your equipment properly.

Glossary of Terms

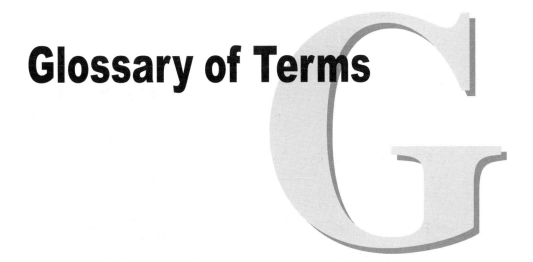

Terms Used in Surveillance Voice Procedure

Expression To Be Used	Meaning Of Expression
ADVANCE WARNING BACK UP	Given in the text of 'Advance Warning, traffic lights, the lights are at red', or 'Advance Warning 'T' junction'.
BACKING	Second vehicle in the convoy, supporting Eyeball. Used by the backing vehicle that is supporting the Call Sign (C/S) that 'HAS' the eyeball.
BUS REQUEST	To be used instead of the term 'Bus Stop' in order to eliminate confusion.
CAN YOU AT...?	Asking the backing C/S to handover at a specific place.
CAN YOU NOW	Initiates the actual handover.
CANCEL MY LAST	Ignore my last message.
COME THROUGH	Given after 'Hang Back' to bring convoy through.

COMMITTED, COMMITTED Means the target is committed to still travelling on a motorway.

COMPLETE Returned or Inside. For example 'India Complete' indicates that call sign India has returned to his vehicle after he has been on foot. Also used to indicate when a person has entered a building.

CONTACT, CONTACT Indicates eyeball is regained by one of the vehicles in the convoy, following search procedure. Point of contact is relayed to the team specifying direction and speed of target. This term is NOT to be used in   military operations.

CONTINUING STRAIGHT Used when the subject is committed to the same road without any deviation.

CONVOY All vehicles comprising the surveillance team.

EYEBALL Vehicle or Operative having primary visual contact with the target and who is directing the operation for the time being.

FOXTROT When someone is walking they are referred to as going 'Foxtrot'.

GO AHEAD Used by a mobile asking another mobile to pass a message. The single term "GO" should not be used as it is too easily confused with "NO". The word SEND has the same meaning.

GOING ROUND AGAIN Indicates that target vehicle is commencing a second, or subsequent circuit of a roundabout. Thereafter, the commentary will continue as for the first circuit in relation to the exits he does or does not take.

GONE... Indicating movement, such as, 'Gone Left Left' or 'Gone towards'.

HANDLING

The person driving a vehicle is said to be 'Handling'.

HANG BACK

Transmission from Eyeball, indicating to convoy that they should 'hang back' as the target vehicle is slowing and may stop.

HELD

Held is a temporary halt such as at a set of traffic lights. Not to be confused with STOP.

I HAVE

Used to indicate that an operator has control of the target and will provide a commentary.

INTENDING

Indicates in which direction the subject is pointing or intending to move or likely to travel.

LEFT, LEFT

Indicates that the target vehicle has turned left.

LEFT, LEFT at...

Indicates where the target has gone Left, or used to identify which junction on a motorway the target has taken off.

LIGHTS AWAY

At night, if you are unsure that it is the target's vehicle that has moved, Lights Away is called in order for another operator to check and confirm it is the target.

LIMA CHARLIE

Loud and Clear, in response to a radio check.

LOOK ALIKE

Used to alert the team there is a similar vehicle/person in the vicinity close to the target. Used to avoid following the wrong person.

MANOEUVRING

Warning issued by eyeball, indicating that the target vehicle is manoeuvring in a car park or on the road.

MAKING GROUND

Call from another C/S who is attempting to get back to the team after being out of it.

NEARSIDE, OFFSIDE INDICATION   States nearside/offside indicator is flashing on the subject vehicle.

NO DEVIATION   Indicates target vehicle is continuing straight ahead, as at a crossroads.

NO LONGER BACKING   Call from the backing C/S to the C/S that 'HAS' to let him know that he is not in a position to actually back due to being held or blocked by traffic.

NOT ONE, NOT TWO   Indicates that the target vehicle negotiating a roundabout has passed first and second exit. 'No Entry' roads are not counted as exits.

OFF, OFF   Transmission by Eyeball, indicating that the target is now on the move. **MOBILE** is also used as a substitute.

ONE UP, TWO UP   Indicating the amount of people in a vehicle.

ONE EIGHTY (180)   Indicates that target had done a 'U' turn and is returning along the same route. 'Reciprocal' is also used.

ORIGINAL   The term used when the target has resumed moving after a stop and is continuing in the Original (same) direction prior to the stop.

OPTION   Indicates a possible turning or route that the subject can go. Such as '2nd Option on the nearside'.

OUT, OUT   Indicates that the target is alighting from a vehicle or is leaving premises.

OUT OF IT   A call to say that you are detached from the team.

PERMISSION   Where an operator asks the Eyeball for 'Permission' to interrupt the commentary to pass on a message.

POSSIBLE	To be used on a Standby if you are unsure (50/50) that the person seen, is the target, team should not react until clarified.
PROBABLE	To be used on a Standby if you are unsure that the person seen is the target, but it is 90% certain that it is. The team should react and check to confirm.
RADIO CHECK	Request from Eyeball to test comms with the remainder of the team. Call signs should respond in alpha/numerical order.
RECEIVED	Used to acknowledge a message. ROGER can also have the same meaning.
RECIPROCAL	Indicates that target had done a 'U' turn and is returning along the same route. May be abbreviated to 'RECIP'.
REGAINED	Indicates target again in view, following temporary unsighted.
RELAY	The vehicle with the responsibility of relaying OR repeating the eyeball footman's messages.
RIGHT, RIGHT	Indicates that target vehicle has turned right.
ROGER	Used to acknowledge a message.
SHADOW CAR	Vehicle being used to back up a footman and act as relay.
SHOWN OUT	If an operator is compromised they have 'shown out'.
SO FAR?	When transmitting long messages, the term "So Far?" is used to break up a message.
STAND DOWN	Indicates cancellation of whole operation.
STOP, STOP, STOP	Indicates that target vehicle has stopped in circumstances other than a 'held' situation.

STRIKE, STRIKE, STRIKE
Indicates designated operators will move in and effect arrest or searches.

STANDBY, STANDBY
Instruction issued by Eyeball or Trigger, alerting the team to possible movement of the target. Can also be used after a loss, when contact has been regained.

SUBJECT
Person subject of the surveillance. Target should not really be used.

TAIL END CHARLIE
Rearmost vehicle in convoy.

TAKEN FIRST, TAKEN SECOND
Indicates that target vehicle has taken first, second or third exit off roundabout.

TEMPORARY UNSIGHTED
Indicates a temporary loss of eyeball, due to terrain, traffic or other conditions.

TOTAL LOSS
When the target is out of sight and control is lost. A total loss will normally be followed by a pre-planned search procedure.

TOUCH RED
A call asking a team member to 'double tap' his brake pedal so that operators behind can see his position at night.

TRIGGER
Term used for eyeball when the Eyeball has to trigger or start the surveillance.

UNSIGHTED TO ME
Indicates that the target is out of your view and so the Eyeball is up for grabs.

WAIT...
Used to indicate that operators should not transmit for the time being and to wait for further transmissions. The normal radio term "STAND BY" has a clearly defined meaning within surveillance and this should never be used instead of 'Wait'.

WHITE 1, 2, 3
Indicates the upper floors of a building or a car park.

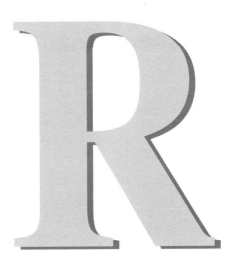

Surveillance Resources

17 Anvil Street
Brighouse
West Yorkshire
HD6 1TP
United Kingdom
Tel: 00 44 (0) 1484 720710
Email: training@rh-assoc.co.uk

Providers of Legal and Security Training

Employment Law
Interview Skills
Police & Criminal Evidence Act
Court Procedure
Criminal Procedure & Investigations Act
Regulation of Investigatory Powers Act
Statement Taking

www.rh-assoc.co.uk

SONIC COMMUNICATIONS (INT) LTD

Sonic Communications Ltd
Brimingham International Park
Starley Way
Bickenhill
Birmingham
B37 7HB
Tel: 00 44 (0) 121 781 4400
Fax: 00 44 (0) 121781 4404
Email: info@sonic-comms.co.uk

www.sonic-comms.co.uk

Specialist Communications and Video Systems for
Law Enforcement, Security Agencies and the Security Industry.

FLIGHT IMAGES

Flight Images
Studio B7, West Entrance
Fairoaks Airport
Cobham, Woking
Surrey, GU24 8HU
United Kingdom
Tel: 00 44 (0) 1276 856222
Fax: 00 44 (0) 1276 855455
Email: info@flightimages.co.uk

www.flightimages.co.uk

Professional Aerial Photography

SECTOR PROTECTION (Europe) AB

Sector Protection (Europe) AB
Box 7212
402 34 Gothenburg
Sweden
Tel: 00 46 31 20 30 00
Fax: 00 46 31 335 95 57
Email: info@sectorprotection.com

www.sector-protection.com

Close Protection Officers : Event Security
Corporate Investigation : Surveillance Teams

STEVE MCMANUS PHOTOGRAPHY
P h o t o   J o u r n a l i s m

The Law Enforcement Picture Library
PO Box 33699
London
N16 6YT
United Kingdom
Tel: 00 44 (0) 208 806 3037
Email: Machardboiled@aol.com

Specialist in law enforcement and related images

Public order situations, demonstrations and protests

www.lawenforcementpicturelibrary.com

THE COVERT WORLD OF
ESPIONAGE

From London to New York to Cairo

The World's most popular newsstand magazine covering
intelligence, espionage, black projects, terrorism, covert operations

Subscribe to EYE SPY Intelligence Magazine and you will find it very useful
in providing a topical digest of what is happening on the fast-moving world
security and intelligence scene. For further information write to:-

EYE SPY
INTELLIGENCE MAGAZINE

Eye Spy Publishing Limited
P.O Box 10
Skipton
North Yorkshire
BD23 5US
United Kingdom

Tel: 00 44 (0) 1756 770199
Email: editor@eyespymag.com

www.eyespymag.com

www.eyespymag.com

Association of British Investigators Ltd

48 Queens Road
Basingstoke
Hampshire
RG21 7RE
United Kingdom
Tel: 01256 816390
Email: abi@globalnet.co.uk

www.theABI.org.uk